Undergraduate Topics in Computer Science

Undergraduate Topics in Computer Science (UTiCS) delivers high-quality instructional content for undergraduates studying in all areas of computing and information science. From core foundational and theoretical material to final-year topics and applications, UTiCS books take a fresh, concise, and modern approach and are ideal for self-study or for a one- or two-semester course. The texts are all authored by established experts in their fields, reviewed by an international advisory board, and contain numerous examples and problems. Many include fully worked solutions.

For further volumes:
http://www.springer.com/series/7592

Gerard O'Regan

Introduction to Software Quality

 Springer

Gerard O'Regan
SQC Consulting
Mallow, Cork, Ireland

Series Editor
Ian Mackie

ISSN 1863-7310   ISSN 2197-1781 (electronic)
ISBN 978-3-319-06105-4   ISBN 978-3-319-06106-1 (eBook)
DOI 10.1007/978-3-319-06106-1
Springer Cham Heidelberg New York Dordrecht London

Library of Congress Control Number: 2014936841

To
Kevin and Maura and the four princesses
(Eve, Grace, Jane and Tara)

Preface

Overview

The objective of this book is to provide an introduction to the software quality field to students and practitioners, and it is based on the author's experience in software quality and software process improvement at leading industrial companies. The principles of software quality management and software process improvement are discussed.

The goal is to cover both theory and practice, and to give the reader a grasp of the fundamentals of the software quality field, as well as guidance on how to apply the theory in an industrial environment.

Organization and Features

The first chapter provides an introduction to the fundamentals of the quality management field, and provides historical background on several pioneers such as Deming, Juran, and Crosby.

Chapter 2 provides a broad overview of software engineering and discusses various software lifecycles and the phases in software development. It includes a discussion on requirements elicitation, software design, implementation, testing, and maintenance.

Chapter 3 provides an introduction to project management and discusses project estimation, project planning and scheduling, project monitoring and control, risk management, and managing project quality.

Chapter 4 discusses requirements and design and is concerned with requirements engineering and management, architectural design, and design and development.

Chapter 5 discusses configuration management and discusses the fundamental concept of a baseline. Configuration management is concerned with identifying those deliverables that must be subject to change control, and controlling changes to them.

Chapter 6 discusses software inspections which play a key role in building quality into a product. The well-known Fagan inspection process which was developed at IBM in the 1970s is discussed, as well as lighter review and walk-through methodologies.

Chapter 7 is concerned with software testing and discusses the various types of testing that may be carried out. It includes a discussion on test planning, test case definition, test tracking, test metrics, test reporting, and testing in an e-commerce environment.

Chapter 8 is concerned with the selection and management of a software supplier. It discusses how candidate suppliers may be formally evaluated, and how the selected supplier may be managed during the project.

Chapter 9 nine discusses software quality assurance and the importance of process quality. It is a premise in the quality field that conformance to the defined process is essential in the delivery of high-quality product, and this chapter discusses audits, and describes how they are carried out.

Chapter 10 is concerned with metrics and problem solving, and this includes a discussion of the balanced score card which assists in identifying appropriate metrics for the organization. The Goal, Question, Metrics (GQM) approach is discussed, and this is useful in defining metrics that are related to the organization goals. This chapter includes a collection of sample metrics for an organization. Problem solving tools such as fishbone diagrams, pareto charts, and trend charts are also discussed.

Chapter 11 discusses the ISO 9000 standard, which is an important standard for product and service delivery. This family of standards includes ISO 9001 and ISO 9004. The main features of the standard are discussed as well as guidance on its implementation.

Chapter 12 discusses software process improvement. It begins with a discussion of a software process, and discusses the benefits that may be gained from a software process improvement initiative. Various models that support software process improvement are discussed, and these include the CMMI, ISO 9000, PSP, and TSP.

Chapter 13 gives an overview of the CMMI model and discusses its five maturity levels and their constituent process areas. It includes a discussion of both the staged and continuous representations.

Chapter 14 describes the activities and teams required to set up a CMMI improvement initiative for an organization. These include the CMMI Steering Group, the SEPG team, and process specific teams.

Chapter 15 discusses the SCAMPI appraisal methodology. This includes the formal SCAMPI Class A appraisal often employed by large organizations to obtain a CMMI rating that allows them to benchmark themselves against other organizations, and SCAMPI Class B and C appraisals that are less expensive and time consuming but may not be used for benchmarking.

Chapter 16 discusses various tools to support the organizations in the various software engineering activities. The focus is first to define the process, and then to find tools to support the process. Tools to support project management are discussed as well as tools to support requirements engineering, configuration management, design and development activities, and software testing.

Chapter 17 discusses formal methods, which consist of a set of mathematical techniques to specify and derive a program from its specification. Formal methods may be employed to rigorously state the requirements of the proposed system; they may be employed to derive a program from its mathematical specification; and they provide a rigorous proof that the implemented program satisfies its specification. They have been mainly applied to the safety critical field.

Chapter 18 presents the Z specification language, which is one of the most widely used formal methods. It was developed at Oxford University in the UK.

Chapter 19 presents the unified modelling language (UML) which is used to present several views of the system architecture. Chapter 20 is the concluding chapter in which we summarize the journey that we have travelled in this book.

Audience

The main audience of this book are computer science students who are interested in learning about software quality, and in learning on how to build high-quality and reliable software on time and on budget. It will also be of interest to industrialists including software engineers, quality professionals, and software managers as well as the motivated general reader.

Mallow, Cork, Ireland   Gerard O'Regan

Acknowledgments

I am deeply indebted to family and friends who supported my efforts in this endeavour.

Contents

List of Figures

List of Tables

Introduction

1

Key Topics

Software Engineering
Shewhart
Deming
Juran
Crosby
Watts Humphries
Metrics
Problem Solving
Cost of Quality
Process Improvement
Customer Satisfaction

1.1 Introduction

The mission of a software company is to develop high-quality innovative products and services at a competitive price to its customers, and to do so ahead of its competitors. This requires a clear vision of the business, a culture of innovation, an emphasis on quality, detailed knowledge of the business domain, and a sound product development strategy.

It also requires a focus on customer satisfaction and software quality to ensure that the desired quality is built into the software product, and that customers remain loyal to the company. Customers today have very high expectations on quality, and expect high-quality software products to be consistently delivered on time. The focus on quality requires that the organization define a sound software development infrastructure to enable quality software to be consistently produced.

G. O'Regan, *Introduction to Software Quality*, Undergraduate Topics
in Computer Science, DOI 10.1007/978-3-319-06106-1_1,
© Springer International Publishing Switzerland 2014

This book describes approaches used in current software engineering to build quality into software. This involves project planning and tracking, software lifecycles, software inspections and testing, configuration management, software quality assurance, etc. The capability maturity model integrated (CMMI) is discussed in detail and the CMMI provides a framework that assists organizations in software process improvement. It allows them to assess the current capability or maturity of selected software processes and to prioritize improvements.

The assessment (or *SCAMPI appraisal*) of an organization against the CMMI reveals strengths and weaknesses of the management and engineering processes in the organization. The output from the appraisal is used to formulate an improvement plan, which is then tracked to completion. The execution of the plan may take 1 or more years of effort.

Quality improvement also requires that the organization be actively aware of industrial best practice, as well as emerging technologies from various research programs. Piloting or technology transfer of innovative technology is a key part of continuous improvement.

The history of quality and some of the key people who have contributed to the quality movement are discussed later in the chapter. This includes well-known quality gurus such as Shewhart, Deming, Juran, and Crosby, and these grandfathers of quality played an important role in promoting quality in business. Watts Humphrey is considered the father of software quality, and his important contributions to software process improvement are discussed.

1.1.1   The Software Engineering Challenge

The challenge in software engineering is to deliver high-quality software on time to customers. The Standish Group research [64] (Fig. 1.1) on project cost overruns in the US during 1998 indicate that 33 % of projects are between 21 and 50 % over estimate, 18 % are between 51 and 100 % over estimate, and 11 % of projects are between 101 and 200 % overestimate.[1]

Project management and estimating project cost, effort and schedule accurately are software engineering challenges. Consequently, organizations need to determine how good their estimation process actually and to improve it. The actual project effort versus estimated project estimate and the actual project schedule versus projected project schedule are determined.

Risk management is a key part of project management, and the objective is to identify potential risks early in the project, to determine the probability of their occurrence and their impact should they occur. The management of a risk involves actions to eliminate or reduce the probability of its occurrence or its impact should

---

[1] The study was from the mid/late 1990s and recent reports from the Standish Group show good improvement trends.

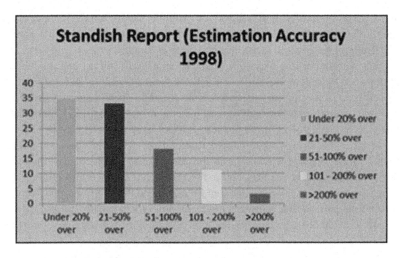

Fig. 1.1 Standish research – Project cost estimation accuracy in 1998

it occur, or to have a contingency plan should the risk materialize. Risks need to be managed throughout the project lifecycle.

Projects sometimes fail and there are many examples of project being abandoned prior to completion. For example, the Taurus project at the London stock exchange is a well-known disaster, and the original budget was £6 million. The project was eventually abandoned, and at that stage it was 11 years late, i.e., 13,200 % late and had cost the city of London hundreds of millions [40].

It is essential that requirements are properly managed as changing requirement (or the introduction of new requirements late in the software development lifecycle) may have a negative effect on the project. It may be necessary to accept the late requirement change if it is demanded by a customer, but there may be risks to the project schedule and quality. However, a good requirements process will ensure that changes to the requirements are minimized and controlled, and the requirements process may include prototyping or joint user reviews to ensure that they match the needs of the customer.

The implementation of the requirements involves design, development and testing activities. It may also involve the production of user manuals and training materials as well as the technical documentation. Changes to requirements may occur, and any change requests must be approved and communicated to the project team. Quality must be built into the software and testing activities are carried out to verify the correctness of the software, and that it correctly implements the requirements. The project manager is responsible for delivering the project on time, and recovering the schedule when the project falls behind schedule.

The challenges in software engineering are also faced in many other disciplines. Bridges have been constructed by engineers for several millennia and bridge building is a mature engineering activity. However, civil engineering projects occasionally fall behind schedule or suffer design flaws; for example, the infamous Tacoma Narrows bridge (or Galloping Gertie as it was known) collapsed in 1940 due to a design flaw.

The Tacoma Narrows Bridge was known for its tendency to sway in windstorms. The shape of the bridge was like that of an aircraft wing, and under windy conditions it would generate sufficient lift to become Unstable. A large windstorm in November, 1940 caused catastrophic failure. The significance of the Tacoma Bridge is its collapse and the subsequent investigation by engineers. They realized that aero-dynamical forces in suspension bridges were not sufficiently understood in the design of the bridge, and that new research was needed. It was recommended that wind tunnel tests be used to aid in the design of the replacement bridge.

Software engineering is a less mature field than civil engineering, and it is only in more recent times that investigations and recommendations from software projects have become part of the software development process. The study of software engineering has led to new theories and understanding of software development.

1.2   History of Software Failures

There are many examples of software failures in the literature. These include the year 2000 (or Y2K) problem which was a design flaw in the representation of the date with two digits; the Intel microprocessor bug which referred to a floating point problem on its microprocessor back in 1994; the Ariane 5 disaster refers to an operand error due to the conversion of a 64 bit floating point number to a 16 bit signed integer number. Software failures may cause major problems and adversely affect the customer's business. It may lead to credibility issues, and damage to the customer relationship.

The Y2K bug is historical and part of computer science folklore. The event on January 1, 2000 had minimal impact on the world economy. However, organizations spent large sums of money in identify all code with a year 2000 impact, changing the representation of the date from 2 digits to 4 digits, and verifying the correctness of the changes made. The worldwide cost of this was in billions of dollars.

The Intel response to a famous microprocessor mathematical bug back in 1994 inflicted (temporary) damage on the company and its reputation. Intel was slow to acknowledge the floating point problem, and to provide adequate information on the problems. This damaged its reputation and there was a financial cost involved in replacing microprocessors.

The Ariane 5 failure caused major embarrassment and damage to the credibility of the European Space Agency (ESA). The maiden flight of the Ariane 5 launcher ended in failure on June 4, 1996, after a flight time of 40 s. The first 37 s of flight proceeded normal. The launcher then veered off its flight path, broke up, and exploded. An independent inquiry board investigated the cause of the failure, and the report and recommendations to prevent a future failure are described in [38].

The inquiry noted that the failure of the inertial reference system was followed immediately by a failure of the backup inertial reference system. The problem was traced to a software failure due to an operand error involving the conversion of a

64 bit floating point number to a 16 bit signed integer value number. The floating point number was too large to be represented in the 16 bit number and this resulted in an operand error.

The inertial reference system and the backup reference system reported failure due to the software exception. The operand error occurred owing to an exceptionally high value related to the horizontal velocity, and this was due to the fact that the early part of the trajectory of the Ariane 5 differed from the earlier Ariane 4, and required a higher horizontal velocity. The inquiry board made a series of recommendations to prevent a reoccurrence of similar problems.

These failures indicate that software quality needs to be a key driving force in any organization. The effect of software failure may result in huge costs to correct the software (e.g., Y2K), negative perception of a company (e.g., Intel microprocessor problem), or the loss of a valuable communications satellite (e.g., Ariane 5).

1.3   Background to Software Quality

Customers today have very high quality and reliability expectations, and expect companies to adhere to very high standards. There are many quality software products in the marketplace; however, the task of producing high-quality software products consistently on time is non-trivial. Even the most respect organizations occasionally deliver software that contains defects, or ship products late due to quality problems. Defects may cause minor irritation to a customer, loss of credibility, or in a worst case scenario they may lead to injury or loss of life.

The late delivery of a product leads to extra costs, and it may adversely affect the customer's revenue, profitability, and business planning. Consequently, it is essential to have a robust process to consistently develop high-quality software on time and within budget. The influential papers by Fred Brooks in [10, 11] suggests that there is no silver bullet to do this, and instead, the focus needs to be on incremental improvement to processes and tools.

1.3.1   What Is Software Quality?

There are various definitions of quality such as the narrow definition proposed by Philip Crosby where quality is defined as "*conformance to the requirements*". This definition does not take the intrinsic difference in quality of products into account in judging the quality of the product. For example, this definition might suggest that a *Mercedes* car is of the same quality as a *Lada* car. Further, the definition does not consider whether the requirements are actually appropriate for the product. Juran defines quality as "*fitness for use*" and this is a better definition, although it does not provide a mechanism to judge better quality when two products are equally fit to be used. The ISO 9126 standard for information technology [31] is a framework for the evaluation of software product quality. It defines six product quality characteristics

Table 1.1 ISO 9126-Quality characteristics

Characteristic	Description
Functionality	This indicates the extent to which the required functionality is available in the software.
Reliability	This indicates the extent to which the software is reliable.
Usability	This indicates the extent to which the users of the software judge it to be easy to use.
Efficiency	This characteristic indicates the efficiency of the software
Maintainability	This indicates the extent to which the software product is easy to modify and maintain.
Portability	This indicates the ease of transferring the software to a different environment.

(Table 1.1) which indicate the extent to which a software product may be judged to be of a high quality.

The extent to which the software product exhibits these quality characteristics will determine whether it will be rated as a high-quality product by customers.

1.3.2 Early Quality Management

In the middle ages a craftsman was responsible for the complete development of a product from conception to delivery to the customer. This led to a strong sense of pride in the quality of the product, and apprentices joined craftsmen to learn the skills of the trade to become successful craftsmen themselves.

The industrial revolution led to a change to this traditional paradigm, and labour became highly organized with workers responsible for a particular part of the manufacturing process. The sense of ownership and the pride of workmanship in the product were diluted, as workers were now responsible only for their portion of the product, and not the product as a whole.

This led to a requirement for more stringent management practices, including planning, organizing, implementation, and control. It inevitably led to a hierarchy of labour with various functions identified, and a reporting structure for the various functions. Supervisor controls were needed to ensure quality and productivity issues were addressed.

1.3.3 Total Quality Management

Total quality management (TQM) is a modern approach to quality management, and this management philosophy involves customer focus, process improvement, developing a culture of quality within the organization and developing a measurement and analysis program. It emphasizes that customers have rights and quality expectations which should be satisfied, and that everyone in the organization is both a customer and has customers.

It is a *holistic approach* and requires that all functions, in the organization follow high standards. Quality needs to be built into the product by ensuring that quality is addressed at every step in the process.

It involves defining *internal* and *external customers*, recognizing that internal and external customers have rights and expectations, identifying the requirements that they have, and meeting these first time and every time. It requires total commitment from the top management, training all staff in quality management, and ensuring that all staff participates in quality improvement. It requires that a commitment to quality be instilled in all staff, and that the focus within the organization change from *fire fighting* to *fire prevention*. Fire prevention involves problem solving to address root causes of problems, and taking corrective action to prevent re-occurrence.

1.3.4   Software Quality Control

Software quality control is concerned with activities to ensure that the end product satisfies the functional and non-functional requirements and is fit for purpose. It includes inspections and testing to verify that the deliverables produced satisfy their requirements. Inspections typically consist of a formal review of a deliverable by independent experts, and the objective is to identify defects within the work product, and to provide confidence in its correctness. Software inspections are discussed in a later chapter.

Inspections in a manufacturing environment are quite different in that they take place at the end of the production cycle, and do not offer a mechanism to build quality into the product. Instead, the defective products are removed from the batch and reworked. There is a growing trend towards quality sampling at the early phases of a manufacturing process to minimize reworking of defective products.

Software testing consists of *"white box"* or *"black box"* testing techniques, and the testing activities include *unit, system, performance*, and *acceptance testing*. The testing is quite methodical, and includes a comprehensive set of manual or automated test cases. The *verification* and *validation* activities involve the execution of the defined tests, and the correction of any failed or blocked tests. It may not always be possible to do sufficient real world testing, and in some cases only limited simulation testing may be possible. In these cases, the simulated environment will need to resemble the real time environment closely to ensure the validity of the testing.

The cost of correction of a defect is directly related to the phase in which it is detected in the lifecycle. Errors detected in phase are the least expensive to correct, and defects detected out of phase become increasingly expensive to correct. The most expensive defect is that detected by the customer, as its correction may require changes to the requirements, design and code. Testing will be required as well as a fix release for the customer. There is further overhead in project management, configuration management, and in communication with the customer.

It is therefore highly desirable to capture defects as early as possible in the software lifecycle, in order to minimize the effort required to re-work the defect.

Modern software engineering places emphasis on defect prevention and in learning lessons from the actual defects. This approach is adopted from manufacturing environments, and consists of formal causal analysis meetings to brainstorm and identify root causes of problems, and the corrective actions necessary to prevent reoccurrence. The actions are then implemented and tracked to completion.

1.4 History of Quality

This section considers the ideas of several pioneers who have influenced the quality field. These include Walter Shewhart, W. Edwards Deming, Joseph Juran, and Philip Crosby. We also discuss the influence of Watts Humphrey who is considered the father of software quality.

1.4.1 Shewhart

Walter Shewhart was a statistician at AT&T Bell Laboratories (or Western Electric Co. as it was known in the 1920s). He is regarded as the founder of statistical process control (SPC), which remains important today in monitoring and controlling a process (Fig. 1.2). He developed a control chart which is a tool that can be used to control the process, with upper and lower limits for process performance specified. The process is under control if it is performing within these limits.

Shewhart's ideas were later applied to the Capability Maturity Model (CMM) in the late 1980s as a way to control key software processes, and statistical process control plays an important role in process improvement. Deming and Juran worked with Shewhart at Bell Labs in the 1920s.

The Shewhart model is a systematic approach to problem solving and process control. It consists of four steps which are used for continuous process improvement, and these are plan, do, check, act, and it is known as the *"PDCA Model"* or Shewhart's model (Fig. 1.3 and Table 1.2).

Shewhart argued that quality and productivity improve as process variability is reduced. His influential book, *The Economic control of quality of manufactured product* [58], was published in 1931, and outlines the methods of statistical process control to reduce process variability. The book prophesized that productivity would improve as process variability was reduced, and this was verified by Japanese engineers in the 1950s.

This lead to a paradigm shift in quality at Japanese companies, and it led to productivity improvements, increased market share, and led to Japanese companies gaining global market share. Today, companies around the world recognize the importance of placing quality at the heart of the organization.

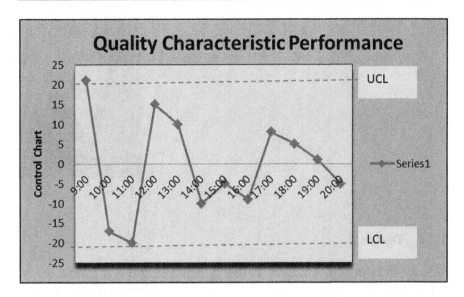

Fig. 1.2 Shewhart's control chart

Fig. 1.3 Shewhart's PDCA
cycle

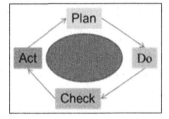

Table 1.2 Shewhart cycle

Step	Description
Plan	This step identifies an improvement opportunity and outlines the problem or process that will be addressed.
	Select the problem to be addressed.
	Describe current process.
	Identify the possible causes of the problem.
	Find the root cause of problems.
	Develop an action plan to correct the root cause.
Do	This step involves carrying out the improvements and it may involve a pilot of the proposed changes to the process.
Check	This step involves checking the results obtained against the expected results to determine their effectiveness.
Act	This step includes the analysis of the results to adjust process performance to achieve the desired results.

Fig. 1.4 W.E. Deming

1.4.2 Deming

W. Edwards Deming (Fig. 1.4) was a major figure in the quality movement. He was influenced by Shewhart's work on statistical process control, and Deming's ideas on quality were adopted in post second world war Japan, and played an important role in transforming Japan industry.

Deming argued that it is not sufficient for everyone in the organization to be doing one's best: instead, what is required is that there be a consistent purpose and direction in the organization. That is, it is first necessary that people know what to do, and there must be a *constancy of purpose* from all individuals to ensure success.

He argued that there is a very strong case for improving quality, as costs will decrease due to less rework of defective products, and productivity will increase as less time is spent in reworking. This will enable the company to increase its market share, with better quality and lower prices, and to stay in business. Conversely, companies which fail to address quality issues will lose market share, and go out of business. Deming was highly critical of the then American approach to quality, and the lack of vision of American management in quality management.

Deming's influential book *Out of the Crisis* [15] proposed 14 principles to transform the western style of management of an organization to a quality and customer focused organization. The implementation of his approach helps an organization to produce high-quality products. It includes:

- Constancy of purpose
- Quality built into the product
- Continuous improvement culture

Statistical process control is employed to minimize variability in process performance, as variability in the process affects product quality. SPC involves the analysis of control charts so that the cause of variability can be identified and eliminated. Deming's ideas are described in more detail in Table 1.3.

Deming argued that there are several diseases that afflict companies in the western world that prevent them for achieving high quality results. The *"five deadly diseases"* noted by Deming include (Table 1.4).

Table 1.3 Deming-14 step programme

Step	Description
Constancy of purpose	Companies face short-term and long-term problems. The problems of tomorrow require long-term planning on new products, training, and innovation. This requires resources invested in research and development and continuous improvement of existing products and services.
Adopt new philosophy	Deming outlined the *five deadly diseases* which afflicted US companies. These included lack of purpose and an excessive interest in short-term profits.
Build quality in	Deming argued that performing mass inspections is equivalent to planning for defects as they are too late to improve quality. Consequently, it is necessary to improve the production process to *build the quality into* the product.
Price and quality	Deming argued against the practice of awarding business on the basis of price alone, as the price of a product or service is meaningless unless there is an objective measure of the quality of the product or service being purchased.
Continuous improvement	There must be *continuous improvement in all areas*, including understanding customer requirements, design, manufacturing and test methods.
Institute training	The organization must be a learning organization and this involves setting up a training program to educate management and staff about the company, customer needs, and pride of workmanship in the products. Supervisors and managers need training on the 14 point program to ensure they fully understand the enhanced contribution that their staff can make if barriers to good work are removed.
Institute leadership	Deming argues that *management is about leadership and not supervision.* Management should work to remove barriers, know the work domain in depth, and seek innovative solutions to resolve quality and other relevant issues.
Eliminate fear	The presence of fear is a barrier to an open discussion of problems and the identification of solutions or changes to prevent problems from arising.
Eliminate barriers	The objective here is to break down barriers between different departments and groups. It is not enough for each group to optimize its own area: instead, what is required is for the organization to be working as one team.
Eliminate slogans	Deming argued that slogans do not help anyone to do a better job. Slogans may potentially alienate staff or encourage cynicism. Deming criticized slogans such as *"Zero Defects"* or *"Do it right the first time"* as inappropriate, as how can it be made right first time if the production machine is defective. Most problems are due to the system rather than the person. A slogan is absolutely inappropriate unless there is a clearly defined strategy to attain it, as otherwise the result is the opposite effect to that intended.
Eliminate numerical quotas	Deming argued that quotas act as an impediment to improvement in quality, as quotas are normally based on what may be achieved by the average worker. People below the average cannot make the rate and the result is dissatisfaction and turnover. Thus, there is a fundamental conflict between quotas and pride of workmanship.
Pride of work	The intention here is to remove barriers that rob people of pride of workmanship (e.g., machines out of order).

(continued)

Table 1.3 (continued)

Step	Description
Self improvement	This involves encouraging education and self-improvement for everyone in the company.
Take action	This requires that management agree on direction using the 14 principles, communicate the reasons for changes to the staff, and train the staff on the 14 principles.

Table 1.4 Deming – Five deadly diseases

Disease	Description
Lack of constancy of purpose	Management is too focused on short term thinking rather than long-term improvements.
Emphasis on short term profit	A company should aim to become the world's most efficient provider of product/service. Profits will then follow.
Evaluation of performance	Deming is against annual performance appraisal and rating
Mobility of management	Mobility of management frequently has a negative impact on quality.
Excessive measurement	Excessive management by measurement.

Comment (Deming): *Deming's program has been quite influential and has many sound points. His views on slogans in the workplace are in direct opposition to the use of slogans like Crosby's "Zero defects". The key point for Deming is that a slogan has no value unless there is a clear method to attain the particular goal described by the slogan.*

1.4.3 Juran

Joseph Juran (Fig. 1.5) was a major figure in the quality movement, and he argued for a top down approach to quality. He defined quality as *"fitness for use"*, and he argued that quality issues are the direct responsibility of management. Management must ensure that quality is planned, controlled, and improved.

The trilogy of *quality planning, control,* and *improvement* is known as the *"Juran Trilogy"*, and is usually described by a diagram with time on the horizontal axis and the cost of poor quality on the vertical axis (Fig. 1.6).

Quality planning consists of setting quality goals, developing plans, and identifying resources to meet the goals. Quality control consists of evaluating performance, setting new goals, and taking action. Quality improvement consists of improving delivery, eliminating wastage and improving customer satisfaction. Juran's 10 step programme is defined in [33], and a summary is in Table 1.5.

Juran defined an approach to achieve a new quality performance level that is termed *"Breakthrough and Control"*, It is described pictorially by a control chart

Fig. 1.5 Joseph Juran

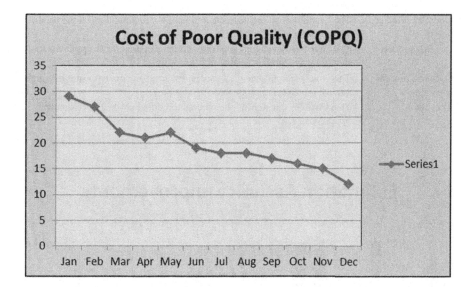

Fig. 1.6 Cost of poor quality – % of sales

showing the old performance level with occasional spikes or random events; what is needed is a breakthrough to a new and more consistent quality performance, i.e., a new performance level with performance achieved at that level.

The example in Fig. 1.7 presents the breakthrough in developing a more accurate estimation process. Initially the variation in estimation accuracy is quite large, but as an improved estimation process is put in place, the control limits are narrowed and more consistent estimation accuracy is achieved.

The breakthrough is achieved by a sustained and coordinated effort, and the old performance standard becomes obsolete. The difference between the old and the

Table 1.5 Juran's ten step programme

Step	Description
Identify customers	This includes the internal and external customers of an organization, e.g., the testing group is an internal customer and the end user of the software is the external customer.
Determine customer needs	Customer needs are generally expressed in the language of the customer's organization. There is a need to elicit and determine the actual desired requirements with further communication with the customer.
Translate	This involves translating the customer needs into the language of the supplier.
Units of measurement	This involves defining the measurement units to be used
Measurement programme	This involves setting up a measurement program in the organization, and includes internal and external measurements of quality and process performance.
Develop product	This step determines the product features to meet the needs of the customer.
Optimize product design	The intention is to optimize the design of the product to meet the needs of the customer and supplier.
Develop process	This involves developing processes which can produce the products to satisfy the customer's needs.
Optimize process capability	This involves optimizing the capability of the process to ensure that high quality products are produced.
Transfer	This involves transferring the process to normal product development operations.

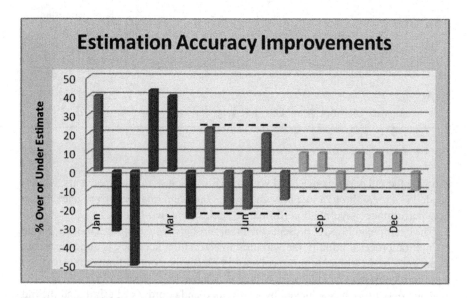

Fig. 1.7 Estimation accuracy – Breakthrough and control

Table 1.6 Juran's breakthrough and control

Step	Description
Breakthrough in attitude	This involves developing a favourable attitude to quality improvement.
Pareto	This involves identifying the key areas affecting quality
Organization	This involves analysing the problem and coordinating a solution.
Control	This is concerned with achieving performance at the new level.
Repeat	This leads to continuous improvement with new performance levels set and breakthroughs made to achieve the new performance levels.

new performance level is known as the *"chronic disease"* which must be diagnosed and cured. His approach to breakthrough and control is (Table 1.6).

1.4.4 Crosby

Philip Crosby was a key figure in the quality movement, and his quality improvement grid influenced the Capability Maturity Model (CMM) developed by the Software Engineering Institute. His influential book *Quality is Free* [14] outlines his philosophy of *doing things right the first time*, i.e., the *zero defects* (ZD) program. Quality is defined as *"conformance to the requirements"* and he argues that people have been conditioned to believe that error is inevitable.

Crosby argued that people in their personal lives do not accept this: for example, it would not be acceptable for nurses to drop a certain percentage of newly born babies. He further argues that the term *"Acceptable Quality Level"* (AQL) is a commitment to produce imperfect material. Crosby notes that defects are due to two main reasons: *lack of knowledge* or a *lack of attention of the individual*.

He argued that lack of knowledge can be measured and addressed by training, but that lack of attention is a mind-set that requires a change of attitude by the individual. The net effect of a successful implementation of a zero defects program is higher productivity due to less reworking of defective products. Thus, *quality*, in effect, *is free*.

Crosby's approach to achieve the desired quality level of zero defects was to put a quality improvement program in place. He outlined a 14 step quality improvement program (Table 1.7). It requires management commitment to be successful, and an organization-wide quality improvement team needs to be set up. A measurement program is put in place to determine the status and cost of quality within the organization. The cost of quality is then shared with the staff and corrective actions are identified and implemented. The zero defect program is communicated to the staff, and 1 day every year is made a *zero defects day*, and is used to emphasize the importance of zero defects to the organization.

Crosby's Quality Management Maturity Grid (Table 1.8) measures the maturity of the current quality system with respect to several quality management categories, and highlights areas which require improvement. Six categories of quality management

Table 1.7 Crosby's 14 step programme

Step	Description
Management commitment	Management commitment and participation is essential for the success of the quality improvement program. The profile of quality is raised within the organization
Quality improvement team	This involves the formation of an organization-wide cross-functional team consisting of representatives from each of the departments.
Quality measurement	The objective of quality measurements is to determine the status of quality in each area of the company and to identify areas where improvements are required
Cost of quality evaluation	The cost of quality is an indication of the financial cost of quality to the organization. The cost is initially high, but as the quality improvement becomes effective there is a reduction in the cost of quality.
Quality awareness	This involves sharing the cost of poor quality with staff, and motivating staff to identify corrective actions to address quality issues.
Corrective action	This involves resolving any problems which have been identified, and bringing any problems which cannot be resolved to the attention of management.
Zero defect program	The next step is to communicate the meaning of zero defects to the employees The key point is that it is not a motivation program: instead, it means doing things right the first time, i.e., zero defects.
Supervisor training	This requires that all supervisors and managers receive training on the 14 step quality improvement program
Zero defects day	This involves setting aside 1 day each year to high-light zero defects, and its importance to the company.
Goal setting	This phase involves getting people to think in terms of goals and achieving the goals
Error cause removal	This phase identifies any roadblocks or problems which prevent employees from performing error-free work.
	The list is produced from the list of problems or road-blocks for each employee.
Recognition	This involves recognizing employees who make out-standing contributions to quality improvement.
Quality councils	This involves bringing quality professionals together on a regular basis to share ideas on action.
Do it over again	The principle of continuous improvement is a key part of the programme. Improvement is continuous.

are considered: *management understanding and attitude towards quality, quality organization status, problem handling, the cost of quality, quality improvement actions and summation of company quality posture.*

Each category is rated on a 1–5 maturity scale and this indicates the maturity of the particular category. Crosby's maturity grid has been adapted and applied to the CMM. The five levels are given in Table 1.8.

Comment (Crosby): *Crosby's program has been quite influential and his maturity grid has been applied to the software CMM. The ZD part of the program is difficult to*

Table 1.8 Crosby's maturity grid

Level	Name	Description
1.	Uncertainty:	Management has no understanding of quality, and is likely to blame quality problems on the quality department. Fire fighting is prevalent and problems are fought as they occur. Root causes of problems are not investigated, and there are few organized quality improvement activities.
2.	Awakening:	Management is beginning to recognize that quality management may be of value, but is unwilling to devote time and money to it. Instead, the emphasis is on appraisal rather than prevention. Teams are set up to address major problems, but long-term solutions are rarely sought.
3.	Enlightenment:	Management is learning more about quality, and is becoming more supportive of quality improvement. The quality department reports to senior management, and implementation of the 14 step quality improvement program is underway. There is a culture of openness where problems are faced openly and resolved in an orderly way.
4.	Wisdom:	Management is fully participating in the program, and fully understands the importance of quality management. All functions within the organization are open to suggestions for improvement, and problems are identified earlier. Defect prevention is now part of the culture.
5.	Certainty:	The whole organization is involved in continuous improvement

apply to the complex world of software development, where the complexities of the systems to be developed are often the cause of defects rather than the mind-set of software professionals (who are generally dedicated to quality). Slogans may be dangerous and potentially unsuitable to some cultures and a zero defects day may potentially have the effect of de-motivating staff.

1.4.5 Watts Humphrey

Watts Humphrey was an American software engineer and vice president of technical development at IBM. He made important contributions to the software engineering field, and is considered the *father of software quality*. He dedicated much of his career to addressing the problems of software development including schedule delays, cost overruns, software quality and productivity (Fig. 1.8).

He was born in Michigan in 1927 and served in the US Navy and completed a bachelor's degree in physics at the University of Chicago in 1949. He obtained a Master's degree in physics from the Illinois Institute of Technology (IIT) and an MBA from the University of Chicago.

He took a position with Sylvania in Boston in the early 1950s, and he became manager of the circuit design group in the company. He recognized the importance of planning and management early in his career, and he later made important contributions to the management aspects of software development at IBM and the Software Engineering Institute (SEI). He joined IBM in 1959 initially as a hardware architect, but most of his IBM career was in management. He was eventually to become a vice president of technical development, where he oversaw 4,000

Fig. 1.8 Watts Humphrey
(Courtesy of Watts
Humphrey)

engineers in 15 development centres in over 7 countries. He was influenced by others at IBM including Fred Brooks who was project manager of the IBM 360 project; Michael Fagan who developed the Fagan Inspection Methodology; and Harlan Mills who developed the Cleanroom methodology. Humphries ran the software quality and process group at IBM towards the end of his IBM career, and became very interested in software quality.

He retired from IBM in 1986 and joined the newly formed SEI at Carnegie Mellon University. He made a commitment to change the software engineering world by developing sound management principles for the software industry. The SEI has largely fulfilled this commitment, and it has played an important role in enhancing the capability of software organizations throughout the world.

The SEI had a contract from the Department of Defence (DOD) to provide guidance to the military in the selection of capable software subcontractors. This evolved into the book "Managing the Software Process" [29] which describes technical and managerial topics essential for good software engineering. The book was influenced by the ideas of Deming and Juran in statistical process control.

Humphries established the software process programme at the SEI, and this led to the development of the software Capability Maturity Model (CMM) and its successors. Humphries asked questions such as:

– How good is the current software process?
– What must I do to improve it?
– Where do I start?

The CMM is a framework to help an organization to understand its current process maturity, and to prioritize improvements. The SEI introduced software process assessment and software capability evaluation methods, and these include CBA/IPI and CBA/SCE. The CMM model and the associated assessment methods were widely adopted by organizations around the world, and their successors are the CMMI Model and the SCAMPI appraisal methodology.

Humphries focused his later efforts to developing the Personal Software Process (PSP) and the Team Software Process (TSP). These are approaches that teach engineers the skills they need to make and track plans, and to produce high-quality software with zero defects. The PSP helps the individual engineer to collect relevant data for statistical process control, whereas the TSP focuses on teams, and the goal is to assist teams to understand and improve their current productivity and quality of their work.

He received many awards for his contributions to the computing field. He was named the first SEI fellow in 1995 in recognition of his outstanding contribution to the software quality field. He received the 2003 National Medal in Technology from President George Bush, and was named an ACM fellow in 2009 for his outstanding contributions to computing and information technology. He was the author of 12 books in the software engineering field. He died in 2010.

1.4.6 Miscellaneous Quality Gurus

There are several other important pioneers in the quality field including *Shingo* who developed his own version of zero defects termed *"Poka yoke"* (or *defects* $= 0$). This involves identifying potential error sources in the process, and monitoring these for errors. Causal analysis is performed on any errors found, and the root causes are eliminated. This approach leads to the elimination of all errors likely to occur, and thus only exceptional errors should occur. These exceptional errors and their causes are then eliminated. The failure mode and effects analysis (FMEA) methodology is a variant of this. Potential failures to the system or sub-system are identified and analysed, and the causes and effects and probability of failure documented.

Genichi Taguchi's definition of quality is quite different. Quality is defined as *"the loss a product causes to society after being shipped, other than losses caused by its intrinsic function"*. Taguchi defines a *loss function* as a measure of the cost of quality; $L(x) = c(x - T)^2 + k$. Taguchi also developed a method for determining the optimum value of process variables which will minimize the variation in a process while keeping a process mean on target.

Kaoru Ishikawa is well known for his work in *quality control circles* (QCC). A quality control circle is a small group of employees who do similar work, and meet regularly to identify and analyse work-related problems. This involves brainstorming, recommending and implementing solutions. The problem solving tools employed include *pareto analysis*, *fishbone diagrams*, *histograms*, *scatter diagrams*, and *control charts*. A facilitator will train the quality circle team leaders, and the activities in a quality circle include:

- Select problem
- State and re-state problem
- Collect facts
- Brain-storm
- Build on each other's ideas
- Choose course of action
- Presentation

Armand Feigenbaum is well known for this work in *total quality control* which concerns quality assurance applied to all functions in the organization. It is distinct from total quality management: total quality control is concerned with controlling quality throughout, whereas TQM embodies a philosophy of quality management and improvement involving all staff and functions throughout the organization.

1.5   Modern Software Quality Management

The cost of correction of a defect increases the later that it is detected in the life cycle. Consequently, it is desirable to detect an error as early as possible and preferably within the phase in which it was created. This involves setting up a software quality infrastructure to assist in error detection within the phase in which the defect is created or at worst to detect the defect shortly after it exits the particular phase. The development of high quality software requires a good software development process to be in place, and this includes best practices in software engineering for:

- Project management
- Estimation methodology
- Risk management process.
- Requirements Development and Management
- Design and Development
- Software development lifecycles
- Quality assurance/management
- Software inspections
- Software testing
- Supplier Selection and Management
- Configuration management
- Customer satisfaction process
- Continuous improvement

Mature software organizations are learning organizations and the goal is to learn from defects to prevent their re-occurrence. Software inspections play a key role in detecting defects in-phase, and they are discussed in the next section.

1.5.1   Software Inspections

The Fagan Inspection process was developed by Michael Fagan of IBM [20], and it aims to identify and remove errors in work products. There is a strong economic case for identifying defects as early as possible, as the cost of correction of a defect increases the later that it is discovered. The process mandates that requirement documents, design documents, source code, and test plans all be formally inspected by experts independent of the author of the deliverable.

There are various *roles* defined in the process including the *moderator* who chairs the inspection. The moderator ensures that all of the inspectors are trained and receive the appropriate materials for the inspection. S/he ensures that sufficient preparation is done, and that the speed of the inspection does not exceed the recommended guidelines. The *reader* reads or paraphrases the particular deliverable; the *author* is the creator of the deliverable and has a special interest in ensuring that it is correct. The *tester* role is concerned with the test viewpoint.

The inspection process will consider whether the design is correct with respect to the requirements, and whether the source code is correct with respect to the design. The errors identified are classified into various types and the data are generally recorded to enable analysis to be performed on the most common types of errors. The analysis will yield actions to be performed to minimize the re-occurrence of the most common defect types. Software inspections are described in more detail in Chap. 6.

1.5.2   Software Testing

Software testing plays a key role in verifying that the software is fit for purpose, and two key types of software testing are *black box* and *white box* testing. White box testing involves checking that every path in a module has been tested, and involves defining and executing test cases to ensure code and branch coverage. The goal of black box testing is to verify the functionality of a module or feature or the complete system itself. Testing is both a constructive activity in that it is verifying the correctness of functionality, and it may be a destructive activity in that the objective is to find defects in the implemented software. Testing verifies that the requirements are correctly implemented, and it yields the presence or absence of defects.

The test cases are reviewed by independent experts to ensure that they are sufficient to verify the correctness of the software. There are various types of testing including, unit, system, performance and usability testing. The effectiveness of the testing is influenced by the maturity of the test process employed. Testing is described in more detail in Chap. 7.

1.5.3   Software Quality Assurance

The IEEE definition of software quality assurance is "*the planned and systematic pattern of all actions necessary to provide adequate confidence that the software performs to established technical requirements*" [41]. The software quality assurance department provides visibility into the quality of the work products being built, and the processes being used to create them. The quality assurance group may be just one person operating part time or it may be a team of quality engineers. The activities of the quality assurance group typically include software testing activities to verify the correctness of the software, and also quality audits of the various groups involved in software development. This section discusses the role of an independent quality assurance group.

The quality group promotes quality in the organization and is independent of the development group. It provides an independent assessment of the quality of the product being built, and this viewpoint is independent of the project manager and development viewpoint. The quality assurance group acts as the voice of the customer, and aims to ensure that quality is considered at each step in the process.

The quality group will perform audits of various projects, groups and departments, and will determine the extent to which the process is followed and report any weaknesses in the processes and non-compliances identified. The quality group will usually have a reporting channel to senior management, and any non-compliance issues which are not addressed at the project level may be escalated to the next level of management for resolution. The key responsibilities of the quality assurance group are:

- Promotes quality in organization
- Customer Advocate
- Conducts audits to verify Compliance
- Reports audit results to management
- Provides visibility to Management on processes followed
- Facilitates software process improvement
- Release sign-offs

The quality audit provides visibility into the work products and processes used to develop the work products. The audit consists of an interview with the project team, and the auditor examines the processes followed and deliverables produced by each team member, considers any issues which have arisen during the work, and assesses if there are any quality risks associated with the project based on the information provided.

The *auditor* needs good written and verbal communication skills, and gathers information via open and closed questions. S/he will need to observe behaviour and body language and be able to deal effectively with any resistance. The auditor will consider the role that the participant is performing, and relate this to the defined process for their area. The entry and exit criteria to the defined processes are generally examined to verify that the criteria have been satisfied at the various milestones. The auditor writes a report detailing the findings from the audit and the recommended corrective actions with respect to any identified non-compliance to the defined procedures. S/he will perform follow-up activity at a later stage to verify that the corrective actions have been carried out. The audit activities include planning activities, the audit meeting, gathering data, reporting the findings and assigning actions, and following the actions through to closure. The audit process is described in more detail Chap. 9.

1.5.4   Problem Solving Techniques

There is a relationship between the quality of the process and the quality of the products built from the process. The defects identified during testing are very valuable in that they enable the organization to learn and improve from the defect. Defects are often caused by the incorrect execution of a process, or due to a defect in the process itself. Consequently, the lessons learned from a particular defect should be used to correct systemic defects in the process.

Problem-solving teams are formed to analyse various problems and to identify corrective actions. They agree on the problem to be solved, the collection and analysis of the facts, and determine the appropriate solution to solve the problem. There are various tools to assist problem solving and these include fishbone diagrams, histograms, trend charts, pareto diagrams, and bar charts. Problem solving is discussed in detail in Chap. 10.

1.5.4.1 Fishbone Diagrams

This well-known cause-and-effect diagram is in the shape of the backbone of a fish. The approach is to identify the possible causes of some particular quality effect. These may include people, materials, methods, and timing. Each of the main causes may then be broken down into sub-causes. The root cause is then identified, as often 80 % of problems are due to 20 % of causes (the 80:20 rule).

1.5.4.2 Histograms

A histogram is a way of representing data via a frequency distribution in bar chart format, and it is a graphical representation of the underlying distribution of the data. It illustrates the shape, variation, and centring of the underlying distribution. The data is divided into a number of buckets, where a bucket is a particular range of data values, and the relative frequency of each bucket is displayed in bar format. The shape of the process and its spread from the mean is evident from the histogram.

1.5.4.3 Pareto Chart

The objective of a pareto chart is to identify the key problems and to focus on these. Problems are classified into various types or categories, and the frequency of each category of problem is then determined. The chart is displayed in a descending sequence of frequency, with the most significant category detailed first, and the least significant category detailed last. The success in problem-solving activities over a period of time may be judged from the trends in the pareto chart, and if problem solving activities are successful, then the key problem categories in the old chart should show a noticeable improvement in the new pareto chart.

1.5.4.4 Trend Graph

A trend graph is a graph of a variable over time and is a study of observed data for trends or patterns over time.

1.5.4.5 Scatter Graphs

The scatter diagram is used to measure the relationship between variables, and to determine whether there is a correlation between the variables. The results may be a positive correlation, negative correlation or no correlation between the data. The scatter diagram provides a means to confirm a hypothesis that two variables are related, and provides a visual means to illustrate the potential relationship.

Table 1.9 Cost of quality categories

Type of cost	Description
Cost external	This includes the cost of external failure and includes engineering repair, warranties, and a customer support function
Cost internal	This includes the internal failure cost and includes the cost of reworking and re-testing of any defects found internally.
Cost prevention	This includes the cost of maintaining a quality system to prevent the occurrence of problems, and includes the cost of software quality assurance, the cost of training, etc.
Cost appraisal	This includes the cost of verifying the conformance of a product to the requirements and includes the cost of provision of software inspections and testing processes.

1.5.4.6 Failure Mode Effect Analysis

This involves identifying all of the possible failures of the system, and the impact of each failure. Each possible failure mode is documented, as well as the impact of failure, the cause of failure, the frequency of occurrence, its severity, the estimate of detection of the failure, the risk and corrective action to minimize the risk. FMEAs are usually applied at the design stage.

The problem solving techniques discussed here are tools for the teams to analyse and identify corrective actions. Problem-solving teams may be formed to solve a particular problem, and the team may be disbanded after successful resolution.

1.5.5 Cost of Quality

Crosby argued that the most meaningful measurement of quality is the cost of quality, and the emphasis on the improvement activities in the organization is therefore to reduce the *cost of poor quality* (COPQ). The cost of quality includes the cost of external and internal failure, the cost of providing an infrastructure to prevent the occurrence of problems, and the cost of the infrastructure to verify the correctness of the product. The cost of quality was divided into four subcategories (Table 1.9) by Feigenbaum in the 1950s, and evolved further by James Harrington of IBM.

The cost of quality graph (Fig. 1.9) will initially show high external and internal costs and very low prevention costs, and the total quality costs will be high. However, as an effective quality system is put in place and becomes fully operational there will be a noticeable decrease in the external and internal cost of quality, and a gradual increase in the cost of prevention and appraisal. The total cost of quality will substantially decrease, as the cost of provision of the quality system is substantially below the savings gained from lower cost of internal and external failure. The COPQ curve will indicate where the organization is in relation to the cost of poor quality, and the organization will need to derive a plan to achieve the desired results to minimize the cost of poor quality.

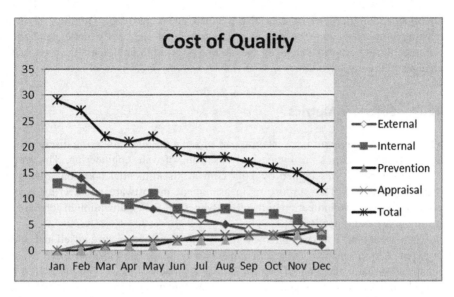

Fig. 1.9 Cost of quality

1.5.6   Software Process Improvement

Software process improvement initiatives support the organization in achieving its key business goals such as delivering software faster to the market, improving quality, reducing or eliminating waste. The objective is to work smarter and to build software better, faster, and cheaper than competitors. It makes business sense and provides a tangible return on investment.

An improvement program is a project in its own right and needs to be managed as such. Model based approaches to process improvement involve using models such as the CMM, CMMI, ISO 9000, PSP or TSP. A maturity model provides a set of best practices in software engineering, and an internal or external assessment of the organization against the model will yield the current strengths and weaknesses of the organization with respect to the model. The organization needs to prioritize the improvements which will give the greatest business gain.

The employees of the company are, in effect, the owners of the process infrastructure within the organization, as they work with the processes and procedures on a daily basis, and have an interest in having the best possible processes and templates for the organization. A good improvement program will empower employees to make suggestions for continuous improvement, and a reward and recognition mechanism helps to make process improvement part of the organization culture.

Improvement tends to be most successful when performed in small steps rather than trying to do too much initially. It is generally easier for an organization to adjust to a series of small changes rather than one big major change. Changes within an organization need to be carefully planned and controlled. Training for the existing employees may be required to ensure that they fully understand the rationale for the proposed changes and are in a position to implement the proposed changes in the organization.

1.5.7 Software Metrics

The use of measurement is an integral part of science and engineering disciplines, and software measures are increasingly used in software engineering. The term *"software metric"* was coined by Tom Gilb in his influential book on software measurement [23]. The purpose of measurement in software engineering is to provide an objective indication of the effectiveness of the organization in achieving its key goals and objectives.

There is, of course, no point in measuring for the sake of measuring itself and care is required to ensure that the measurements to be made are closely related to an organization particular goal. The well-known approach of *Goal, Question, Metric* (GQM) suggests that the organization first needs to identify the key goals which it is trying to achieve; then it identifies relevant questions which need to be answered to assess the extent to which the goal is being satisfied, and then to formulate a metric to give an objective answer to the particular question. This approach was formulated by Victor Basilli and others, and is described in [2].

The use of measurement is invaluable in determining whether an organization has actually improved, as actual quantitative data before and after the improvement initiative can be compared and used to determine the extent of the improvements. The initial measurements prior to the improvement program serve as the baseline measurement, and these indicate the current capability and results of the organization. A successful improvement programs will lead to improvements, and this will be reflected in the metrics. The implementation of metrics involves:

- Business goals
- Questions related to goals
- Metrics
- Data gathering
- Presentation of charts
- Trends
- Action plans

Software metrics are discussed in Chap. 10, and the chapter includes a collection of sample metrics for the various functional areas in the organization. The metrics are only as good as the underlying data, and data gathering is a key part of a metrics program.

1.5.8 Customer Satisfaction

The effectiveness of the quality management system in delivering high-quality software will ultimately be judged by the customer, and the level of customer

Fig. 1.10 Customer
satisfaction process

satisfaction will determine whether the customer will purchase again from the company, or recommend the company. Consumer research and customer satisfaction surveys are used to determine the level of customer satisfaction with the company.

A customer satisfaction survey involves the customer rating the organization in several key areas such as the quality of the software, its reliability, the timeliness of the project, and so on. The customer satisfaction process takes the form of a closed feedback loop, and the customer satisfaction feedback will be analysed and acted upon appropriately.

The customer satisfaction survey is conducted, and the feedback analysed and used to prepare the action plan. The actions are executed and the customer is surveyed again at later date (Fig. 1.10). The follow up activity may involve a telephone conversation with the customer or a visit to the customer to discuss the specific issues. The issues are shared with engineering groups as appropriate. The objective is to ensure that customers are totally satisfied with the product and service, and a loyal customer will re-purchase and recommend the company to other potential customers.

The customer satisfaction process is summarized as follows:
• Define customer surveys
• Send customer surveys
• Customer Satisfaction Ratings
• Customer meeting and key issues
• Action plans and follow-up
• Metrics for customer satisfaction

The definition of the questionnaire will vary depending on the nature of the business. It is essential that the questionnaire is usable, and covers the relevant questions to determine where the organization is weak (and in need of improvement), and also to identify areas where it is strong. The questions typically employ a rating scheme to allow the customer to give quantitative feedback on satisfaction, and the survey will also enable the customer to go into more detail on issues.

Table 1.10 Sample customer satisfaction questionnaire

No	/Question	Unacceptable	Poor	Fair	Satisfied	Excellent	N/A
1.	Quality of software	☐	☐	☐	☐	☐	☐
2.	Ability to meet agreed dates	☐	☐	☐	☐	☐	☐
3.	Timeliness of projects	☐	☐	☐	☐	☐	☐
4.	Effective testing of software	☐	☐	☐	☐	☐	☐
5.	Expertise of staff	☐	☐	☐	☐	☐	☐
6.	Value for money	☐	☐	☐	☐	☐	☐
7.	Quality of support	☐	☐	☐	☐	☐	☐
8.	Ease of installation	☐	☐	☐	☐	☐	☐
9.	Ease of use	☐	☐	☐	☐	☐	☐
10.	Timely problem resolution	☐	☐	☐	☐	☐	☐

Fig. 1.11 Customer satisfaction metrics

Software companies will be interested in the customer's perception of the quality of software, reliability, usability, timeliness of delivery, value for money, etc., and a sample survey form is included in Table 1.10. This includes ten questions and may be expanded as appropriate. A survey form will typically include open-ended questions to enable the customer to give feedback in more detail.

Customer satisfaction metrics provide visibility into the level of customer satisfaction with the software company, and enable trends to be determined. A sample customer satisfaction metric is provided in Fig. 1.11, and it provides a quantitative understanding of the level of customer satisfaction with the company.

1.5.9 Assessments (Appraisals)

The objective of an assessment (or *appraisal*) of an organization is to determine its maturity with respect to a maturity model such as the CMMI or SPICE, or against an international quality standard such as ISO 9000:2000.

The appraisal is performed by an external or internal assessment team, and yields the strengths and weaknesses of the organization with respect to the model. The appraisal report is used to plan and prioritize future improvements.

The appraisal is a major review of the organization and it needs to be carefully planned. The assessment team needs sufficient expertise and experience, and the appraisal may take 1–2 weeks. It involves interviews with the project managers and project teams as well as the review of relevant documentation. The assessment report will detail the extent to which the model is implemented, and any gaps and improvement opportunities are highlighted in the report.

The SCAMPI methodology is used for CMMI appraisals, and it is discussed in Chap. 15.

1.5.10 Total Quality Management

Total quality management (TQM) is a management philosophy to focus attention on quality and to develop a culture of quality within the organization. Quality is a company-wide objective, and the organization goal is total customer satisfaction. The organization aims to deliver products and services that totally satisfy the customer needs. It is a holistic approach and it applies to all levels and functions within the organization.

TQM employs many of the ideas of the pioneers in the quality movement. Management are required to take charge of the implementation of quality management, and all staff will need to be trained in quality improvement activities.

The implementation of TQM involves a focus on all areas within the organization, and in identifying areas for improvement. The problems in the particular area are evaluated and data is collected and analysed. An action plan is then derived and the actions implemented and monitored. This is then repeated for continuous improvement. The implementation is summarized as follows:

- Identify improvement area
- Problem evaluation
- Data collection
- Data analysis
- Action plan
- Implementation of actions
- Monitor effectiveness
- Repeat

There are four main parts of TQM (Table 1.11).

Table 1.11 Total quality management

Part	Description
Customer focus	This involves identifying internal and external customers and recognizing that all customers have expectations and rights which need to be satisfied first time and every time. Quality must be considered in every aspect of the business, and the focus is on fire prevention.
Process	This involves a focus on the process and improvement to the process via problem solving. The improvements will reduce waste and eliminate error.
Measurement and analysis	This involves setting up a measurement program within the organization to enable objective and effective analysis of the quality of the process and product
Human factors	This involves developing a culture of quality and customer satisfaction throughout the organization. The core values of quality and customer satisfaction need to be instilled in the organization. This requires training for the employees on quality, customer satisfaction, and continuous improvement.

The ISO 9000 standard (see Chap. 11) is a structured approach to the implementation of TQM. Its clauses are guidelines for what needs to be done, and include requirements to be satisfied for the organization to satisfy ISO 9000.

1.6 Miscellaneous

Software quality management is, in many ways, the application of common sense to software engineering. It makes sense to plan and track a project, identify potential risks early and attempt to eliminate or reduce their impact; determine the requirements, produce a design, review the design and development activities for correctness. It is sensible to test the software against the requirements, to record any problems identified, and to correct them. It is sensible to have objective criteria to determine if the software is ready to be released to the customer, and to learn any lessons from the project and to survey customers to obtain valuable feedback.

1.6.1 Organization Culture and Change

Every organization has a distinct culture and this reflects the way in which things are done in the company. Organization culture includes the ethos of the organization, its core values, its history, its success stories, its people, amusing incidents, and so on. The culture of the organization may be favourable or unfavourable to developing high-quality software.

Occasionally a change to the organization culture is required, and this may be difficult as it could involve changing its fundamental approach to software development, and there may be a resistance to this. Successful change management often involves the following:
- Kick-off meeting
- Motivate rationale for changes

- Present plan
- Training
- Implement changes
- Monitor implementation
- Institutionalize

The culture of an organization is often illustrated by the phrase: *"That's the way we do things around here"*. For example, the evolution from one level of the CMM to another often involves a change the way that things are done in the organization. The focus on prevention requires a change in mind-set to focus on *problem solving* and *fire prevention*, rather than on *fire fighting*.

1.6.2 Law of Negligence

The impact of a flaw in software may be catastrophic, and several software failures were discussed earlier in this chapter. Clearly, every organization must take all reasonable precautions to prevent the occurrence of defects, especially in the safety critical domain where defects may cause major damage or even loss of life. Reasonable precautions consist of having appropriate software engineering practices in place to allow the organization to consistently produce high quality software.

A quality management system indicates that the organization takes software quality seriously. The objective of the quality management system is to put a sound software development process in place that serves the needs of the organization and its customers. Modem quality assurance systems include processes for software inspections, testing, quality audits, customer satisfaction, software development, project planning, etc.

The organization will require evidence or records to prove that the quality management system is in place, that it is appropriate for the organization, and that it is fully operational within the organization. The proof that the quality system is actually operational typically takes the form of records of the various activities. The records also enable the organization to prepare a legal defence to show that it took all reasonable precautions in software development, especially if a customer decides to take legal action for negligence against the software provider following a serious problem in the software at the customer environment.

The presence of records may be used to indicate that all reasonable steps were taken, and the records typically include lists of all the deliverables in the project; minutes of project meetings; records of reviews of requirements, design, and software code, records of test plans and test results; and so on.

1.6.3 Quality and the WEB

The explosive growth of the World Wide Web and electronic commerce has made the quality of web sites a key concern. Web technology is rapidly becoming ubiquitous in society, and is quite distinct from other software systems in that:

- It may be accessed from anywhere in the world.
- It may be accessed by many different browsers.
- The usability and look and feel of the application is a key concern.
- The performance of the web site is a key concern.
- Security is a key concern.
- The web site must be capable of dealing with a large number of transactions at any time.
- The web site has very strict availability constraints (typically 24×365).
- The web site needs to be highly reliable.

It is inappropriate to employ the waterfall lifecycle for this domain, and usually a spiral lifecycle will be employed as the requirements are often incomplete at project initiation and evolve to the agreed set during the project. Often, Rapid Application Development (RAD) or Joint Application Development (JAD) lifecycle are employed.

1.7   Review Questions

1. Discuss the contributions of Deming and Juran.
2. Describe Crosby's maturity grid and discuss how it influenced the Capability Maturity Model?
3. Explain why Watts Humphrey is considered the father of software quality.
4. Explain the difference between software inspections and testing?
5. What is an assessment (appraisal) and explain how it forms part of the improvement cycle.
6. Explain the importance of the cost of poor quality.
7. Discuss the importance of software metrics in problem solving.
8. Explain the importance of customer satisfaction and describe how it may be measured.

1.8   Summary

This chapter provided a short introduction to the software quality field, and the discussion covered the contributions of various pioneers such as Shewhart, Deming, Juran and Crosby. The contributions of Watts Humphrey, who is considered the father of software quality, were also discussed.

We examined various definitions of quality such as Crosby's "conformance to the requirements" and Juran's "fitness for purpose", as well as considering the various dimensions of software product quality listed in ISO 9126.

We considered various software failures such as the Ariane 5 disaster, the year 2000 problem, and a maths bug in the Intel microprocessor in the mid-1990s. A software failure may lead to loss of life, a telecoms outage, the loss of a rocket and its satellite cargo, and the loss of credibility of the company. Consequently, there is a strong economic case to consistently develop high-quality software.

We discussed modern software quality management including software inspections that are used to build quality into the software; software testing to verify that the software is of high quality as well as finding defects in the software; software quality assurance to provide visibility into the processes and the extent to which they are followed; problem solving techniques to prevent problems from re-occurring; the cost of poor quality to the organization; software process improvement to improve the key processes in the organization; and customer satisfaction to determine the level of customer satisfaction with the organization.

Software Engineering

2

Key Topics

Standish Chaos Report
Software Lifecycles
Waterfall Model
Spiral Model
Rational Unified Process
Agile Development
Software Inspections
Software Testing
Project Management

2.1 Introduction

The approach to software development in the 1950s and 1960s has been described as the *"Mongolian Hordes Approach"* by Ince and Andrews [30]. The "method" or lack of method was characterized by:
The completed code will always be full of defects.
The coding should be finished quickly to correct these defects.
Design as you code approach.

This philosophy accepted defeat in software development, and suggested that irrespective of a solid engineering approach, that the completed software would always contain lots of defects, and that it therefore made sense to code as quickly as possible, and to then identify the defects that would be present, so as to correct them as soon as possible.

G. O'Regan, *Introduction to Software Quality*, Undergraduate Topics
in Computer Science, DOI 10.1007/978-3-319-06106-1_2,
© Springer International Publishing Switzerland 2014

In the late 1960s it was clear that the existing approaches to software development were deeply flawed, and that there was an urgent need for change. The NATO Science Committee organized two famous conferences to discuss critical issues in software development [12], with the first conference held at Garmisch, Germany, in 1968, and it was followed by a second conference in Rome in 1969.

Over 50 people from 11 countries attended the Garmisch conference, including Edsger Djkstra, who did important theoretical work on formal specification and verification. The NATO conferences highlighted problems that existed in the software sector in the late 1960s, and the term *"software crisis"* was coined to refer to these problems. These included budget and schedule overruns, as well as problems with the quality and reliability of the delivered software.

The conference led to the birth of *software engineering* as a discipline in its own right, and the realization that programming is quite distinct from science and mathematics. Programmers are like engineers in that they build software products, and they therefore need education in traditional engineering as well as the latest technologies. The education of a classical engineer includes product design and mathematics. However, often computer science education places an emphasis on the latest technologies rather than the important engineering foundations of designing and building high-quality products that are safe for the public to use.

Programmers therefore need to learn the key engineering skills to enable them to build products that are safe for the public to use. This includes a solid foundation on design and the mathematics required for building safe software products. Mathematics plays a key role in engineering and may assist software engineers in the delivery of high-quality software products. Several mathematical approaches to assist software engineers are described in [48].

There are parallels between the software crisis in the late 1960s, and serious problems with bridge construction in the nineteenth century. Several bridges collapsed or were delivered late or over-budget due to the fact that people involved in their design and construction did not have the required engineering knowledge. This led to bridges that were inadequately designed and constructed, leading to their collapse with the loss of life and endangering the lives of the public.

This led to legislation requiring engineers to be licensed by the Professional Engineering Association prior to practicing as engineers. This organization identified a core body of knowledge that the engineer is required to possess, and the licensing body verifies that the engineer has the required qualifications and experience. This helps to ensure that only personnel competent to design and build products actually do so. Engineers have a professional responsibility to ensure that the products are properly built and are safe for the public to use.

The Standish group has conducted research (Fig. 2.1) on the extent of problems with IT projects since the mid-1990s. These studies were conducted in the United States, but there is no reason to believe that European or Asian companies perform any better. The results indicate serious problems with on-time delivery of projects or projects being cancelled prior to completion.[1] However, the comparison between

---

[1] These are IT projects covering diverse sectors including banking, telecommunications, etc., rather than pure software companies. Software companies following maturity frameworks such as the CMMI generally achieve more consistent project, and the CMMI focuses on the management side of software engineering.

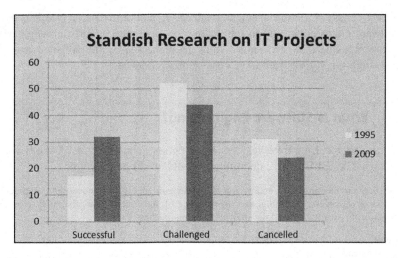

Fig. 2.1 Standish report – Results of 1995 and 2009 survey

1995 and 2009 suggests that there have been some improvements with a greater percentage of projects being delivered successfully, and a reduction in the percentage of projects being cancelled.

Fred Brooks argues that software is inherently complex, and that there is no *silver bullet* that will resolve all of the problems associated with software development such as schedule or budget overruns [10, 11]. Problems with poor software quality can lead to software flaws that may seriously impact the work of an organization or even loss of life. It is therefore essential that software development organizations place sufficient emphasis on quality throughout the software development lifecycle.

The Y2K problem was caused by a two digit representation of dates, and it required major rework of legacy software for the new millennium. Clearly, well-designed programs would have hidden the representation of the date, and would have required minimal changes for year 2000 compliance. Instead, companies spent vast sums of money to rectify the problem.

The quality of software produced by some companies is impressive.[2] These companies employ mature software processes, and are committed to continuous improvement. Today, there is a lot of industrial interest in software process maturity models for software organizations, and various approaches to assess and mature software companies are described in [47, 49].[3] These models focus on improving

---

[2] I recall projects at Motorola that regularly achieved 5.6σ-quality in a L4 CMM environment (i.e., approx. 20 defects per million lines of code. This represents very high quality).

[3] Approaches such as the CMM or SPICE (ISO 15504) focus mainly on the management and organizational practices required in software engineering. The emphasis is on defining software processes that are fit for purpose and consistently following them. The process maturity models focus on what needs to be done rather how it should be done. This gives the organization the freedom to choose the appropriate implementation to meet its needs. The models provide useful information on practices to consider in the implementation.

the effectiveness of the management, engineering and organization practices related to software engineering, and in introducing best practice in software engineering. The disciplined use of the mature software processes by the software engineers enables high-quality software to be consistently produced.

2.2   What Is Software Engineering?

Software engineering involves the multi-person construction of multi-version programs. The IEEE 610.12 definition of Software Engineering is:

> Software engineering is the application of a systematic, disciplined, quantifiable approach to the development, operation, and maintenance of software; that is, the application of engineering to software, and the study of such approaches.

Software engineering includes:

1. Methodologies to design, develop, and test software to meet customers' needs.
2. Software is engineered. That is, the software products are properly designed, developed, and tested in accordance with engineering principles.
3. Quality and safety are properly addressed.
4. Mathematics may be employed to assist with the design and verification of software products. The level of mathematics employed will depend on the *safety critical* nature of the product. Systematic peer reviews and rigorous testing will often be sufficient to build quality into the software, with heavy *mathematical techniques reserved for safety and security critical software.*
5. Sound project management and quality management practices are employed.
6. Support and maintenance of the software is properly addressed.

Software engineering is not just programming. It requires the engineer to state precisely the requirements that the software product is to satisfy, and then to produce designs that will meet these requirements. The project needs to be planned and delivered on time and budget. The requirements must provide a precise description of the problem to be solved: i.e., *it should be evident from the requirements what is and what is not required.* The requirements need to be rigorously reviewed to ensure that they are stated clearly and unambiguously and are exactly what the customer wants. The next step is then to create the design that will solve the problem, and it is essential to validate the correctness of the design. Next, the software to implement the design is written, and peer reviews and software testing are employed to verify and validate the correctness of the software.

The verification and validation of the design is rigorously performed for safety critical systems, and it is sometimes appropriate to employ mathematical techniques for these systems. However, it will usually be sufficient to employ peer reviews or software inspections as these methodologies provide a high degree of rigour. This may include approaches such as Fagan inspections [20], Gilb inspections [24], or Prince 2's approach to quality reviews [51].

The term *"engineer"* is a title that is awarded on merit in classical engineering. It is generally applied only to people who have attained the necessary education and competence to be called engineers, and who base their practice on classical engineering principles. The title places responsibilities on its holder such as to behave professionally and ethically. Often in computer science the term "*software engineer*" is employed loosely to refer to anyone who builds things, rather than to an individual with a core set of knowledge, experience, and competence.

Several computer scientists (such as Parnas[4]) have argued that computer scientists should be educated as engineers to enable them to apply appropriate scientific principles to their work. They argue that computer scientists should receive a solid foundation in mathematics and design, to enable them to have the professional competence to perform as engineers in building high-quality products that are safe for the public to use. The use of mathematics is an integral part of the engineer's work in other engineering disciplines, and so the *software engineer* should be able to use mathematics to assist in the modelling or understanding of the behaviour or properties of a proposed software system.

Software engineers need education[5] on specification, design, turning designs into programs, software inspections, and testing. The education should enable the software engineer to produce well-structured programs that are fit for purpose.

Parnas has argued that software engineers have responsibilities as professional engineers.[6] They are responsible for designing and implementing high-quality and reliable software that is safe to use. They are also accountable for their decisions and actions,[7] and have a responsibility to object to decisions that violate professional

---

[4] Parnas has made important contributions to computer science. He advocates a solid engineering approach with the extensive use of classical mathematical techniques to software development. He also introduced information hiding in the 1970s which is now a part of object-oriented development.

[5] Software Companies that are following approaches such as the CMM or ISO 9001 consider the education and qualification of staff prior to assigning staff to performing specific tasks. The appropriate qualifications and experience for the specific role are considered prior to appointing a person to carry out the role. Many companies are committed to the education and continuous development of their staff, and on introducing best practice in software engineering into their organization..

[6] The concept of accountability was used by the ancient Babylonians, and they employed a code of laws (known as the Hammurabi Code) c. 1750 B.C. It included a law that stated that if a house collapsed and killed the owner then the builder of the house would be executed.

[7] However, it is unlikely that an individual programmer would be subject to litigation in the case of a flaw in a program causing damage or loss of life. A comprehensive disclaimer of responsibility for problems rather than a guarantee of quality accompany most software products. Software engineering is a team-based activity involving many engineers in various parts of the project, and it would be potentially difficult for an outside party to prove that the cause of a particular problem is due to the professional negligence of a particular software engineer, as there are many others involved in the process such as reviewers of documentation and code and the various test groups. Companies are more likely to be subject to litigation, as a company is legally responsible for the actions of their employees in the workplace, and a company is a wealthier entity than one of its employees. The legal aspects of licensing software may protect software companies from litigation. However, greater legal protection for the customer can be built into the contract between the supplier and the customer for bespoke-software development.

standards. Engineers are required to behave professionally and ethically with their clients. The membership of the professional engineering body requires the member to adhere to the code of ethics[8] of the profession. Engineers in other professions are licensed, and therefore Parnas argues that a similar licensing approach be adopted for professional software engineers[9] to provide confidence that they are competent for the particular assignment. Professional software engineers are required to follow best practice in software engineering and the defined software processes.[10]

Many software companies invest heavily in training as the education and knowledge of its staff are essential to delivering high-quality products and services. Employees in receive professional training related to the roles that they are performing, such as project management, service management, and software testing. The fact that the employees are professionally qualified increases confidence in the ability of the company to deliver high-quality products and services. A company that pays little attention to the competence and continuous development of its staff will suffer a loss of reputation and market share.

2.3   Challenges in Software Engineering

The challenge in software engineering is to deliver high-quality software on time and on budget to customers. The research done by the Standish Group was discussed earlier in this chapter, and the results of their 1998 research (Fig. 2.2) on project cost overruns in the US indicated that 33 % of projects are between 21 and 50 % over estimate, 18 % are between 51 and 100 % over estimate, and 11 % of projects are between 101 and 200 % overestimate.

The accurate estimation of project cost, effort and schedule is a challenge in software engineering. Therefore, project managers need to determine how good their estimation process actually is and to make appropriate improvements. The use of software metrics is an objective way to do this, and improvements in estimation will be evident from a reduced variance between estimated and actual effort. The project manager will determine and report the actual versus estimated effort and schedule for the project.

Risk management is an important part of project management, and the objective is to identify potential risks early and throughout the project, and to manage them

---

[8] Many software companies have a defined code of ethics that employees are expected to adhere. Larger companies will wish to project a good corporate image and to be respected worldwide.

[9] The British Computer Scientist (BCS) has introduced a qualification system for computer science professionals that it used to show that professionals are properly qualified. The most important of these is the BCS Information Systems Examination Board (ISEB) which allows IT professionals to be qualified in service management, project management, software testing, and so on.

[10] Software companies that are following the CMMI or ISO 9000 standards will employ audits to verify that the processes and procedures have been followed. Auditors report their findings to management and the findings are addressed appropriately by the project team and affected individuals.

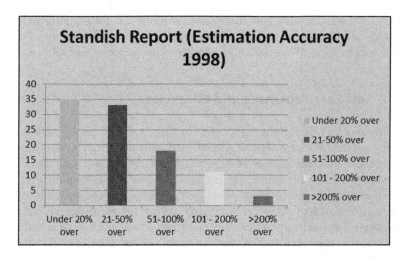

Fig. 2.2   Standish 1998 report – Estimation accuracy

appropriately. The probability of each risk occurring and its impact is determined and the risks are managed during project execution.

Software quality needs to be properly planned to enable the project to deliver a quality product. Flaws with poor quality software lead to a negative perception of the company, and could potentially lead to damage to the customer relationship with a subsequent loss of market share.

There is a strong economic case to building quality into the software, as less time is spent in re-working defective software. The cost of poor quality (COPQ) should be measured and targets set for its reductions. It is important that lessons are learned during the project and acted upon appropriately. This helps to promote a culture of continuous improvement.

We discussed a number of high-profile software failures in the previous chapter. These included the millennium bug (Y2K) problem; the floating point bug in the Intel microprocessor; the European Space Agency Ariane-5 disaster, and so on. These have caused embarrassment to the organizations as well as the cost of replacement and correction.

The millennium bug was due to the use of two digits to represent dates rather than four digits. The solution involved finding and analysing all code that that had a Y2K impact; planning and making the necessary changes; and verifying the correctness of the changes. The worldwide cost of correcting the millennium bug is estimated to have been in billions of dollars.

The Intel Corporation was slow to acknowledge the floating-point problem in its Pentium microprocessor, and in providing adequate information on its impact to its customers. It incurred a large financial cost in replacing microprocessors for its customers. The Ariane-5 failure caused major embarrassment and damage to the credibility of the European Space Agency (ESA). Its maiden flight ended in failure on June 4, 1996, after a flight time of just 40 s.

These failures indicate that quality needs to be carefully considered when designing and developing software. The effect of software failure may be large costs to correct the software, loss of credibility of the company, or even loss of life.

2.4   Software Processes and Lifecycles

Organizations vary by size and complexity, and the processes employed will reflect the nature of their business. The development of software involves many processes such as those for defining requirements; processes for project management and estimation; processes for design, implementation, testing, and so on.

It is important that the processes employed are fit for purpose, and a key premise in the software quality field is that the quality of the resulting software is influenced by the quality and maturity of the underlying processes, and compliance to them. Therefore, it is necessary to focus on the quality of the processes as well as the quality of the resulting software.

There is, of course, little point in having high-quality processes unless their use is institutionalized in the organization. That is, all employees need to follow the processes consistently. This requires that people are trained on the new processes and that process discipline is instilled by an appropriate audit strategy.

Employees need to be trained on the processes, and audits are conducted to ensure process compliance. Data will be collected to improve the process. The software process assets in an organization generally consist of:
- A software development policy for the organization
- Process maps that describe the flow of activities
- Procedures and guidelines that describe the processes in more detail.
- Checklists to assist with the performance of the process
- Templates for the performance of specific activities (e.g., Design, Testing)
- Training Materials

The processes employed to develop high-quality software generally include processes for:
- Project Management Process
- Requirements process
- Design Process
- Coding Process
- Peer Review Process
- Testing Process
- Supplier Selection and Management processes
- Configuration Management process
- Audit process
- Measurement Process.
- Improvement Process
- Customer Support and Maintenance processes

The software development process has an associated lifecycle that consists of various phases. There are several well-known lifecycles employed such as the

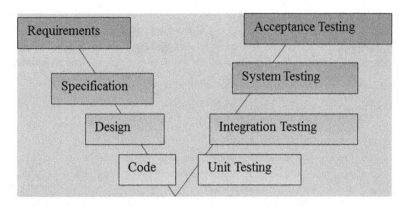

Fig. 2.3 Waterfall V lifecycle model

waterfall model [56]; the spiral model [8], the Rational Unified Process [57] and the Agile methodology [3] which has become popular in recent years. The choice of a particular software development lifecycle is determined from the particular needs of the specific project. The various lifecycles are described in more detail in the following Sections.

2.4.1 Waterfall Lifecycle

The waterfall model[11] (Fig. 2.3) starts with requirements gathering and definition. It is followed by the functional specification, the design and implementation of the software, and comprehensive testing. The testing generally includes unit, system and user acceptance testing.

It is employed for projects where the requirements can be identified early in the project lifecycle or are known in advance. It is also called the "V" life cycle model, with the left-hand side of the "V" detailing requirements, specification, design, and coding and the right-hand side detailing unit tests, integration tests, system tests and acceptance testing. Each phase has entry and exit criteria that must be satisfied before the next phase commences. There are several variations to the waterfall model.

Many companies employ a set of templates to enable the activities in the various phases to be consistently performed. Templates may be employed for project planning and reporting; requirements definition; design; testing and so on. These templates may be based on the IEEE standards or industrial best practice.

---

[11] We treat the waterfall model as identical to the V model in this text.

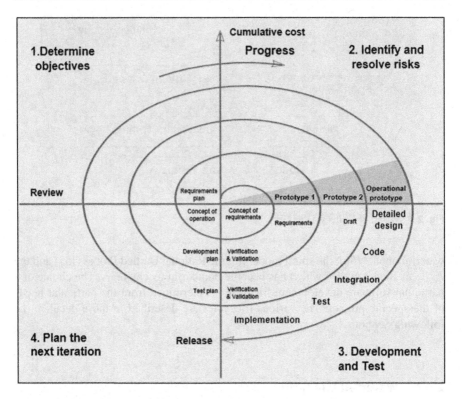

Fig. 2.4 SPIRAL lifecycle model ... Public domain

2.4.2   Spiral Lifecycles

The spiral model (Fig. 2.4) was developed by Barry Boehm in the mid-1980s, and is useful for a project in which the requirements are not fully known at project initiation, or where the requirements evolve as a part of the development lifecycle. The development proceeds in a number of spirals, where each spiral typically involves objectives and an analysis of the risks, updates to the requirements, design, code, testing, and a user review of the particular iteration or spiral.

The spiral is, in effect, a re-usable prototype with the business analysts and the customer reviewing the current iteration, and providing feedback to the development team. The feedback is analysed and used to plan the next iteration. This approach is often used in joint application development, where the usability and look and feel of the application is a key concern. This is important in web-based development and in the development of a graphical user interface (GUI). The implementation of part of the system helps in gaining a better understanding of the requirements of the system, and this feeds into subsequent development cycle. The process repeats until the requirements and the software product are fully complete.

There are several variations of the spiral model including Rapid Application Development (RAD); Joint Application Development (JAD) models; and the Dynamic Systems Development Method (DSDM) model. Agile methods have become popular in recent years and these generally employ sprints (or iterations) of 2 weeks duration to implement a number of user stories. A sample spiral model is shown in Fig. 2.4.

There are other life-cycle models, for example, the iterative development process that combines the waterfall and spiral lifecycle model. The Cleanroom approach developed by Harlan Mills at IBM includes a phase for formal specification, and its approach to software testing is based on the predicted usage of the software product. The Rational Unified Process has become popular in recent years, and it is discussed in the next section.

2.4.3 Rational Unified Process

The *Rational Unified Process* [57] was developed at the Rational Corporation (now part of IBM). It uses the Unified Modelling Language (UML) as a tool for specification and design, and UML is a visual modelling language for software systems which provides a means of specifying, constructing, and documenting the object-oriented system. It was developed by James Rumbaugh, Grady Booch, and Ivar Jacobson, and it facilitates the understanding of the architecture and complexity of the system.

RUP is *use case driven, architecture centric, iterative* and *incremental*, and includes cycles, phases, workflows, risk mitigation, quality control, project management, and configuration control. Software projects may be very complex, and there are risks that requirements may be incomplete, or that the interpretation of a requirement may differ between the customer and the project team.

Requirements are gathered as use cases, and the *use cases describe the functional requirements from the point of view of the user of the system.* They describe what the system will do at a high level, and ensure that there is an appropriate focus on the user when defining the scope of the project. *Use cases also drive the development process,* as the developers create a series of design and implementation models that realize the use cases. The developers review each successive model for conformance to the use-case model, and the test team verifies that the implementation correctly implements the use cases.

The software architecture concept embodies the most significant static and dynamic aspects of the system. The architecture grows out of the use cases and factors such as the platform that the software is to run on, deployment considerations, legacy systems, and non-functional requirements.

RUP decomposes the work in a large project into smaller slices or mini-projects, and *each mini-project is an iteration that results in an increment to the product.* The iteration consists of one or more steps in the workflow, and generally leads to the growth of the product. If there is a need to repeat an iteration, then all that is lost is the misdirected effort of one iteration, rather that the entire product. Another words, RUP is a way to mitigate risk in software engineering.

2.4.4 Agile Development

There has been a growth of popularity among software developers in lightweight methodologies such as *Agile*. This is a software development methodology that claims to be more responsive to customer needs than traditional methods such as the waterfall model. *The waterfall development model is similar to a wide and slow moving value stream*, and halfway through the project 100 % if the requirements are typically 50 % done. *However, for agile development 50 % of requirements are typically 100 % done halfway through the project.*

This methodology has a strong collaborative style of working and its approach includes:

- Aim is to achieve a narrow fast flowing value stream
- Feedback and adaptation employed in decision making
- User Stories and sprints are employed
- Stories are either done are not done
- Iterative and Incremental development is employed
- A project is divided into iterations
- An iteration has a fixed length (i.e., Time boxing is employed)
- Entire software development lifecycle is employed for the implementation of each story
- Change is accepted as a normal part of life in the Agile world
- Delivery is made as early as possible.
- Maintenance is seen as part of the development process
- Refactoring and Evolutionary Design Employed
- Continuous Integration is employed
- Short Cycle Times
- Emphasis on Quality
- Stand Up Meetings
- Plan regularly
- Direct interaction preferred over documentation
- Rapid conversion of requirements into working functionality
- Demonstrate value early
- Early decision making

Ongoing changes to requirements are considered normal in the Agile world, and it is believed to be more realistic to change requirements regularly throughout the project rather than attempting to define all of the requirements at the start of the project. The methodology includes controls to manage changes to the requirements, and good communication and early regular feedback is an essential part of the process.

A story may be a new feature or a modification to an existing feature. It is reduced to the minimum scope that can deliver business value, and a feature may give rise to several stories. Stories often build upon other stories and the entire software development lifecycle is employed for the implementation of each story. *Stories are either done or not done*: i.e., *there is such thing as a story being 80 % done.*

The story is complete only when it passes its acceptance tests. Stories are prioritized based on a number of factors including:
- Business Value of Story
- Mitigation of risk
- Dependencies on other stories.

Sprint planning is performed before the start of the iteration, and stories are assigned to the iteration to fill the available time. The estimates for each story and their priority are determined, and the prioritized stories are assigned to the iteration. *A short morning stand up meeting is held daily* during the iteration, and attended by the project manager and the project team. It discusses the progress made the previous day, problem reporting and tracking, and the work planned for the day ahead. A separate meeting is held for issues that require more detailed discussion.

Once the iteration is complete the latest product increment is demonstrated to an audience including the product owner. This is to receive feedback and to identify new requirements. The team also conducts a retrospective meeting to identify what went well and what went poorly during the iteration. This is to for continuous improvement for future iterations.

Agile employs pair programming and a collaborative style of working with the philosophy that two heads are better than one. This allows multiple perspectives in decision making and a broader understanding of the issues.

Software testing is very important and Agile generally employs automated testing for unit, acceptance, performance and integration testing. Tests are run frequently with the goal of catching programming errors early. They are generally run on a separate build server to ensure that all dependencies are checked. Tests are re-run before making a release. *Agile employs test driven development with tests written before the code.* The developers write code to make a test pass with ideally developers only coding against failing tests. This approach forces the developer to write testable code.

Refactoring is employed in Agile as a design and coding practice. The objective is to change how the software is written without changing what it does. Refactoring is a tool for evolutionary design where the design is regularly evaluated, and improvements are implemented as they are identified. The automated test suite is essential in showing that the integrity of the software is maintained following refactoring.

Continuous integration allows the system to be built with every change. Early and regular integration allows early feedback to be provided. It also allows all of the automated tests to be run thereby identifying problems earlier.

2.5 Activities in Waterfall Lifecycle

The waterfall software development lifecycle consists of various activities including:
- Business Requirements Definition
- Specification of System Requirements
- Design

- Implementation
- Unit Testing
- System Testing
- UAT Testing
- Support and Maintenance

These activities are discussed in the following sections.

2.5.1 Business Requirements Definition

The requirements specify what the customer wants and define what the software system is required to do (*as distinct from how this is to be done*). The requirements are the foundation for the system, and if they are incorrect, then the implemented system will be incorrect. *Prototyping may be employed* to assist in the definition and validation of the requirements.

The specification of the requirements needs to be unambiguous to ensure that all parties involved in the development of the system share a common understanding of what is to be developed and tested.

Requirements gathering involve meetings with the stakeholders to gather all relevant information for the proposed product. The stakeholders are interviewed, and requirements workshops conducted to elicit the requirements from them. An early working system (prototype) is often used to identify gaps and misunderstandings between developers and users. The prototype may serve as a basis for writing the specification.

The requirements workshops with the stakeholders are used to discuss and prioritize the requirements, as well as identifying and resolving any conflicting requirements. The collected information is consolidated into a coherent set of requirements.

The requirements are validated by the stakeholders to ensure that they are actually those desired, and to establish their feasibility. This may involve several reviews of the requirements until all stakeholders are ready to approve the requirements document. Changes to the requirements may occur during the project, and these need to be controlled. It is essential to understand the impacts of a change request prior to its approval.

The requirements for a system are generally documented in a natural language such as "English". Other notations that may be employed to express the requirements include the visual modelling language UML [32], and formal specification languages such as VDM or Z.

2.5.2 Specification of System Requirements

The specification of the system requirements of the product is essentially a statement of what the software development organization will provide to meet the business requirements. That is, the detailed business requirements are a statement of what the customer wants, whereas the specification of the system requirements is a statement of what will be delivered by the software development organization.

It is essential that the system requirements are valid with respect to the business requirements, and they are reviewed by the stakeholders to ensure that their validity with respect to the business requirements. Traceability may be employed to show that the business requirements are addressed by the system requirements

There are two categories of system requirements: namely, functional and non-functional requirements. The *functional requirements* define the functionality that is required of the system, and it may include screen shots, report layouts or desired functionality specified as use cases. The *non-functional requirements* will generally include security, reliability, performance and portability requirements, as well as usability and maintainability requirements.

2.5.3   Design

The design of the system consists of engineering activities to describe the architecture or structure of the system, as well as activities to describe the algorithms and functions required to implement the system requirements. It is a creative process concerned with how the system will be implemented, and its activities include architecture design, interface design, and data structure design. There are often several possible design solutions for a particular system, and the designer will need to decide on the most appropriate solution.

The design may be specified in various ways such as graphical notations that display the relationships between the components making up the design. The notation may include flow charts, or various UML diagrams such as sequence diagrams, state charts, and so on. Program description languages or pseudo code may be employed to define the algorithms and data structures that are the basis for implementation.

Functional design involves starting with a high-level view of the system and refining it into a more detailed design. The system state is centralized and shared between the functions operating on that state.

Object-oriented design has become popular in recent years and is based on the concept of *information hiding* developed by Parnas [52]. The system is viewed as a collection of objects rather than functions, with each object managing its own state information. The system state is decentralized and an object is a member of a class. The definition of a class includes attributes and operations on class members, and these may be inherited from super classes. Objects communicate by exchanging messages

It is essential to verify and validate the design with respect to the system requirements, and this will be done by traceability of the design to the system requirements and design reviews.

2.5.4   Implementation

This phase is concerned with implementing the design in the target language and environment (e.g., C++ or Java), and involves writing or generating the actual code. The development team divides up the work to be done, with each programmer responsible for one or more modules. The coding activities often include code reviews or walkthroughs to ensure that quality code is produced, and to verify its correctness. The code reviews will verify that the source code conforms to the coding standards and that maintainability issues are addressed. They will also verify that the code produced is a valid implementation of the software design.

Software reuse has become more important in recent times as it provides a way to speed up the development process. Components or objects that may be reused need to be identified and handled accordingly. The implemented code may use software components that have either being developed internally or purchased off the shelf. Open source software has become popular in recent years, and it allows software developed by others to be used (*under an open source license*) in the development of applications.

The benefits of software reuse include increased productivity and a faster time to market. There are inherent risks with customized-off-the shelf (COTS) software, as the supplier may decide to no longer support the software, or there is no guarantee that software that has worked successfully in one domain will work correctly in a different domain. It is therefore important to consider the risks as well as the benefits of software reuse and open source software.

2.5.5   Software Testing

Software testing is employed to verify that the requirements have been correctly implemented, and that the software is fit for purpose, as well as identifying defects present in the software. There are various types of testing that may be conducted including *unit testing, integration testing, system testing, performance testing and user acceptance testing*. These are described below:

2.5.5.1 Unit Testing
Unit testing is performed by the programmer on the completed unit (or module), and prior to its integration with other modules. These tests are written by the programmer, and the objective is to show that the code satisfies the design. Each unit test case is documented and it should include a test objective and the expected result.

Code coverage and branch coverage metrics are often recorded to give an indication of how comprehensive the unit testing has been. These metrics provide visibility into the number of lines of code executed as well as the branches covered during unit testing.

The developer executes the unit tests; records the results; corrects any identified defects and re-tests the software. *Test driven development* has become popular in recent years (e.g., in the Agile world), and this involves writing the unit test case before the code, and the code is written to pass the unit test cases.

2.5.5.2 Integration Test

The development team performs this type of testing on the integrated system, once all of the individual units work correctly in isolation. The objective is to verify that all of the modules and their interfaces work correctly together, and to identify and resolve any issues. Modules that work correctly in isolation may fail when integrated with other modules.

2.5.5.3 System Test

The purpose of system testing is to verify that the implementation is valid with respect to the system requirements. It involves the specification of system test cases, and the execution of the test cases will verify that the system requirements have been correctly implemented. An independent test group generally conducts this type of testing, and the system tests are traceable to the system requirements.

Any system requirements that have been incorrectly implemented will be identified, and defects logged and reported to the developers. The test group will verify that the new version of the software is correct, and regression testing is conducted to verify system integrity. System testing may include security testing, usability testing and performance testing.

The preparation of the test environment requires detailed planning, and it may involve ordering special hardware and tools. It is important that the test environment is set up as early as possible to allow the timely execution of the test cases.

2.5.5.4 Performance Test

The purpose of performance testing is to ensure that the performance of the system is within the bounds specified in the non-functional requirements. It may include *load performance testing*, where the system is subjected to heavy loads over a long period of time, and *stress testing*, where the system is subjected to heavy loads during a short time interval.

Performance testing often involves the simulation of many users using the system, and involves measuring the response times for various activities. Test tools are employed to simulate a large number of users and heavy loads. It is also employed to determine is the system is scalable to support future growth.

2.5.5.5 User Acceptance Test

UAT testing is usually performed under controlled conditions at the customer site, and its operation will closely resemble the real life behaviour of the system. The customer will see the product in operation, and can judge whether or not the system is fit for purpose.

The objective is to demonstrate that the product satisfies the business requirements and meets the customer expectations. Upon its successful completion the customer is happy to accept the product.

2.5.6   Maintenance

This phase continues after the release of the software product to the customer. Any problems that the customer notes with the software are reported as per the customer support and maintenance agreement. The support issues will require investigation, and the issue may be *a defect in the software, an enhancement to the software*, or *due to a misunderstanding*. The support and maintenance team will identify the causes of any identified defects, and will implement an appropriate solution to resolve. Testing is conducted to verify that the solution is correct, and that the changes made have not adversely affected other parts of the system. Mature organizations will conduct post mortems to learn lessons from the defect,[12] and will take corrective action to prevent a re-occurrence.

The presence of a maintenance phase suggests an acceptance of the reality that problems with the software will be identified post release. The goal of building a correct and reliable software product the first time is very difficult to achieve, and the customer is always likely to find some issues with the released software product. It is accepted today that quality needs to be built into each step in the development process, with the role of software inspections and testing to identify as many defects as possible prior to release, and minimize the risk that that serious defects will be found post-release.

The more effective the in-phase inspections of deliverables, the higher the quality of the resulting implementation, with a corresponding reduction in the number of defects detected by the test groups. The testing group plays a key role in verifying that the system is correct, and in providing confidence that the software is fit for purpose. The approach to software correctness almost seems to be a *"brute force"* approach, where quality is achieved by testing and re-testing, until the testing group is confident that all defects have been eliminated. Dijkstra [16] noted that:

> Testing a program demonstrates that it contains errors, never that it is correct.

That is, irrespective of the amount of time spent testing, it can never be said with absolute confidence that the program is correct, and, at best, statistical techniques may be employed to give a measure of the confidence in its correctness. That is, there is no guarantee that all defects have been found in the software.

---

[12] This is essential for serious defects that have caused significant inconvenience to customers (e.g., a major telecoms outage). The software development organization will wish to learn lessons to determine what went wrong in its processes that prevented the defect from been identified during peer reviews and testing. Actions to prevent a reoccurrence will be identified and implemented.

Many software companies may consider one defect per thousand lines of code (KLOC) to be reasonable quality. However, if the system contains one million lines of code this is equivalent to a thousand post-release defects, which is unacceptable.

Some mature organizations have a quality objective of three defects per million lines of code. This goal is known as six-sigma (6σ) and it was developed by Motorola. It was originally applied it to its manufacturing businesses and subsequently applied to its software organizations. The goal is to reduce variability in manufacturing processes and to ensure that the processes performed within strict process control limits. Motorola was awarded the first Malcom Baldridge Quality award for its six-sigma initiative and its commitment to quality.

2.6   Software Inspections

Software inspections were discussed in Chap. 1 and they are used to build quality into software products. There are a number of well-known approaches such as the Fagan Methodology [20]; Gilb's approach [24]; and Prince 2's approach.

Fagan inspections were developed by Michael Fagan of IBM It is a seven-step process that identifies and removes errors in work products. The process mandates that requirement documents, design documents, source code, and test plans are all formally inspected by experts independent of the author of the deliverable to ensure quality.

There are various *roles* defined in the process including the *moderator* who chairs the inspection. The *reader's* responsibility is to read or paraphrase the particular deliverable, and *the author* is the creator of the deliverable and has a special interest in ensuring that it is correct. The *tester* role is concerned with the test viewpoint.

The inspection process will consider whether the design is correct with respect to the requirements, and whether the source code is correct with respect to the design. Software inspections play an important role in reducing the cost of poor quality in the organization.

2.7   Software Project Management

The timely delivery of quality software requires good management and engineering processes. Software projects have a history of being delivered late or over budget, and good project management practices include the following activities:
– Estimation of cost, effort and schedule for the project
– Identifying and managing risks
– Preparing the project plan
– Preparing the initial project schedule and key milestones
– Obtaining approval for the project plan and schedule
– Staffing the project

- Monitoring progress, budget, schedule, effort, risks, issues, change requests and quality
- Taking corrective action
- Re-planning and re-scheduling
- Communicating progress to affected stakeholders
- Preparing status reports and presentations

The project plan will contain or reference several other plans such as the project quality plan; the communication plan; the configuration management plan; and the test plan.

Project estimation and scheduling are difficult as often software projects are breaking new ground and differ from previous projects. That is, previous estimates may often not be a good basis for estimation for the current project. Often, unanticipated problems can arise for technically advanced projects, and the estimates may often be optimistic. Gantt charts are often employed for project scheduling, and these show the work breakdown for the project, as well as task dependencies and allocation of staff to the various tasks.

The effective management of risk during a project is essential to project success. Risks arise due to uncertainty and the risk management cycle involves[13] risk identification; risk analysis and evaluation; identifying responses to risks; selecting and planning a response to the risk; and risk monitoring. The risks are logged, and the likelihood of each risk arising and its impact is then determined. The risk is assigned an owner and an appropriate response to the risk determined.

2.8   CMMI Maturity Model

The CMMI is a framework to assist an organization in the implementation of best practice in software and systems engineering. It is an internationally recognized model for process improvement and assessment, and is used world-wide by thousands of organizations. It provides a solid engineering approach to the development of software, and helps in the definition of high-quality processes for the various software engineering and management activities.

It was developed by the Software Engineering Institute (SEI) who adapted the process improvement principles used in the manufacturing field to the software field. They developed the original CMM model and its successor the CMMI. The CMMI states *what the organization needs to do* to mature its processes rather than *how this should be done.*

The CMMI consists of five maturity levels with each maturity level consisting of several process areas. Each process area consists of a set of goals, and these goals are implemented by practices related to that process area. Level two is focused on management practices; level three is focused on engineering and organization practices; level four is concerned with ensuring that key processes are performing

---

[13] These are the risk management activities in the Prince 2 methodology.

within strict quantitative limits; level five is concerned with continuous process improvement. Maturity levels may not be skipped in the staged implementation of the CMMI, as each maturity level is the foundation for the next level.

The CMMI allows organizations to benchmark themselves against other organizations. This is done by a formal appraisal conducted by an authorized lead appraiser. The results of the appraisal are generally reported back to the SEI, and there is a strict qualification process to become an *authorized lead appraiser*. An appraisal is useful in verifying that an organization has improved, and it enables the organization to prioritize improvements for the next improvement cycle. The CMMI is discussed in more detail in a later chapter.

2.9 Formal Methods

Dijkstra and Hoare have argued that the way to develop correct software is to derive the program from its specifications using mathematics, and to employ *mathematical proof* to demonstrate its correctness with respect to the specification. This offers a rigorous framework to develop programs adhering to the highest quality constraints. However, in practice mathematical techniques have proved to be cumbersome to use, and their widespread deployment in industry is unlikely at this time.

The *safety-critical area* is one domain to which mathematical techniques have been successfully applied: for example, demonstrating the presence or absence of safety properties such as "*when a train is in a level crossing, then the gate is closed*". There is a need for extra rigour in the software development process used in the safety critical field, and mathematical techniques can demonstrate the presence or absence of certain desirable or undesirable properties.

Spivey [62] defines a "*formal specification*" as the use of mathematical notation to describe in a precise way the properties which an information system must have, without unduly constraining the way in which these properties are achieved. It describes *what* the system must do, as distinct from *how* it is to be done. This abstraction away from implementation enables questions about what the system does to be answered, independently of the detailed code. Furthermore the unambiguous nature of mathematical notation avoids the problem of speculation about the meaning of phrases in an imprecisely worded natural language description of a system.

The formal specification thus becomes the key reference point for the different parties concerned with the construction of the system, and is a useful way of promoting a common understanding for all those concerned with the system.

The term "*formal methods*" is used to describe a formal specification language and a method for the design and implementation of computer systems. The specification is written in a mathematical language, and avoids the problem of ambiguity inherent in a natural language specification. The derivation of an implementation from the specification may be achieved via *step-wise refinement*. Each refinement step makes the specification more concrete and closer to the actual implementation.

There is an associated *proof obligation* that the refinement be valid, and that the concrete state preserves the properties of the more abstract state. Thus, assuming the original specification is correct and the proofs of correctness of each refinement step are valid, then there is a very high degree of confidence in the correctness of the implemented software.

Formal methods have been applied to a diverse range of applications, including circuit design, artificial intelligence, specification of standards, specification and verification of programs, etc. They are described in more detail Chap. 17.

2.10 Review Questions

1. Discuss the research results of the Standish Group the current state of IT project delivery?
2. What are the main challenges in software engineering?
3. Describe various software lifecycles such as the waterfall model and the spiral model.
4. Discuss the benefits of Agile over conventional approaches. List any risks and disadvantages?
5. Describe the purpose of software inspections? What are the benefits?
6. Describe the main activities that take place in software testing.
7. Describe the main activities in project management?

2.11 Summary

The birth of software engineering was at the NATO conference held in 1968 in Germany. This conference highlighted the problems that existed in the software sector in the late 1960s, and the term "*software crisis*" was coined to refer to these. This led to the realization that programming is quite distinct from science and mathematics, and that software engineers need to be properly trained to enable them to build high-quality products that are safe to use.

The Standish group conducts research on the extent of problems with the delivery of projects on time and budget. Their research indicates that it remains a challenge to deliver projects on time, on budget and with the right quality.

Programmers are like engineers in the sense that they build products. Therefore, programmers need to receive an appropriate education in engineering as part of their training. The education of traditional engineers includes training on product design, and an appropriate level of mathematics.

Software engineering involves multi-person construction of multi-version programs. It is a systematic approach to the development and maintenance of the software, and it requires a precise statement of the requirements of the software product, and then the design and development of a solution to meet these requirements. It includes methodologies to design, develop, implement and test software as well as sound project management, quality management and configuration management practices. Support and maintenance of the software is properly addressed.

Software process maturity models such as the CMMI have become popular in recent years. They place an emphasis on understanding and improving the software process to enable software engineers to be more effective in their work.

Project Management

3

Key Topics

Project Planning
Estimation
Scheduling
Risk Management
Project Governance
Project Board
Business Case
Project Reports
Project Metrics
Project Monitoring and Control
Quality Management
Prince 2
PMP and PMBOK

3.1   Introduction

Software projects have a history of being delivered late or over budget, and the timely delivery of high-quality software requires good estimation and planning, and good management and engineering processes. Project management is concerned with the effective management of projects to ensure successful delivery of a high-quality product, on time and on budget, to the customer. *A project is a temporary group activity designed to accomplish a specific goal such as the delivery of a product to a customer. It has a clearly defined beginning and end in time.*

Project management involves good project planning and estimation; the management of resources; the management of issues and change requests that arise during

G. O'Regan, *Introduction to Software Quality*, Undergraduate Topics
in Computer Science, DOI 10.1007/978-3-319-06106-1_3,
© Springer International Publishing Switzerland 2014

the project; managing quality; managing risks; managing the budget; monitoring progress; taking appropriate action when progress deviates from expectations; communicating progress to the various stakeholders; and delivering a high-quality product to the customer. It involves:

- Defining the scope of the project and what it is to achieve
- Estimation of the cost, effort and schedule
- Determining the start and end dates for the project
- Determining the resources required
- Assigning resources to the various tasks and activities
- Determining the project lifecycle and phases of the project
- Staffing the project
- Preparing the project plan
- Scheduling the various tasks and activities in the schedule
- Preparing the initial project schedule and key milestones
- Obtaining approval for the project plan and schedule
- Identifying and managing risks
- Monitoring progress, budget, schedule, effort, risks, issues, change requests and quality
- Taking corrective action
- Re-planning and re-scheduling
- Communicating progress to affected stakeholders
- Preparing status reports and presentations

The scope of the project needs to be determined and effort and schedule estimates should be established. The project plan should then be developed and approved by the stakeholders. The project plan will need to be maintained during the project.

The project plan will contain or reference several other plans such as the project quality plan; the communication plan; the configuration management plan; and the test plan.

Project estimation and scheduling are difficult as software projects are often breaking new ground and differ from previous projects. That is, previous estimates may often not be a good basis for estimation for the current project. Often, unanticipated problems may arise for technically advanced projects, and the estimates may be overly optimistic.

Gantt charts are generally employed for project scheduling, and these show the work breakdown for the project as well as task dependencies and allocation of staff to the various tasks.

The effective management of risk during a project is essential to project success. Risks arise due to uncertainty and the risk management cycle involves[1] risk identification; risk analysis and evaluation; identifying responses to risks; selecting and planning a response to the risk; and risk monitoring.

---

[1] These are the risk management activities in the Prince 2 methodology.

Once the risks have been identified they are logged (e.g., in the Risk Log). The likelihood of each risk arising and its impact is then determined. The risk is assigned an owner and an appropriate response to the risk determined.

Once the planning is complete the project execution commences, and the focus moves to monitoring progress, re-planning as appropriate, managing risks and issues, re-planning as appropriate, providing regular progress reports to the project board, and so on.

The two most popular project management methodologies are the *Prince* 2 methodology which was developed in the U.K., and *Project Management Professional (PMP)* and its associated project management body of knowledge (PMBOK) from the *Project Management Institute* (PMI) in the United States.

3.2   Project Start Up and Initiation

There are various ways in which a project may arise: for example, a telecoms company may wish to develop a new version of its software with attractive features to dazzle its customers and to gain market share; an internal IT department may receive a request from its business users to alter its business software in order to satisfy new legal or regulatory requirements. A software development company may be contacted by a business to develop a bespoke solution to meet its needs, and so on.

All parties must be clear on what the project is to achieve, and how it will be achieved. It is fundamental that there is a *business case* for the project, as it clearly does not make sense for the organization to spend a large amount of money unless the project makes business sense. At the project start up the initial scope and costing for the project are determined, and the feasibility of the project is established.[2] The project is authorised,[3] and a project board is set up for project governance. The project board verifies that there is a sound business case for the project, and a *project manager* is appointed to manage the project.

The *project board* (or steering group) includes the key stakeholders, and is accountable for the success of the project. The project manager provides regular status reports to the project board during the project, and the project board is consulted when key project decisions need to be made.

The project manager is responsible for the day-to-day management of the project, and good planning is essential to its success. The approach to the project is decided,[4] and the project manager *kicks off the project* and mobilises the project team. The detailed requirements and estimates for the project are determined, the schedule of activities and tasks established, and resources are assigned to the

---

[2] This refers to whether the project is technically and financially feasible.

[3] Organizations have limited resources, and as many projects may be proposed it will not be possible to authorise every project, and so several projects with weak business cases will be rejected.

[4] For example, it may be decided to outsource the development to a third party provider, purchase an off-the-shelf solution, or develop the solution internally.

various tasks and activities.[5] The project manager prepares the project plan which is subject to the approval of the key stakeholders. The initial risks are identified and managed, and a risk log (or repository) is set up for the project. Once the planning is complete project execution commences.

3.3   Estimation

Estimation is a key part of project management, and the accurate estimates of effort, cost and schedule are essential to delivering a project the on time and on budget, and with the right quality.[6] Estimation is employed in the planning process to determine the resources and effort required, and it feeds into the scheduling of the project. The problems with over or under-estimation of projects are well-known, and good estimates allow:
– Accurate calculation of the project cost and its feasibility.
– Accurate scheduling of the project
– The measurement of progress and costs against the estimates.
– Determining the resources required for the project
  Poor estimation leads to:
– Projects being over or under-estimated.
– Projects being over or under-resourced (impacting staff morale)
– Negative impression of the project manager.
  Consequently, estimation needs to be rigorous, and there are several well-known estimation techniques available (e.g., work-breakdown structures, function points, and so on). Estimation applies to both the early and later parts of the project, with the later phases of the project refining the initial estimates, as a more detailed understanding of the project activities is then available. The new estimates are used to re-schedule and to predict the eventual effort, delivery date and cost of the project. The following are guidelines for estimation:
– Sufficient time needs to be allowed to do estimation.
– Estimates are produced for each phase of software development.
– The initial estimates are high-level.
– The estimates for the next phase should be solid whereas estimates for the later phases may be high-level.
– The estimates should be conservative rather than optimistic.
– Estimates will usually include contingency
– Estimates should be reviewed to ensure their adequacy.
– Estimates from independent experts may be useful.
– It may be useful to prepare estimates using various methods and to compare.

---

[5] The project scheduling is usually done with the Microsoft Project tool.
[6] The consequences of under estimating a project include the project being delivered late, with the project team working late nights and weekends to recover the schedule, quality being compromised with steps in the process omitted, and so on.

Table 3.1 Estimation techniques

Technique	Description
Work breakdown structure	Identify the project deliverables to be produced during the project. Estimate the size of each deliverable (in pages or LOC). Estimate the effort (number of days) required to complete the deliverable based on its complexity and size. Estimate the cost of the completed deliverable.
Analogy method	This involves comparing the proposed project with a previously completed project (that is similar to the proposed project) The historical data and metrics for schedule, effort and budget estimation accuracy are considered, as well as similarities and differences between the projects to provide effort, schedule and budget estimates.
Expert judgment	This involves consultation with experienced personnel to derive the estimate. The expert(s) can factor in differences between past project experiences, knowledge of existing systems as well as the specific requirements of the project.
Delphi method	The *Delphi Method* is a consensus method used to produce accurate schedules and estimates. It was developed by the Rand Corporation and improved by Barry Boehm and others. It provides extra confidence in the project estimates by using experts independent of the project manager or third party supplier.
Cost predictor models	These include various cost prediction modes such as *Cocomo* and Slim. The Costar tool supports Cocomo, and the Qsm tool supports Slim.
Function points	*Function Points* were developed by Allan Albrecht at IBM in the late 1970s, and involve analysing each functional requirement and assigning a number of function points based on its size and complexity. This total number of function points is a measure of the estimate.

Project metrics may be employed to measure the accuracy of the estimates. These metrics are reported during the project and include:
– Effort Estimation Accuracy
– Budget Estimation Accuracy
– Schedule Estimation Accuracy
Next, we discuss various estimation techniques including the work-breakdown structure, the analogy method, and the Delphi method.

3.3.1   Estimation Techniques

Estimates need to be produced consistently, and it would be inappropriate to have an estimation procedure such as "*Go ask Fred*",[7] as this clearly relies on an individual and is not a repeatable process. The estimates may be based on a work-breakdown structure, function points, or another appropriate methodology. There are several approaches to project estimation including those given in Table 3.1.

---

[7] Unless "Go Ask Fred" is the name of the estimation methodology or the estimation tool employed.

Table 3.2 Example work-breakdown structure

Lifecycle phase	Project deliverable or task description	Est. size	Est. effort	Est. cost
Planning and requirements	Project plan	40	10 days	$5,000
	Project schedule	20	5 days	$2,500
	Business requirements	20	10 days	$5,000
	Test plan	15	5 days	$2,500
	Issue/risk log	3	2 days	$1,000
	Lessons learned log	1	1 day	$500
Design	System requirements	15	5 days	$2,500
	Technical/DB design	30	10 days	$5,000
Coding	Source code	5,000 (LOC)	10 days	$5,000
	Unit tests/results	200	2 days	$1,000
Testing	ST specs	30	10 days	$5,000
	System testing		10 days	$5,000
	UAT specs	30	10 days	$5,000
	UAT testing		10 days	$5,000
Deployment	Release notes/procedures	20	5 days	$2,500
	User manuals	50	10 days	$5,000
	Support procedures	15	10 days	$5,000
	Training plan	25	5 days	$2,500
Project closure	End project report	10	2 days	$1,000
	Lessons learned report	5	2 days	$1,000
Contingency	10 %		13.4	$6,700
Total			147.4	$73,700

3.3.2   Work Breakdown Structure

This is a popular approach to project estimation (*it is also known as decomposition*) and involves the following:
– Identify the project deliverables to be produced during the project
– Estimate the size of each deliverable (in pages or LOC)
– Estimate the effort (number of days) required to complete the deliverable based on its complexity and size, and experience of team.
– Estimate the cost of the completed deliverable.
– The estimate for the project is the sum of the individual estimates.

   The approach often uses productivity data that is available from preciously completed projects. The effort required for a complex deliverable is higher than that of a simple deliverable (where both are of the same size). The project planning section in the project plan (or a separate estimation plan) will include the lifecycle phases, and the deliverables/tasks to be carried out in each phase, as given in Table 3.2.

3.4 Project Planning and Scheduling

A well-managed project has an increased chance of success, and good planning is an essential part of project management. There is the well-known adage which states *"Fail to plan, plan to fail"*. The project manager and the relevant stakeholders will consider the appropriate approach for the project, and determine whether a solution should be purchased off the shelf, whether to outsource the software development to a third party supplier, or whether to develop the solution internally. A simple process map for project planning is in Fig. 3.1.

Estimation is a key part of project planning, and the effort estimates are used for scheduling of the tasks and activities in a project scheduling tool such as *Microsoft Project* (Fig. 3.2).

The schedule will detail the phases in the project, the key project milestones, the activities and tasks to be performed in each phase as well as their associated timescales, and the resources required to carry out each task. The project manager will update the project schedule regularly during the project.

Projects vary in size and complexity and the formality of the software development process employed needs to reflect this. The project plan defines how the project will be carried out, and it generally includes:
- Business Case
- Project Scope
- Project Goals & Objectives
- Key Milestones
- Project Planning and Estimates
- Key Stakeholders
- Project Team and Responsibilities

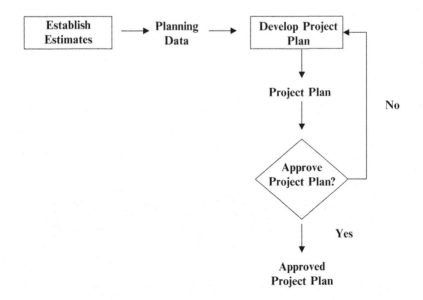

Fig. 3.1 Simple process map for project planning

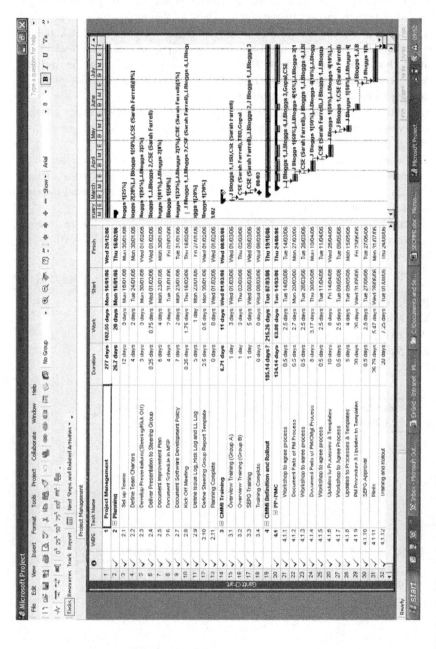

Fig. 3.2 Sample Microsoft project schedule

Table 3.3 Sample project management checklist

No.	Item to check
1.	Is the project plan complete and approved by the stakeholders?
2.	Are the Risk Log, Issue Log and Lessons Learned Log set up?
3.	Are the responses to the risks and issues appropriate?
4.	Is the Microsoft Schedule defined for the project?
5.	Is the project schedule kept up to date?
6.	Is the project appropriately resourced?
7.	Are estimates available for the project? Are they realistic?
8.	Has quality planning been completed for the project?
9.	Does the project have a business case?
10.	Has the change control mechanism been set up for the project?
11.	Are all deliverables under configuration management control?
12.	Has project communication been appropriately planned?
13.	Is the project directory set up for the project?
14.	Are the key milestones defined in the project plan?

- Knowledge and Skills Required
- Communication Planning
- Financial Planning
- Quality and Test Planning
- Configuration Management

Communication planning describes how communication will be carried out during the project, and this includes the various project meetings and reports that will be produced; financial planning is concerned with budget planning for the project; quality and test planning is concerned with the planning required to ensure that a high-quality product is delivered; and configuration management is concerned with identifying the configuration items to be controlled, and systematically controlling changes to them throughout the lifecycle. It ensures that all deliverables are kept consistent following approved changes.

The project plan is a key project document, and it needs to be approved by all stakeholders. The project manager needs to ensure that the project plan, schedule and technical work products are kept consistent with the requirements.

Checklists are useful in verifying that the tasks have been completed. The sample project management checklist in Table 3.3 verifies that project planning has been appropriately performed and that controls are in place.

3.5 Risk Management

Risks arise due to uncertainty, and *risk management is concerned with managing uncertainty*, and especially the management of any undesired events. Risks need to be identified, analysed and controlled in order for the project to be successful.

Once the initial set of risks to the project has been identified, they are analysed to determine their *likelihood of occurrence* and their *impact* (e.g. on cost, schedule or

Table 3.4 Risk management activities

Activity	Description
Risk management strategy	This defines how the risks will be identified, monitored, reviewed and reported during the project, as well as the frequency of monitoring and reporting.
Risk identification	This involves identifying the risks to the project and recording them in a risk repository (e.g., Risk Log). It continues throughout the project lifecycle. The Prince 2 methodology classifies risks into five main types:
	Business (e.g., collapse of subcontractors)
	Legal and Regulatory
	Organisational (e.g., availability of skilled resources and management).
	Technical (e.g., scope creep, architecture, design)
	Environmental (e.g., flooding or fires)
Evaluating the risks	This involves assessing the likelihood of occurrence of a particular risk and its impact (on cost, schedule, etc.) should it materialise. These two parameters result in the risk category.
Identifying risk responses	The project manager (and other stakeholders) will determine the appropriate response to a risk depending on its severity. The response may reduce the probability of its occurrence or its impact should it occur. This includes:
	Prevention which aims to prevent it from occurring
	Reduction aim to reduce the probability of occurrence or impact should it occur.
	Transfer aims to transfer the risk to a 3rd party.
	Acceptance is when nothing can be done about it
	Contingency are actions that are carried out should the risk materialise.
Risk monitoring and reporting	This involves monitoring existing risks to verify that the actions taken to manage the risks are effective, as well as identifying new risks. It provides an early warning that an identified risk is going to materialise.
Lessons learned	This is concerned with determining the effectiveness of risk management during the project and to learn any lessons for future projects.

quality). These two parameters determine the *risk category* of the risk, and the most serious risk category refers to a risk with a high probability of occurrence and a high impact on occurrence.

Countermeasures are defined to reduce the likelihood of occurrence and impact of the risks, and contingency plans are prepared to deal with the situation of the risk actually occurring. Additional risks may become evident during the project, and the project manager needs to be proactive in their identification and management.

Risks need to be reviewed regularly especially following changes in the project. These could be changes to the business case or the business requirements, loss of key personnel, and so on. Events that occur may affect existing risks (including the probability of their occurrence and their impact), and may lead to new risks. Countermeasures need to be kept up to date during the project. Risks are reported regularly throughout the project.

The risk management cycle is concerned with identifying and managing risks throughout the project lifecycle. It involves identifying risks; identifying their probability of occurrence and impact should they occur; identifying responses to the risks; and monitoring and reporting. Table 3.4 describes these activities in greater detail.

The project manager will maintain a risk repository (this may be a tool or a risk log) to record details of each risk, including its type and description; its likelihood and its impact (yielding the risk category); as well as the response to the risk.

3.6   Quality Management in Projects

There are various definitions of "quality" such as Juran's definition that quality is "*fitness for purpose*". Crosby defined quality as "*conformance to the requirements*", and this definition is often useful in the quality management of projects.

It is fundamental premise in the quality field that it is more cost effective to build quality into the product, rather than adding it later during the testing phase. Therefore, quality needs to be considered at every step during the project, and every deliverable needs to be reviewed to ensure its fitness for purpose. The review may be similar to a *software inspection*, a *structured walkthrough* or another appropriate methodology.

The project plan will include a section on quality planning for the project (this may be a separate plan). The quality plan will define how the project plans to deliver a high quality project, as well as the quality controls and quality assurance activities that will take place during project execution. The quality planning needs to ensure that the customer's quality expectations will be achieved.

The project manager has overall responsibility for project quality, and the quality department (if one exists) will assign a quality engineer to the project, and the quality engineer will promote quality and its importance to the project team, as well as facilitating quality improvement. The project manager needs to ensure that sound software engineering processes are employed on the project, as well as standards and templates for the various deliverables.

Process quality is important, as it is an accepted principle in the quality field that conformance to the defined process is essential in the delivery of a high-quality product. The quality engineer will conduct process audits to ensure that the processes and standards are followed consistently during the project. An audit report is published, and any audit actions are tracked to closure.

Software Testing is conducted to verify that the software corresponds to the requirements and a separate test plan will define the various types of testing to be performed. This will typically include unit, integration, system, performance and acceptance testing. The test results play an important role in determining whether the software is ready to be released or not.

The project manager will report various metrics (including the quality metrics) in the regular status reports, and the quality metrics provide an objective indication of the quality of the product.

The cost of poor quality may be determined at the end of the project, and this may require a time recording system for the various project activities. The effort involved in detecting and correcting defects may be recorded, and a chart similar to Fig. 1.9 presented.

Poor quality may be due to various reasons. For example, it may be caused by inadequate reviews or testing of the software; inadequate skills or experience of the project team; or poorly defined or understood requirements.

3.7   Project Monitoring and Control

Project monitoring and control is concerned with monitoring project execution, and taking corrective action when project performance deviates from expectations. The progress of the project should be monitored against the plan, and corrective actions taken as appropriate. The key project parameters such as budget, effort and schedule as well as risks and issues are monitored, and the status of the project communicated regularly to the effected stakeholders. The project manager will conduct progress and milestone reviews to determine actual progress, new issues are identified and monitored, and the corrective actions identified are tracked to closure. The main focus of project monitoring and control is:

- Monitor the project plan and schedule and take action to ensure that the project schedule remains on track.
- Monitor the key project parameters
- Conduct progress and milestone reviews to determine the actual status.
- Monitor risks, issues and change requests, and take appropriate action.
- Monitor resources and manage any resource issues.
- Report the project status to management and project board
- Analyse issues and take corrective action
- Track corrective action to closure

A sample process map is provided in Fig. 3.3.

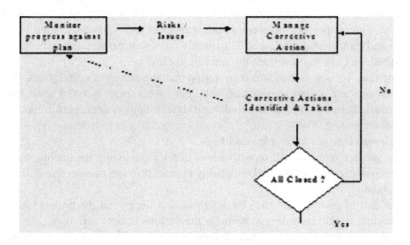

Fig. 3.3 Simple process map for project monitoring and control

The project manager will monitor progress, risks and issues during the project, and take appropriate corrective action. The status of the project will be reported in the regular status reports sent to management and the project board, with the status reviewed with management regularly during the project.

3.8   Managing Issues and Change Requests

The management of issues and change requests is a normal part of project management. An *issue* can arise at any time during the project (e.g., a supplier to the project may go out of business, an employee may resign, specialized hardware for testing may not arrive in time, and so on), and it refers to a problem that has occurred which may have a negative impact on the project. The severity of the issue is an indication of its impact, and the project manager has responsibility for managing it. The issue needs to be properly dealt with to enable the project to be delivered on time and on budget and with the right quality.

A *change request* is a stakeholder request for a change to the scope of the project, and it may arise at any time during the project. The impacts of the change request (e.g., technical, cost and schedule) need to be carefully considered, as a change introduces new risks to the project, and may adversely affect cost, schedule and quality. It is therefore essential to fully understand the impacts in order to make an informed decision on whether to authorise or reject the change request. The project manager may directly approve small change requests, and the impacts of a larger change requests are considered by the *change control board* (CCB), who make an informed decision to authorise or reject it.

The activities involved in managing issues and change requests are summarised in Table 3.5.

Table 3.5   Activities in managing issues and change requests

Activity	Description of issue/change request
Log issue or change request	The issue or change request is logged by the project manager. It is assigned a unique reference number and severity and categorised into a problem or change request.
Assess impact	This involves analysis to determine the technical impacts, as well as the impacts on cost, schedule and quality for the issue or change request. The risks need to be identified.
Decision on implementation	A decision is made on how to deal with the issue or change request. The CCB is usually involved in the decision to authorise a change request.
Implement solution	The affected project documents and software modules are identified, and modified accordingly.
Verify solution	Testing (Unit, System and UAT) are employed to verify the correctness of the solution.
Close issue/CR	The issue or change request is closed.

3.9   Project Board and Governance

The *project board*[8] (or steering group) is responsible for directing the project, and is directly accountable for the success of the project. It consists of senior managers and staff in the organization that have the authority to make resources available, to remove roadblocks, and to get things done.

It is consulted whenever key project decisions need to be made, and it plays a key role in project governance. The project board ensures that there is a clear business case for the project, and that the capital funding for the project is adequate and well spent. The project board may cancel the project at any stage during project execution should there cease to be a business case, or should project spending exceed tolerance and go out of control.[9]

The project manager reports to the project board, and sends regular status reports to highlight progress made as well as key project risks and issues. The project board meets at an appropriate frequency during the project (with extra sessions held should serious project issues arise) (Fig. 3.4).

There are several roles on the project board (an individual could perform more than one role) and their responsibilities are given in Table 3.6.

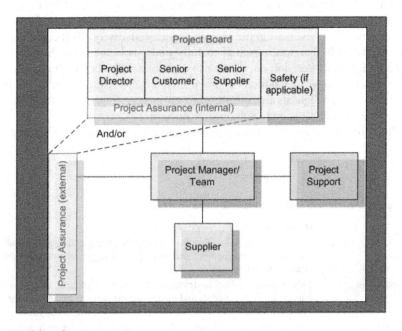

Fig. 3.4 Prince 2 project board

---

[8] The project board in the Prince 2 methodology includes roles such as the project executive, senior supplier, senior user, project assurance, and the project manager. These roles have distinct responsibilities.

[9] The project plan will usually specify a *tolerance level* for schedule and spending, where the project may spend (perhaps less than 10 %) in excess of the allocated capital for the project before seeking authorization for further capital funding for the project.

Table 3.6 Project board roles and responsibilities

Project Director	Ultimately responsible for the project. Provides overall guidance to the project.
Senior Customer	Represents the interests of users.
Senior Supplier	Represents the resources responsible for implementation (e.g., IS manager).
Project Manager	Link between project board and project team.
Project Assurance	Internal role (optional) that provides independent objective of the project.
Safety	Ensure adherence to health and safety standards (optional role).

3.10   Project Reporting

The frequency of project reporting is defined in the project plan (or the communications plan). The project report advises management and the key stakeholders of the current status of the project, and includes key project information such as:

- Completed Deliverables (during period)
- New risks and issues
- Schedule, Effort and Budget Status (RAG metrics[10])
- Quality and Test Status
- Key Risks and Issues
- Milestone Status
- Deliverables planned (next period)

The project manager discusses the project report with management and the project board, and states how the key risks and issues will be dealt with. The project manager will present a recovery plan to deal with the circumstances where the project has fallen significantly behind schedule or over budget.

The key risks and issues will be discussed, and the project manager will explain how the key issues are being dealt with, and how the key risks will be managed. The new risks and issues will also be discussed, and the project board will carefully consider how the project manager plans to deal with these, and will provide appropriate support to the project manager.

The project board will carefully consider the status of the project as well as the input from the project manager before deciding the appropriate course of action (which could include the immediate termination of the project).

3.11   Project Closure

A project is a temporary activity, and once the project goals have been achieved and the product handed over to the customer and support group, it is ready to be closed. The project manager will prepare an end of project report detailing the extent to

---

[10] Often, a colour coding mechanism is employed with a red flag indicating a serious issue; amber highlighting a potentially serious issue; and green indicating that everything is on track.

Fig. 3.5 Project
management triangle

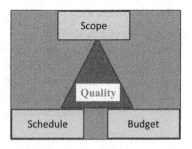

which the project achieved its targeted objectives. The report will include a summary of key project metrics including key quality metrics and the budget and timeliness metrics.

The success of the project is judged on the extent to which the defined objectives have been achieved, and on the extent to which the project has delivered the agreed functionality on schedule, on budget and with the right quality. This is often referred to as the project management triangle (Fig. 3.5).

The project manager presents the end project report to the project board, including any factors (e.g., change requests) that may have affected the timely delivery of the project or the allocated budget. The project is then officially closed.

The project manager then schedules a meeting with the team review the lessons learned from the project. The lessons learned are recorded by the team during the project (typically in a lessons learned log), and the key lessons learned are summarised in the lessons learned report. Any actions identified are assigned to individuals and follower through to closure, and the lessons learned report is made available to other projects (with the goal of learning from experience).

The project team is disbanded and the project team members are assigned to other duties.

3.12   Prince 2 Methodology

Prince 2 (*Projects in controlled environments*) is a popular project management methodology widely used in the U.K. and Europe. It is a structured, process driven approach to project management, with processes for project start up, initiating a project, controlling a stage, managing stage boundaries, closing a project, managing product delivery, planning and directing a project (Fig. 3.6). It has procedures to coordinate people and activities in a project, as well as procedures to monitor and control project activities.

These key processes are described in more detail in Table 3.7, and more detailed information on Prince 2 is in [51].

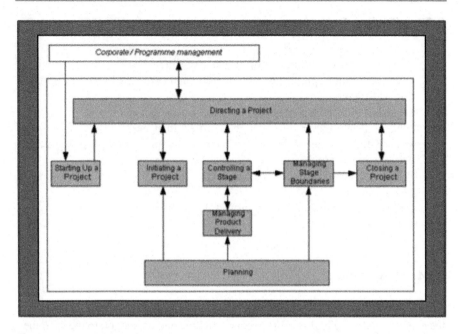

Fig. 3.6 Prince 2 processes

Table 3.7 Key processes in Prince 2

Process	Description
Start-up	Project Manager and project board appointed, project approach and project brief defined.
Controlling a stage	Stage plan prepared, quality and risks/issues managed, progress reviewed & reported.
Managing stage boundary	Stage status reviewed & next stage planned, actual products produced vs. original stage plan compared, stage or exception report produced.
Closing a project	Orderly closure of project with project board, end project report and lessons learned report.
Managing product delivery	Covers product creation by the team or a 3rd party supplier. Ensure that the planned deliverables meet quality criteria.
Planning	Prince 2 employs product based planning which involves identifying the products required, and then activities and resources to provide them. A good project plan gives everyone a common understanding of the work to be done.
Directing a project	Senior management have authority to define what is required from the project, authorization of the project, to commit resources and funds, and to provide management direction. The project board controls the project.

3.13   Review Questions

1. What is a project? What is project management?
2. Describe various approaches to estimation and explain why good estimation is difficult.
3. What activities take place at project start-up and initiation?
4. What skills are required to be a good project manager?
5. What is the purpose of the project board and explain why project governance is important.
6. What is the purpose of risk management? Describe how risks are managed in a project.
7. Describe the main activities in project management.

3.14   Summary

Project management is concerned with the effective management of projects, and the goal is to deliver a high-quality product, on time and on budget, to the customer. It involves good project planning and estimation; managing resources; managing changes and issues that arise during the project; managing quality; managing risks; managing the budget; monitoring progress and taking action when progress deviates from expectations; communicating progress to the various stakeholders; and delivering a high-quality product to their business customers.

The scope of the project needs to be determined, and the effort and schedule estimates should be established. The project plan is then be developed and approved by the stakeholders. It needs to be maintained during the project. The project plan will contain or reference several other plans such as the quality plan; the communication plan; the configuration management plan; and the test plan.

Project estimation and scheduling are difficult as often software projects are breaking new ground and differ from previous projects. Gantt charts are often employed for project scheduling, and these show the work breakdown for the project as well as task dependencies and allocation of staff to the various tasks.

The effective management of risk during a project is essential to project success. Risks arise due to uncertainty and the risk management cycle involves risk identification; risk analysis and evaluation; identifying responses to risks; selecting and planning a response to the risk; and risk monitoring.

Once the planning is complete the project execution commences, and the focus moves to monitoring progress, re-planning as appropriate, managing risks and issues, re-planning as appropriate, providing regular progress reports to the project board, and so on.

Requirements, Design and Development

4

Key Topics

Requirements Elicitation
Requirements Analysis
Traceability
Managing Changes to Requirements
Software Design
Software Reuse

4.1 Introduction

The user requirements specify what the customer wants and define *what* the software system is required to do, as distinct from *how* this is to be done. The requirements are the foundation for the system, and if they are incorrect then irrespective of the best software development process in the world, the implemented system will be incorrect.

Often, the initial requirements for a project arise due to a particular problem that the business or customer needs to solve. This leads to a project to implement an appropriate solution, and the first step is to determine the scope of work and the actual requirements for the project, and whether the project is feasible from the cost, time and technical considerations. The user requirements are determined from discussions with the customer to determine their actual needs, and they are then refined into the system requirements which state the functional and non-functional requirements of the system.

The software design of the system is concerned with the architecture of the system, as well as activities to describe the algorithms and functions required to implement the system requirements. It is a creative process concerned with how the system will

G. O'Regan, *Introduction to Software Quality*, Undergraduate Topics
in Computer Science, DOI 10.1007/978-3-319-06106-1_4,
© Springer International Publishing Switzerland 2014

be implemented, and the architecture may include hardware such as personal computers and servers as well as the various software modules and their interfaces.

The software development is concerned with the actual implementation of the design, and the implementation is in some programming language such as C++ or Java. The software may be developed internally or it may be outsourced to another company, or a solution may be purchased off-the-shelf. It is essential that the design is valid with respect to the requirements, and that the implemented system is valid with respect to the design.

4.2   Requirements Engineering

The specification of the requirements needs to be unambiguous to ensure that all parties involved share a common understanding of the development of the system, and fully agree on what is to be developed and tested. Table 4.1 presents symptoms of a poor requirements process.

Table 4.2 lists characteristics of good requirements.

Prototyping may be employed to assist in the definition and validation of the requirements, and a suitable prototype will include key parts of the system. It will allow users to give early feedback on the proposed system, and on the extent to which it meets their needs. Prototyping is very useful in clarifying the requirements, and helps in reducing the risk of developing the wrong solution.

The implications of the proposed set of requirements needs to be understood, as the choice of a particular requirement may affect the choice of another requirement. For example, in the telecommunications domain, two features may work correctly in isolation, but when present together they interact in an undesirable way. Therefore, feature interactions need to be identified and investigated at the requirements phase to determine how interactions should be resolved.

The following activities are involved in requirements definition and management, and they are discussed in more detail in the following sections:

- Requirements elicitation and specification
- Requirements analysis
- Requirements verification and validation
- Requirements traceability
- Managing changes to the requirements

We distinguish between the user (or business) requirements and the system requirements. The *user requirements* are the high-level requirements for the system, whereas the *system requirements* are a more detailed description of what the system is to do. The user requirements are more abstract than the system requirements, and a user requirement is expanded into several system requirements. The system requirements provide more detailed information on the system to be implemented.

The system requirements include the functional and non-functional requirements. A *functional requirement* is a statement about the functionality of the system: i.e., how the system should behave and how it should respond to particular inputs. A *non-functional requirement* is a constraint on the functionality of the

Table 4.1 Symptoms of poor requirements development and management

No.	Symptoms of poor requirements process
1.	High-level of requirements creep during the project.
2.	Requirements changing regularly during the project.
3.	Missing requirements
4.	Requirements accepted from any source
5.	High-level of rework during the project
6.	Design, Implementation and Test products inconsistently interpret the requirements.
7.	Untestable requirements
8.	Inability to prove that the implementation satisfies the requirements.

Table 4.2 Characteristics of good requirements

No.	Characteristics of good requirements
1.	Each requirement is clear and unambiguous.
2.	Each requirement has a priority to indicate its importance
3.	Each requirement may be implemented.
4.	Each requirement is testable.
5.	Each requirement is necessary.
6.	Any conflicts between the requirements are resolved.
7.	Each requirement is broken down as fully as possible
8.	Each requirement is consistent with the project's objectives.
9.	Each requirement is stated as a stakeholder need (i.e., premature design/solution or implementation information is not included).
10.	The business requirements are traceable (in both directions) throughout the development cycle
11.	The requirements are complete and consistent.

system (e.g., a timing, performance, security or hardware constraint). Next, we discuss the process of determining the requirements for the system.

4.2.1 Requirements Elicitation and Specification

The process of determining the requirements for the proposed system involves discussions with the relevant stakeholders to determine their needs, and to explicitly define what functionality the system should provide, as well as any hardware and performance constraints. The process of eliciting the requirements from the stakeholders is difficult as

- Stakeholders often do not know what they want from the system.
- Stakeholders often do not know what is or what is not technically feasible, and may have unrealistic expectations.
- Stakeholders express the requirements in the language of their domain, which may differ from the language of the business analysts.

– Different stakeholders may want different things from the system resulting in conflicts that need to be resolved.

The project manager/business analyst and relevant stakeholders will conduct a brainstorming session to define the high level requirements for the proposed system (or modification to an existing system). Further requirements workshops will review and analyse the draft requirements, and identify all further relevant information for the proposed system. The workshops involve interviews with the relevant stakeholders to elicit the actual requirements for the proposed system from the stakeholders.

Prototyping helps to identify gaps and misunderstandings in the definition of the requirements. The prototype is an early working version of the system, and it is used to give the users a flavour of what the working system will look like, and its evaluation by the stakeholders helps in clarifying the requirements. The prototype may be thrown away at the end of prototyping, or it may be re-used in the development of the system. It involves:

– Define prototype objectives
– Decide which functional requirements will be prototyped
– Develop the prototype
– Evaluate the prototype

The project manager (or a business analyst) will facilitate the requirements workshop, and the requirements gathered are then consolidated into a coherent set of requirements to form the first draft of the user requirements. Following the initial workshop, the project manager/business analyst prepares a draft of the detailed requirements, and sends the document to the participants for comments. Further requirements workshops are held to discuss and analyse the draft requirements to ensure that they meet the needs of the stakeholders, and this process continues until all participants are in agreement with the user requirements. In some cases, the requirements may already be defined and documented by the customer.

The requirements workshops involve a brainstorming session with the attendees, and this allows the users to discuss their needs and the requirements for the proposed system. The requirements workshops allow the proposed requirements to be discussed, analysed and prioritized. Any conflicts in the requirements are identified and resolved. The requirements document is updated accordingly with the agreed set of user requirements.

The project manager/business analyst may use a checklist to determine that the requirements have been fully specified, and to verify that every requirement specified is actually necessary. The final version of the user requirements document is circulated to all participants for their final review and approval.

Once the user requirements have been agreed by all stakeholders the work on the *system requirements* commences, and the business analyst expands the user requirements into more specific and detailed system requirements. Further system requirements workshops are conducted with the relevant stakeholders until the system requirements are approved.

The requirements for a system are generally documented in a natural language such as "*English*". Natural language is inherently ambiguous, and therefore care needs to be taken to ensure that the definition is precise and unambiguous.

The ambiguity of natural language has led to interest in precise notations to express requirements unambiguously. These include the formal specification notations such as Z or VDM that are often employed in the safety critical or security critical fields. The advantage of these mathematical languages is that they are precise and amenable to proof, and mathematical analysis may be employed in a sense to debug[1] the requirements. This provides increased confidence in the correctness and validity of the requirements. However, these notations are perceived as being difficult to use by industrialists, and they are not widely employed at this time. Formal methods are discussed in Chap. 17.

Other notations to express the requirements include the visual modelling language UML [32] which has become popular in recent years. UML is discussed in Chap. 19.

4.2.2   Requirements Analysis

The requirements are analysed to ensure that they are technically feasible and to identify any conflicts between them. The resolution of any conflicts is through negotiations with the stakeholders. The requirements are prioritized to define the importance of each requirement, and some development models implement the most important requirements first. Requirements analysis is an iterative process with feedback going back to the stakeholders in the requirements elicitation process.

The workshops will verify that the system requirements are valid with respect to the user requirements, and technical workshops will need to be conducted to determine the appropriate approach to their implementation.

4.2.3   Requirements Verification and Validation

The difference between requirements validation and verification is illustrated by the phrase "*Building the right thing*" vs. "*building it right*". In other words *validation* is concerned with ensuring that the correct requirements are being implemented, whereas *verification* is concerned with ensuring that the requirements are being implemented correctly.

The stakeholders validate the requirements to ensure that the defined requirements are actually those desired. This may involve several reviews of the requirements (and prototype) by the stakeholders, with updates made by the author until all stakeholders are ready to approve the requirements of the system.

---

[1] Essentially, the mathematical language provides the facility to prove that certain properties are true of the specification, and that certain undesirable properties are false in the specification.

The validation of the requirements will ensure that the requirements are complete, consistent, and realizable and reflect the needs of the customer. The final validation step is the user acceptance testing, and this is performed by the customer to confirm that the completed system fully meets user requirements. The lifecycle model employed determines the verification and validation activities to be conducted during the project, with models such as joint application development (JAD) and Agile involving a high-level of customer involvement.

Requirements verification is concerned with ensuring that the system as built (from design, to development, to testing) properly implements the defined requirements. A traceability matrix shows how the requirements are implemented and tested, and may be employed for requirements verification.

4.2.4   Managing Changes to Requirements

A *change request* is a stakeholder request for a change to the scope of the project, and it may arise at any time during the project. It is essential that the impacts of a change request on schedule, effort, budget and technical areas are fully considered prior to its authorisation.

Once the system requirements have been approved, any proposed changes to the requirements are subject to formal change control. Change request are considered by the *change control board* (CCB), who make an informed decision to authorise or reject the request based on its impacts.

The need to change the requirements may be due to business or regulatory changes, or to a customer need becoming apparent at a late stage of the project when the system is nearing completion. The impacts of the change request (e.g., technical, cost and schedule) need to be carefully considered, as a change introduces new risks to the project, and may adversely affect cost, schedule and quality. The activities involved in managing change requests are summarised in Table 4.3.

Following the approval of a change request the affected documents such as the system requirements, the design, and software modules are modified. Testing is carried out to verify that the changes have been implemented correctly.

4.2.5   Requirements Traceability

The objective of requirement traceability is to verify that all of the requirements for the project have been implemented and tested. One way to do this is to consider each requirement number and to go through every part of the design document to find where the requirement is being implemented in the design, and similarly to go through the test documents and find any reference to the requirement number to show where it is being tested. This would demonstrate that the particular require-ment number has been implemented and tested.

Table 4.3 Managing change requests

Activity	Change request
Log change request	The change request is logged and a unique reference number and severity assigned.
Assess impact	The cost, schedule, technical and quality impacts are determined and the risks identified.
Decision	The CCB authorises or rejects the change request.
Implement solution	The affected project documents and software modules are identified, and modified accordingly.
Verify solution	Testing (Unit, System and UAT) are employed to verify the correctness of the solution.
Close CR	The change request is closed.

Table 4.4 Sample trace matrix

Requirement no.	Sections in design	Test cases in test plan
R1.1	D1.4, D1.5, D3.2	T1.2, T1.7
R1.2	D1.8, D8.3	T1.4
R1.3	D2.2	T1.3
R1.50	D20.1, D30.4	T20.1 T24.2

A more effective mechanism to do this is to employ a traceability matrix, which may be employed to map the user requirements to the system requirements; the system requirements to the design; the design to the unit test cases; the system test cases; and the UAT test cases. That is, traceability is defined through the project lifecycle, and the matrix provides details of how the requirements have been implemented and tested.

The traceability of the requirements is *bi-directional*, and the traceability matrix may be maintained as a separate document, or as part of the requirements document. The basic idea is that a mapping between the requirement numbers and sections of the design or test plan is defined, and this provides confidence that all of the requirements have been implemented and tested.

Requirements may be numbered and a single requirement number may map on to several sections of the design or to several test cases: i.e., the mapping may be one to many. The traceability matrix (Table 4.4) provides the mapping between individual requirement numbers, and the sections in the design or test plan corresponding to the particular requirement number.

This mapping will typically be *one to many*: i.e., a single requirement number will typically be implemented in several design sections, and verified by several test cases. The traceability matrix will be employed to demonstrate that all of the requirements have been implemented and tested.

It is essential to keep the traceability matrix up to date during the project, and following changes to the requirements. The traceability matrix is useful as a tool whenever there are changes to the requirements as it allows the impacts of the change on the other requirements (and other project deliverables) to be easily determined.

4.3   Architecture Design

The design of the system consists of engineering activities to describe the *architecture model or structure of the system* that will satisfy the functional and non-functional requirements, as well as the *design of the individual programs* to describe the algorithms and functions required to implement the system requirements. *Design is a creative process* concerned with how the system will be organized, and the architecture design is often presented as a set of interacting components. The design activities include architecture design, interface design, component design, algorithm design, and data structure design. There are often several possible design solutions for a particular system, and the designer will need to choose the most appropriate design of the system.

The architectural model of the system is an abstract visual representation of the system, and it is often presented as a set of boxes or block diagrams. The major components of the system and their interactions are identified, and each box represents a component with the architecture showing all the components and their connections. A box within a box represents a sub-component, and arrows are used to represent the flow of data between the components. This abstract description of the system provides a high-level view of the system, and is an effective way to facilitate discussion about the system design with the relevant stakeholders.

The views of C.A.R. Hoare on software design are interesting (Fig. 4.1). He states that there are two ways of constructing a software design.

> One way is to make it so simple that there are obviously no deficiencies.
> The other way is to make it so complex that there are no obvious deficiencies.

He argues that the first method is far more difficult to achieve, and that it requires skill and insight.

The starting point in design is always the problem domain, and it is essential that the problem to be solved is understood from a number of different viewpoints. A number of potential solutions may then be identified, and each potential solution is evaluated. This leads to the chosen solution which may, for example, be the simplest and least costly.

Design is an iterative process and the goal is to describe the system architecture that will satisfy the functional and non-functional requirements. It involves describing the system at a number of different levels of abstraction, with the designer starting off with an informal picture of the design that is then refined by adding more information.

Parnas's ideas on design have been quite influential (Fig. 4.2), and his 1972 paper *"On the criteria to be used in decomposing systems into modules"* [52] is a classic in software engineering. He introduced the revolutionary *information hiding* principle, which allows software to be *designed in a way to deal with change*. A module is characterized by its knowledge of a design decision (*secret*) that it hides from all other modules. Every information-hiding module has an *interface* that provides the only means to access the services provided by the modules. *The*

Fig. 4.1 C.A.R. Hoare
(Public domain)

Fig. 4.2 David Parnas
(Public domain)

interface hides the module's implementation. Information hiding is used in object-oriented programming. Parnas argues in his 1972 paper that:

> It is almost always incorrect to begin the decomposition of a system into modules on the basis of a flowchart. We propose instead that one begins with a list of difficult design decisions or design decisions which are likely to change. Each module is then designed to hide such a decision from the others

The design may be specified in various ways such as graphical notations that display the relationships between the various components making up the design. The notation may include block diagrams, flow charts, or various UML diagrams such as sequence diagrams, state charts, and so on. The design of programs may employ pseudo code to specify the algorithms as well as the data structures that are the basis for implementation. Natural language is often employed to express information that cannot be expressed formally. The design activities include:

- Architecture Design of system (with all sub-systems)
- Abstract specification of each sub-system
- Interface Design (for each subsystem)
- Component Design

Table 4.5 Views of system architecture

View	Description
Logical	This view shows the key abstractions in the system as objects or object classes
Process view	This view shows how the system is composed of interacting processes at run-time.
Development view	This view shows how the software is decomposed into modules/components for development.
Physical view	This view shows the system hardware and how the software components are distributed across the system.

– Data Structure Design
– Algorithm Design

The quality of the software architecture directly impacts the robustness, performance and maintainability of the system. A good software architecture will manage the inherent complexity of the system, and ensures a solid performance of the implemented system, with safety, security, availability and maintainability requirements properly addressed.

There is a need to present multiple views of the system architecture such as how the system is decomposed into modules, how the run-time processes interact, how the hardware is distributed across the processors in the system. These views may include [61] those given in Table 4.5.

The process view could be described by data-flow diagrams (part of the SSADM method) which show the flow of data through a system. UML is a popular design method which gives several views of the architecture of the system. It is essential validate the design with respect to the system requirements.

4.4   Design and Development

The design of the system consists of engineering activities to describe the components of the system as well as the algorithms and functions required to implement the system requirements. Design and development are closely related and are concerned with developing an executable software system.

Functional design involves starting with a high-level view of the system and refining it into a more detailed design. The system state is centralized and shared between the functions operating on that state.

Object-oriented design has become popular in recent years and is based on the concept of information hiding developed by Parnas [52]. The system is viewed as a collection of *objects* rather than functions, with each object managing its own state information. The system state is decentralized and an object is a member of an object class. The definition of a *class* includes *attributes* and *operations* on class members, and these may be inherited from super classes. Objects communicate by exchanging *messages*.

Software design and development are closely linked, and often proceed in parallel. Software design is the creative process that identifies the software components and their relationships, whereas software development is concerned with the implementation of the design in some programming language. The choice of language reflects the problem domain, and may be an object-oriented language such as C++ or Java, or a procedural language such as C or FORTRAN. It is important that the software code is subject to a peer review to ensure that it is of high-quality, and that it is a valid implementation of the requirements and design. The coding standards for the language will also need to be followed, as this assists in the maintainability of the code.

Software reuse has become topical in recent years, and today many organizations approach to development includes software reuse. The advantages of software reuse are that it potentially improves productivity, and delivers higher quality software. *Open source development* is a modern approach to software development in which the source code is published, and software developers from around the world volunteer to participate in the software development process. The idea is that the source code is not proprietary, and that it should be available for software developers to use and modify as they wish. *Customized-off-the-shelf software* (*COTS*) is software (or a system) that may be purchased off-the-shelf, and adapted to the user's requirements. The reader is referred to the classic text in software engineering [61] for a more detailed explanation of the design and development activities.

4.5   Review Questions

1. What is the difference between a functional and non-functional requirement?
2. What is the difference between requirements verification and validation?
3. How are requirement elicited from the customer?
4. Discuss the difference between architecture design and detailed design.
5. How are changes to the requirements managed?
6. What is the purpose of requirements traceability?
7. Explain the differences between COTS, software reuse, and open source software.

4.6   Summary

The success of business is highly influenced by software, and companies may develop their own software internally, or they may acquire software solutions off-the-shelf or from bespoke software development. Cost is a key driver in most organizations and it is essential that software is produced as cheaply and efficiently as possible, and that waste is reduced or eliminated in the software development process. Companies need to produce software that is *better, faster and cheaper* than their competitors in order to survive in the market place.

The user requirements specify what the customer wants and define *what* the software system is required to do, as distinct from *how* this is to be done. The requirements are the foundation for the system, and it is essential that they are correct and reflect the needs of the customer.

Often, the initial requirements for a project arise due to a particular problem that the business or customer needs to solve. The first step is to determine the scope of work and the actual requirements for the project, and whether the project is feasible. The user requirements are determined from discussions with the customer to determine their actual needs, and they are then refined into the system requirements.

The software design of the system is concerned with the architecture of the system, as well as activities to describe the algorithms and functions required to implement the system requirements. It is a creative process concerned with how the system will be implemented, and it may include hardware as well as the various software modules and their interfaces.

The software development is concerned with the actual implementation of the design, and the implementation is in some programming language such as C++ or Java. The software may be developed internally or it may be outsourced to another company, or a solution may be purchased off-the-shelf. It is essential that the design is valid with respect to the requirements, and that the implemented system is valid with respect to the design.

Configuration Management

5

5.1 Introduction

Software configuration management is concerned with identifying the configuration items of a system; controlling changes to them; and maintaining integrity and traceability. The configuration items are generally documents in the early part of the development lifecycle, whereas the focus is on source code control management and software release management in the later parts of development. Configuration management involves:

- Identifying what needs to be controlled
- Ensuring those items are accurately defined and documented
- Ensuring that changes are made in a controlled manner
- Ensuring that the correct version of a work product is being used
- Determining the status of a configuration item at any time
- Ensuring adherence to company standards
- Planning builds and releases

G. O'Regan, *Introduction to Software Quality*, Undergraduate Topics
in Computer Science, DOI 10.1007/978-3-319-06106-1_5,
© Springer International Publishing Switzerland 2014

Table 5.1 Features of good configuration management

Features of good configuration management
What is the correct version of the software module to be updated?
Where can I get a copy of R4.7 of Software System X?
What versions of the Software System X are installed at the various customer sites?
What changes have been introduced in the new release of software (version R4.8 from the previous release of R4.7)?
What version of the Design document corresponds to software system version R3.5?
What customers use R3.5 of the software system?
Are we certain that no undocumented or unapproved changes have been included in released versions of the software?

It allows the orderly development of software, and it ensures that the impacts of proposed changes are considered prior to authorization. It ensures that releases are planned and that only authorized changes to the software are made. The integrity of the system is maintained and the constituents of the software system and their version numbers are known at all times.

Effective configuration management allows questions such as in Table 5.1 to be easily answered.

The symptoms of poor configuration management include corrected defects that suddenly begin to reappear; difficulty in or failure to locate the latest version of source code; or failure to determine the source code that corresponds to a software release. Therefore, it is important to employ sound configuration management practices to enable high-quality software to be consistently produced. Poor configuration management practices lead to quality problems resulting in a loss of the credibility and reputation of a company. Several symptoms of poor configuration management practices are listed in Table 5.2.

Configuration management involves identifying the configuration items to be controlled, and systematically controlling change to them, in order to maintain the integrity and traceability of the configuration throughout the lifecycle. There is a need to manage and control changes to documents and source code, including the project plan, the requirements document, design documents, code, and test plans.

A key concept in configuration management is that of a "*baseline*", which is *a set of work products that have been formally reviewed and agreed upon, and serves as the foundation for future development work.*

A baseline can only be changed through a formal change control procedure which leads to a new baseline. It provides a stable basis for the continuing evolution of the configuration items, and all approved changes move forward from the current baseline leading to the creation of a new baseline. The CCB authorizes the release of baselines, and the content of each baseline is documented. All configuration items must be approved before they are entered into the released baselines.

Therefore, it is necessary to identify the configuration items that need to be placed under formal change control, and to maintain a history of the changes made to the baseline. There are four key parts to software configuration management (Table 5.3).

Table 5.2 Symptoms of poor configuration management

Symptoms of poor configuration management
Defects corrected suddenly begin to re-appear
Cannot find latest version of source code
Unable to match source code and object code
Wrong version of software sent to the customer
Wrong code tested
Cannot replicate previously released code
Simultaneous changes to same source component by multiple developers with some changes lost

Table 5.3 Software configuration management activities

Area	Description
Configuration Identification	This requires identifying the configuration items to be controlled, and implementing a sound configuration management system, including a repository where documents and source code are placed under controlled access. It includes a mechanism for releasing documents or code, a naming convention and version numbering system for documents and code, and baseline/release planning. The version and status of each configuration item should be known.
Configuration Control	This involves tracking and controlling change requests, and controlling changes to the configuration items. Any changes to the work products are controlled, and authorized by a change control board or similar mechanism. Problems or defects reported by the test groups or customer are analysed, and any changes made are subject to change control. The version of the work product is known, and the constituents of a particular release are known and controlled. The previous versions of releases can be recreated as the source code constituents are fully known.
Configuration Auditing	This includes audits of the baselines to verify integrity of the baseline and audits of the configuration management system itself and verification that standards and procedures are followed. The results of the audits are communicated to the affected groups and corrective action taken.
Status Accounting	This involves data collection and report generation. These reports include the software baseline status, the summary of changes to the software baseline, problem report summaries, and change request summaries

A typical software release, e.g., in the telecommunications domain, consists of incremental development where the software to be released consists of a number of release builds where each build initially consists of new functionality, and the later builds consists of fix releases.

Software configuration management is planned for the project and each project will typically have a build plan which will detail the planned delivery of functionality and fix release to the project (Table 5.4).

Each of the R. 1.0.O.k are termed release builds and they consist of functionality and fixes to problems. The content of each release build is known; i.e., the project team and manager will target specific functionality and fixes for each build, and the actual content of the particular release baseline is documented. Each release build

Table 5.4 Build plan

Release baseline	Contents
R 1.0.0.0	F_4, F_5, F_7
R. 1.0.0.1	F_1, F_2, F_6 + fixes
R. 1.0.0.2	F_3 + fixes
R. 1.0.0.3	F_8 + fixes (functionality freeze)
R. 1.0.0.4	Fixes
R. 1.0.0.5	Fixes
R. 1.0.0.6	Official release

Table 5.5 CMMI requirements for configuration management

Specific goal	Specific practice	Description of specific practice/goal
SG 1		**Establish baselines**
	SP 1.1	Identify configuration items
	SP 1.2	Establish a configuration management system
	SP 1.3	Create or release baselines
SG 2		**Track and control changes**
	SP 2.1	Track change requests
	SP 2.2	Control configuration items
SG 3		**Establish integrity**
	SP 3.1	Establish configuration management records
	SP 3.2	Perform configuration audits

can be replicated, as the version of source code to create the build is known and the source code is under control management.

There are various tools employed for software configuration management activities, and these include well-known tools such as Clearcase, PVCS, Visual Source Safe (VSS) for source code control management. The PV tracker tool and Clearquest may be used for tracking defects and change requests. A defect tracking tool will list all of the open defects against the software, and a defect may require several change requests to correct the software, as a problem may affect different parts of the software product as well as different versions of the product, and a change request may be necessary for each part. The tool will generally link the change requests to the problem report. The current status of the problem report can be determined, and the targeted release build for the problem identified.

The CMMI provides guidance on practices to be implemented for sound configuration management (Table 5.5).

The CMMI requirements are concerned with establishing a configuration management system; identifying the work products that need to be subject to change control; controlling changes to these work products over time; controlling releases of work products; creating baselines; maintaining the integrity of baselines; providing accurate configuration data to stakeholders; recording and reporting the status of configuration items and change requests; and verifying the correctness and completeness of configuration items with configuration audits. We shall discuss the key parts of configuration management in the following Sections.

5.2 Configuration Management System

The configuration management system enables the controlled evolution of the documents and the software modules produced during the project. It includes
- Configuration management planning.
- A document repository with check in/check out features
- A source code repository with check in/check out features
- A configuration manager (may be a part time role)
- File naming convention for documents and source code.
- Project directory structure
- Version Numbering System for documents
- Standard templates for documents
- Facility to create a baseline
- A release procedure
- A group (change control board) to manage changes to baseline
- A change control procedure
- Configuration management audits to verify integrity of baseline

5.2.1 Identify Configuration Items

The configuration items are the work products to be placed under configuration management control, and they include project documents, source code and data files. They may also include compilers as well as any supporting tools employed in the project.

The project documentation will typically include project plans; the business requirements document; the system specification; the architecture and technical design documents; the test plans, etc.

The items to be placed under configuration management control are identified and documented early in the project lifecycle. Each configuration item needs to be uniquely identified and controlled. This may be done with a naming convention for the project deliverables and source code, and applying it consistently. For example, a simple approach is to employ mnemonics labels and version numbers to uniquely identify project deliverables. For example, a business requirements specification for project 005 in the Finance business area may be represented simply by:

FIN_005_BRS

5.2.2 Document Control Management

The project documents are stored in a document repository using a configuration management tool such as PVCS or VSS. For consistency, a standard directory structure is often employed for projects, as this makes it easier to locate particular configuration items. A single repository may be employed for both documents and software code, or a separate repository for each.

Clearly, it is undesirable for two individuals to modify the same document at the same time, and the document repository will include *check in/check out* procedures. The document must be checked out prior to its modification, and once it is checked out it may not be modified by another until it is checked back in. An audit trail of all modifications made to a particular document is maintained, including who made the change, the date the change was made, and the rationale for the change.

5.2.2.1 Version Numbering of Documents

A simple version numbering system may be employed to record the versions of documents: e.g., v0.1, v0.2, v0.3 is often used for draft documents, with version v1.0 being the first approved version of the document. Each time a document is modified its version number is incremented, and the document history records the reasons for modification.

- V0.1 Initial draft of document
- V0.x Revised draft $(x > 0)$
- V1.0 Approved baseline version
- V1.x Approved minor revision $(x > 0)$
- Vn.0 Approved major revision $(n > 1)$
- Vn.x Approved minor revision $(x > 0, n > 1)$

The configuration management system will provide records of the configuration management activities as well as the status of the configuration items and the status of the change requests. The revision history of the configuration items will be maintained.

5.2.3   Source Code Control Management

The source code and data files are stored in a source code repository using a tool such as PVCS, VSS or Clearcase, and the repository provides an audit trail of all the changes made to the source code. An item must first be checked out for modification, the changes are made, and it is then checked back in to the repository. The source code management system provides security and control of the configuration items, and the procedures include:

- Access controls
- Checking in/out configuration items
- Merging and Branching
- Labels
- Reporting

This ensures that the integrity of the work product is preserved, and prevents more than one person from altering the work product at the same time.

5.2.4 Configuration Management Plan

A software *configuration management plan* is prepared early in the project, and defines the configuration management activities for the project. It may be a section of the overall project plan or a separate plan. It will detail the items to be placed under configuration management control, the standards for naming configuration items, the version numbering system, as well as version control and release management.[1] The configuration management plan is placed under configuration management control.

The contents of each software release need to be documented as well as installation and rollback instructions. It will detail the requirements and change requests implemented, as well as the defects corrected and the version of the new release. A list will be maintained customer sites of where the release has been installed. All software releases are tested appropriately prior to their approval. The CM plan will include:
- Roles and responsibilities
- Configuration Items
- Naming Conventions
- Version Control
- Filing Structure for project

The stakeholders and roles involved are identified and documented in the CM plan. Often, the role of a *software configuration manager* is employed, and this may be a full or part time role[2] depending on the size of the organization and projects. The CM manager ensures that the configuration management activities are carried out correctly, and will conduct and report the results of the CM audits.

5.3 Change Control

A change request database[3] is set up to record requests for changes during the project. The change requests are documented and considered by the change control board (CCB). The CCB may just consist of the project manager and the system owner for small projects. The impacts and risks of the proposed change are considered, and the CCB rejects or approves the request. The impacts may be on the schedule and budget, as well technical. It is important to keep change to a minimum at the later stages of the project in order to reduce risks to quality.

Figure 5.1 describes a simple process for raising a change request; performing an impact assessment; deciding on whether to approve or reject the change request; and proceeding with implementation (where applicable).

The results of the CCB review of each change request (including the rationale of the decision made) will be recorded. Change requests and problem reports for all

---

[1] These may be defined in a Configuration Management procedure and referenced in the CM plan.

[2] The project manager may perform the CM manager role for small organizations and projects.

[3] This may just be a simple Excel spread sheet or a sophisticated tool.

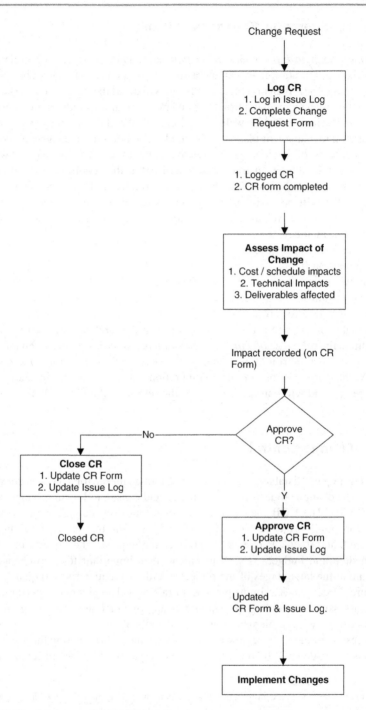

Fig. 5.1 Simple process map for change requests

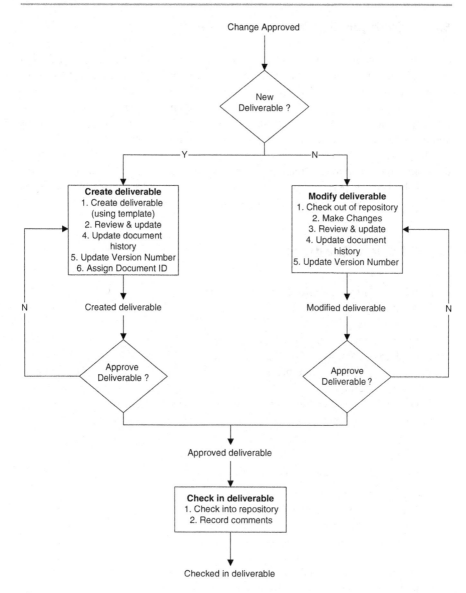

Fig. 5.2 Simple process map for configuration management

configuration items are recorded and analysed, reviewed, approved (or rejected) and tracked to closure.

A sample configuration management process map is detailed in Fig. 5.2, and it shows the process for updates to configuration information following an approved change request. The deliverable is checked out of the repository; modifications are made and the changes approved; configuration information is updated and the deliverable is checked back into the repository.

5.4   Configuration Management Audits

Configuration management audits are conducted during the project to verify that the configuration is consistent and complete. Every project should have at least one configuration audit, and the objective is to verify the completeness and correctness of the configuration system for the project. The audit will check that the records correctly identify the configuration, and that the configuration management standards and procedures have been followed. Table 5.6 presents a sample checklist.

There may also be a *librarian role* to set up the filing structure for the project, or the configuration manager may perform this role. The project manager assigns responsibilities for performing configuration management activities. All involved in the process receive appropriate training on the process.

5.5   Review Questions

1. What is software configuration management?
2. What is change control?
3. What is a baseline?
4. Explain source code control management.
5. Explain document control management.
6. What is a configuration management audit and explain how it differs from a standard audit?
7. Describe the role of the configuration manager and librarian.
8. What is a baseline?

Table 5.6 Sample configuration management audit checklist

No.	Item to check
1.	Is the Directory Structure set up for the project?
2.	Are the configuration items identified and listed?
3.	Have the latest versions of the templates been used?
4.	Is a unique document Id employed for each document?
5.	Is the standard version numbering system followed for the project?
6.	Are all versions of documents and software modules in the document/source code repository?
7.	Is the Configuration Management plan up to date?
8.	Are the roles defined in the Configuration Management Plan performing their assigned responsibilities?
9.	Are changes to the approved documents formally controlled?
10.	Is the version number of a document incremented following an agreed change to an approved document?
11.	Is there a change control board set up to approve change requests?
12.	Is there a record of which releases are installed at the various customer sites?
13.	Are all documents/software modules produced by vendors under appropriate configuration management control?

5.6 Summary

Software configuration management is concerned with the orderly development and evolution of the software. It involves identifying the configuration items that are subject to change control, controlling changes to them, and maintaining integrity and traceability. The configuration items are generally documents in the early part of the development lifecycle, whereas the focus is on source code control management and software release management in the later parts of development.

The company standards need to be adhered to, and the correct version of a work product should be known at all time. There is a need for a document and source code repository, which has access controls, checking in and checking out procedures; and labelling of releases.

A project will have a configuration management plan, and the configuration manager role is responsible for ensuring that the configuration management activities are carried out correctly. Configuration audits will be conducted to verify that the CM activities have been carried out correctly.

Configuration management ensures that the impacts of proposed changes are considered prior to authorization. It ensures that releases are planned and that only authorized changes to the software are made. The integrity of the system is maintained, and the constituents of the software system and their version numbers are known at all times.

Summary

Software Inspections

6

6.1 Introduction

The objective of software inspections is to build quality into the software product, rather than adding quality later. There is clear evidence that the cost of correction of a defect increases the later that it is detected, and it is therefore more cost effective to build quality in rather than adding it later in the development cycle. Software inspections are an effective way of doing this.

There are several approaches to software inspections, and these vary in the level of formality employed. A simple informal approach consists of a walkthrough of the document or code by an individual other than the author. The meeting usually takes place at the author's desk or in a meeting room, and the reviewer and author discuss the document or code informally.

There are formal software inspection methodologies such as the well-known *Fagan inspection* methodology [20] and the Gilb methodology [24]. These methodologies include pre-inspection activity, an inspection meeting, and post-inspection

G. O'Regan, *Introduction to Software Quality*, Undergraduate Topics
in Computer Science, DOI 10.1007/978-3-319-06106-1_6,
© Springer International Publishing Switzerland 2014

Fig. 6.1 Michael Fagan

activity. Several inspection roles are typically employed, including an *author* role, an *inspector* role, a *tester* role, and a *moderator* role.

The Fagan inspection methodology was developed by Michael Fagan (Fig. 6.1) at IBM in the mid-1970s, and the Gilb methodology was developed by Tom Gilb. The formality of the inspection methodology used by an organization is dependent on its type of business. The impact of a defect may have a major adverse effect on the customer's business: for example, an incorrect one-line change to telecoms software could create a major telecommunications outage and major disruption to customers. There may be financial impacts, as the service level agreement details the service level that will be provided, and the compensation given for service disruption. Consequently, a telecommunications company needs to ensure that its software is fit for purpose, and a formal inspection process tends to be employed. This means that requirement documents, high-level and detailed design documents, and code are inspected, and generally inspections are explicitly planned in the project schedule.

An organization will need to devise an inspection process which is suitable for its particular needs. The level of formality is influenced by its business, its culture, and the potential impact of a software defect on its customers. It may adopt a formal approach such as the Fagan or Gilb methodology, or it may devise a less formal process tailored to its needs. It may not be possible to have all of the participants present in a room, and participation by conference call or video link may be employed. A formal inspection process may not suit some organization cultures, and an informal approach such as a structured walkthrough may be the adopted approach.

Software inspections play an important role in building quality into each phase, and in ensuring that the quality of the delivered product is good. The quality of the delivered software product is only as good as the quality at the end each phase, and therefore a phase should be exited only when the desired quality has been achieved.

The effectiveness of an inspection is influenced by the expertise of the inspectors, adequate preparation, the speed of the inspection, and compliance to the inspection process. The inspection methodology provides guidelines on the inspection and preparation rates for an inspection, and guidelines on the entry and exit criteria for an inspection.

There are typically at least two roles in the inspection methodology. These include the *author* role and the *inspector* role. The *moderator, tester,* and the *reader* role may also be present in the methodology.

The next section describes the benefits of software inspections, and this is followed by a discussion of a simple review methodology where the reviewers send comments directly to the author. Then, a slightly more formal inspection process is described, and finally the Fagan inspection process is described in detail.

6.2   Economic Benefits of Software Inspections

A software inspection program has tangible benefits in terms of productivity, quality, time to market, and customer satisfaction. For example, IBM Houston employed software inspections for the Space Shuttle missions: 85 % of the defects were found by inspections and 15 % were found by testing. There were no defects found on the space missions, and about two million lines of computer software were employed. IBM, North Harbour in the UK quoted a 9 % increase in productivity with 93 % of defects found by software inspections.

Software inspections are useful for educating new employees on the product, and on the standards and procedures used in the organization. They ensure that knowledge is shared among the employees, rather than understood by just one individual. Inspections improve software productivity, as less time is spent in correcting defective software.

The cost of correction of a defect increases the later that it is identified in the lifecycle. Boehm [7] states that the *cost of correction of a requirements defect identified in the field is over 40 times more expensive than if it were detected at the requirements phase,* and so it is most economical to detect and fix the defect in phase. The cost of correction of a requirements defect identified at the customer site includes the cost of correcting the requirements, the cost of design, coding, unit testing, system testing, and regression testing. It may be necessary to send an engineer on site to fix the problem, and there may be hidden costs in the negative perception of the company with a subsequent loss of sales. There is a powerful argument to identify defects as early as possible, and software inspections are a cost effective way to achieve this.

There are various estimates of the *cost of poor quality* (COPQ) in an organization (Fig. 1.9), and estimates suggest that it may be 20–40 % of sales. The exact calculation may be determined by a time sheet accountancy system, which details the cost of internal and external failure, and the cost of appraisal and prevention. The return on investment from an introduction of software inspections may be calculated, and the evidence available suggests that they are a cost-effective way of improving quality and productivity.

Table 6.1 Informal review

Step	Description
1.	The author circulates the deliverable (either physically or electronically) to the review audience.
2.	The author advises the review audience of the due date for comments
3.	The due date for comments is typically 1 week or longer.
4.	The author checks that all comments have been received by the due date
5.	Any reviewers who have not provided feedback are contacted by the author, and comments are requested.
6.	The author analyses all comments and implements the appropriate changes.
7.	The deliverable is circulated to the review audience for sign-off.
8.	The reviewers signoff (with any final comments) indicating that the document has been correctly amended by the author
9.	The author/project leader stores the comments received

6.3   Informal Reviews

This type of review involves reviewers sending comments directly to the author, and there is no actual review meeting. It is not as effective as the Fagan inspection process, but it helps in identifying some defects in the work products.

The author is responsible for making sure that the review happens, and advises the participants that comments are due by a certain date. The author analyses the comments received, makes the required changes, and circulates the document for approval. The activities involved are described in Table 6.1.

comment: *The informal review process may help to improve quality in an organization. It is dependent on the participants adequately reviewing the deliverable and sending comments to the author. The author can only request the reviewer to send comments. There is no independent monitoring of the author to ensure that the review actually happens and is effective, and that comments are requested, received, and implemented.*

6.4   Structured Walkthrough

A structured walkthrough is a peer review in which the author of a deliverable (e.g., a project document or actual code) brings one or more reviewers through the deliverable. The objective is to get feedback from the reviewers on the quality of the document or code, and to familiarize the review audience with the author's work. The walkthrough includes several roles namely the *review leader* (usually the author), the *author*, the *scribe* (may be the author) and the *review audience* (Table 6.2).

Table 6.2 Structured walkthroughs

Step	Description
1.	The author circulates the deliverable (either physically or electronically) to the review audience.
2.	The author schedules a meeting with the reviewers.
3.	The reviewers familiarize themselves with the deliverable.
4.	The review leader (usually the author) chairs the meeting.
5.	The author brings the review audience through the deliverable, explaining what each section is aiming to achieve, and requesting comments from them as to its correctness.
6.	The scribe (usually the author) records errors, decisions and any action items.
7.	A meeting outcome is agreed and the author addresses all agreed items. If the meeting outcome is that a second review should be held then go to step 1.
8.	The deliverable is circulated to reviewers for signoff and the reviewers signoff (with any final comments) indicating that the deliverable has been correctly amended by the author.
9.	The author/project leader stores the comments and sign-offs.

6.5   Semi-formal Review Meeting

A semi-formal review is a moderated review meeting chaired by the review leader. The leader may be the author, and the role involves chairing the meeting and verifying that the follow-up activity has been completed. The material in this section is adapted from [46].

The author selects the reviewers and appoints a review leader (who may be the author). The author distributes the deliverable to be reviewed, and provides a brief overview where appropriate.

The leader schedules the review meeting which includes the reviewers (with possible participation via a conference call). The review leader chairs the meeting and is responsible for keeping the meeting focused and running smoothly, resolving any conflicts, recording actions and completing the review form.

The review leader checks that all participants, including conference call participants are present, and that all have done adequate preparation. Each reviewer is invited to give general comments, as this will determine whether the deliverable is ready to be reviewed, and whether the review should take place. Participants who are unable to attend are required to send their comments to the review leader prior to the review, and the review leader will present these comments at the meeting. The material is typically reviewed page per page for a document review, and each reviewer is invited to comment on the current page. Code reviews may focus on coding standards only or may focus on finding defects in the software code. The issues noted during the review are recorded, and these may include items requiring further investigation.

The review outcome is decided at the end of the review (i.e., whether the deliverable needs a second review). The author then carries out the necessary corrections and investigation, and this is verified by the review leader. The document is then circulated to the review audience for sign-off.

Table 6.3   Activities for semi-formal review meeting

Phase	Review task	Roles
Planning	Ensure document/code is ready to be reviewed	Author
	Appoint *review leader* (may be author)	Leader
	Select reviewers with appropriate knowledge/experience and assign roles	
Distribution	Distribute document/code and other material to reviewers at least 3 days before the meeting	Author
	Schedule the meeting	Leader
Optional	Give overview of deliverable to be reviewed	Author
meeting	Allow reviewers to ask any questions	Reviewers
Preparation	Read through document/code, marking up issues/questions	Reviewers
	Mark minor issues on their copy of the document/code	
Review meeting	Review Leaders chairs the meeting	Leader
	Explains purpose of the review and how it will proceed	
	Set time limit for meeting	
	Keep review meeting focused and moving	
	Review document page by page	
	Code reviews may focus on standards/defects	
	Resolve any conflicts or defer as investigates	
	Note comments/shortcomings on review form	
	Raise issues – *(Do not fix them)*	Reviewers
	Present comments/suggestions/questions	
	Pass review documents/code with marked up minor issues directly to the author	
	Respond to any questions or issues raised	Author
	Propose outcome of review meeting	Leader
	Complete review summary form/return to Author	
	Keep a record of the review form	
Post re-view	Investigate and resolve any issues or shortcomings identified at the review	Author
	Verify that the author has made the required corrections	Leader

comment: *The semi-formal review process works well for an organization when the review leader is not the author. This ensures that the review is conducted effectively, and that the follow up activity takes place. It may work with the author acting as review leader provided the author has received the right training on software inspections, and follows the review process.*

The process for semi-formal reviews is summarized in Table 6.3. Figure 6.2 presents a template to record the issues identified during the review.

Deliverable _____   Review Reference ____
Date _____   Version No. ____
Author _____   No. of Reviews _____
Reviewers _____

Issue   Page/Line No.   Description   Action No

Unresolved Issued / Investigates
Issue   Reason unresolved   Verified.

Review Outcome (Tick one of the following)
    No changes required
    Verification by Review Leader only   _____
    Full review required   _____
    Review incomplete   _____

Review Summary (Optional)
#Major Defects_____ # Minor Defects _____ Estimated Rework time _____
Hours Preparation _____ #Hours Review _____ Amount Reviewed _____

Fig. 6.2 Template for semi-formal review

6.6   Fagan Inspections

The Fagan methodology (Table 6.4) is a well-known software inspection methodology. It is a seven-step process and includes planning, overview, preparation, inspection meeting, process improvement, re-work, and follow-up activity. Its objectives are to identify and remove errors in the work products, and also to identify any systemic defects in the processes used to create the work products.

The Fagan inspection process stipulates that requirement documents, design documents, source code and test plans all be formally inspected by experts independent of the author, and the inspection is conducted from different viewpoints such as requirements, design, test, etc.

There are various roles defined in the inspection process, including the *moderator*, who chairs the inspection, the *reader*, who paraphrases the particular

Table 6.4 Overview Fagan inspection process

Activity	Role/ responsibility	Objective
Planning	Moderator	Identify inspectors and roles.
		Verify material is ready for inspection.
		Distribute inspection material
		Book a room for the inspection.
Overview	Author	Brief participants on material.
		Give background information.
Preparation	Inspectors	Prepare for the meeting and role to be performed. Checklist may be employed.
		Read through the deliverable and mark up issues/questions.
Inspection meeting	Moderator/ inspectors	The moderator will cancel the inspection if inadequate preparation is done.
		Time limit set for inspection
		Moderator keeps meeting focused.
		The inspectors perform their roles
		Emphasis on finding defects not solutions.
		Defects are recorded and classified.
		Author responds to any questions.
		The duration of the meeting is recorded.
		An inspection outcome is agreed
Process improvement	Inspectors	Continuous improvement of development and inspection process.
		The causes of major defects are recorded
		A root cause analysis is performed to identify any systemic defect with the software development process or inspection process.
		Recommendations are made to the process improvement team.
Re-work	Author	The author corrects the defects and carries out any necessary investigations.
Follow-up	Moderator/ author	The moderator verifies that the author has resolved the defects and investigations.

deliverable, the *author*, who is the creator of the deliverable; and the *tester*, who is concerned with the testing viewpoint. The inspection process will consider whether a design is correct with respect to the requirements, and whether the source code is correct with respect to the design.

The goal is to identify as many defects as possible, and to confirm the correctness of a particular deliverable. Inspection data are recorded and may be used to assess the effectiveness of the organization in detecting and preventing defects.

The moderator records the defects identified during the inspection, and the defects are classified according to their type and severity. Mature organizations typically enter defects into an inspection database to allow metrics to be generated, and to enable analysis to be performed. The severity of the defect is recorded, and the major defects are classified according to the Fagan defect classification scheme. Some organizations use other classification schemes, e.g., the *orthogonal defect classification* scheme (ODC).

The next section describes the Fagan inspection guidelines, and these include the recommended time to be spent on the various inspection activities. An organization may need to tailor the Fagan inspection process to suit its needs, and the recommended times in the Fagan process may need to be adjusted accordingly. The tailored guidelines will need empirical evidence to confirm that they are effective in defect detection.

6.6.1 Fagan Inspection Guidelines

The Fagan inspection guidelines are based on studies by Michael Fagan, and provide recommendations on the time to spend on the various inspection activities. The goal is to spend sufficient time to enable the inspection to be effective, and identify as many major defects as possible. Two tables are presented here: the strict Fagan guidelines as defined by the Fagan methodology (Table 6.5), and more relaxed guidelines that have been shown to be effective.

The effort involved in a strict adherence to the Fagan guidelines is substantial, and the tailored guidelines presented here have been employed in the telecoms domain. Empirical evidence of the effectiveness of the tailoring is not presented. Tailoring any methodology requires care, and the effectiveness of the tailoring should be demonstrated by a pilot prior to its deployment in the organization. This would generally involve quantitative data on the effectiveness of the inspection and the number of escaped customer reported defects.

It is important to comply with the guidelines once they are deployed in the organization, and trained moderators and inspectors will ensure awareness and compliance. Audits may be employed to verify compliance.

The relaxed guidelines detailed in Table 6.6 do not conform to the strict Fagan inspection methodology.

Table 6.5 Strict Fagan
inspection guidelines

Activity	Area	Amount/Hr	Max/Hr
Preparation time	Requirements	4 pages	6 pages
	Design	4 pages	6 pages
	Code	100 LOC	125 LOC
	Test plans	4 pages	6 pages
Inspection time	Requirements	4 pages	6 pages
	Design	4 pages	6 pages
	Code	100	125 LOC
	Test plans	4 pages	6 pages

Table 6.6 Tailored
(Relaxed) Fagan inspection
guidelines

Activity	Area	Amount/Hr	Max/Hr
Preparation	Requirements	10–15 pages	30 pages
Time	Design	10–15 pages	30 pages
	Code	300 LOC	500 LOC
	Test plans	10–15 pages	30 pages
Inspection	Requirements	10–15 pages	30 pages
Time	Design	10–15 pages	30 pages
	Code	300 LOC	500 LOC
	Test plans	10–15 pages	30 pages

6.6.2   Inspectors and Roles

There are four inspector roles identified in a Fagan Inspection and they are
described in Table 6.7.

6.6.3   Inspection Entry Criteria

There are explicit entry and exit criteria defined for the various types of inspections.
These criteria need to be satisfied to ensure that the inspection is effective. The
entry criteria for the various inspections are given in Table 6.8.

6.6.4   Preparation

Preparation is a key part of the inspection process, as the inspection will be
ineffective if the inspectors are insufficiently prepared. The moderator is required
to cancel the inspection if any of the inspectors has been unable to do appropriate
preparation.

Table 6.7 Inspector roles

Role	Responsibilities
Moderator	Manages the inspection process and ensures compliance to the process.
	Plans the inspection and chairs the meeting
	Keeps the meeting focused and resolves any conflicts
	Keeps to the inspection guidelines
	Verifies that the deliverables are ready to be inspected
	Verifies that the inspectors have done adequate preparation.
	Records the defects on the inspection sheet
	Verifies that the agreed follow-up work has been completed.
	Skilled in the inspection process and appropriately trained.
	Skilful, diplomatic, and occasionally forceful.
Reader	Paraphrases the deliverable and gives an independent view of it
	Actively participates in the inspection.
Author	Creator of the work product being inspected
	Has an interest in finding all defects present in the deliverable.
	Ensures that the work product is ready to be inspected.
	Gives an overview to inspectors (if required)
	Participates actively during inspection and answers all questions.
	Resolves all identified defects and carries out any required investigation.
Tester	Role is focused on how the product would be tested
	Role often employed in requirements inspection/test plan inspection
	The tester participates actively in the inspection.

Table 6.8 Fagan entry criteria

Inspection type	Entry criteria	Inspectors/roles
Requirements	Inspector(s) with sufficient expertise available	Moderator/inspectors
	Preparation done by inspectors	
	Correct requirements template used.	
Design inspection	Requirements inspected and signed off	Moderator/inspectors
	Correct design template used to produce design	
	Inspector(s) have sufficient domain knowledge.	
	Preparation done by inspectors	
Code inspection	Requirements/design inspected and signed off	Moderator/inspectors
	Overview provided	
	Preparation done by inspectors	
	Code Listing available	
	Clean compile of source code	
	Coding standards satisfied	
	Inspector(s) have sufficient domain knowledge	
Test plan inspection	Requirements/design signed off	Moderator/inspectors
	Preparation done by inspectors	
	Inspector(s) have sufficient domain knowledge	
	Correct Test Plan template employed	

Table 6.9 Inspection meeting

Inspection type	Purpose	Procedure
Requirements	Find requirements defects. Confirm requirements correct and reflect customer's needs.	Inspectors review each page of requirements and raise questions or concerns. Defects recorded by Moderator
Design	Find defects in design and confirm its correctness with respect to requirements	Inspectors review each page of design (compare to requirements) and raise questions or concerns. Defects recorded by Moderator
Code	Find defects in the code and confirm its correctness with respect to the design and requirements.	Inspectors review the code and compare to requirements/design, and raise questions or concerns. Defects recorded by Moderator.
Test	Find defects in test cases/test plan. Confirm test cases sufficient to verify the design/requirements.	Inspectors review each page of test plan/spec., compare to requirements/ design and raise questions or concerns. Defects recorded by moderator.

6.6.5   The Inspection Meeting

The inspection meeting (Table 6.9) consists of a formal meeting between the author and at least one inspector. It is concerned with finding major defects in the particular deliverable, and verifying the correctness of the inspected material. The effectiveness of the inspection is influenced by

– The expertise and experience of the inspector(s)
– Preparation done by inspector(s)
– The speed of the inspection

These factors are quite clear since an inexperienced inspector will lack the appropriate domain knowledge to understand the material in depth. Second, an inspector who has inadequately prepared will be unable to make a substantial contribution during the inspection. Third, the inspection is ineffective if it tries to cover too much material in a short space of time. The moderator will complete the inspection form (Fig. 6.3) to record the results from the inspection.

The final part of the inspection is concerned with process improvement. The inspector(s) and author examine the major defects, identify the root causes of the defect, and determine corrective action to address any systemic defects in the software process. The moderator is responsible for completing the inspection summary form and the defect log form, and for entering the inspection data into the inspection database. The moderator will give any process improvement suggestions directly to the process improvement team.

Inspection Type_____ **Deliverable** _____ **Project**_____
Date_____ **Amount Inspected** _____ **Version No.** ____
Author_____ **Moderator**_____ **No. of Reviews** ____
Inspectors _____
#Hours Preparation _____ **# Hours Inspection** _____ **#Hours Rework** ____
Summary of Findings: **# Majors** _____ **# Minors** ____ **# PIs** _____ **# INVs** ____
ODC Summary (Majors): #CHK _#ASS__#ALG__#TIM__#INT_#FUN___#DOC__#BLD__

No. Page/Line No. Severity   Type Description

Top 3 Root Causes of Major Defects/ Process Improvement Actions
1.
2.
3.

Review Outcome
No changes □ Verification by Moderator □   Full Review   □ Review Incomplete □
Defects per KLOC _____ Defects per page _____ Verification of Rework _____
Date Verified _____ Inspection Data in Database ____

Fig. 6.3 Template for Fagan inspection

Table 6.10 Fagan exit criteria

Inspection type	Exit criteria
Requirements	Requirements satisfy the customer's needs
	All requirements defects are corrected
Design inspection	Design satisfies the requirements.
	All identified defects are corrected
	Design satisfies the design standards
Code inspection	Code satisfies the design and requirements
	Code follows coding standards
	Code compiles cleanly
	All identified defects corrected
Test plan	Test plan sufficient to test the requirements
	Test plan follows test standards
	All identified defects corrected

Table 6.11 Issue severity

Issue severity	Definition
Major (M)	A defect in the work product that would lead to a customer reported problem if undetected
Minor (m)	A minor issue in the work product
Process (PI)	A process improvement suggestion based on analysis of
Improvement (PI)	major defects
Investigate (INV)	An item to be investigated. It is not clear whether it is a defect or not

6.6.6   Inspection Exit Criteria

The exit criteria for the various inspections are given in Table 6.10.

6.6.7   Issue Severity

The severity of an issue identified in the Fagan inspection may be classified as major, minor, a process improvement item, or an item requiring further investigation. It is classified as *major* if its non-detection would lead to a defect report being raised later in the development cycle, whereas a defect report would not be raised for a *minor* issue. An issue classified as an investigate item requires further study, and an issue classified as process improvement is used to improve the software development process (Table 6.11).

6.6.8   Defect Type

There are several defect-type classification schemes employed in software inspections. These include the Fagan inspection defect classification (Table 6.12) and the Orthogonal Defect Classification scheme (Table 6.13).

Table 6.12 Classification of defects in Fagan inspections

Code inspection	Type	Design inspections	Type	Requirements Inspections	Type
Logic (code)	LO	Usability	UY	Product objectives	PO
Design	DE	Requirements	RQ	Documentation	DS
Requirements	RQ	Logic	LO	Hardware interface	HI
Maintainable	MN	Systems interface	IS	Competition analysis	CO
Interface	IF				
Data usage	DA	Portability	PY	Function	FU
Performance	PE	Reliability	RY	Software interface	SI
Standards	ST	Maintainability	MN	Performance	PE
Code	CC	Error handling	EH	Reliability	RL
Comments		Other	OT	Spelling	GS

Table 6.13 Classification of ODC defect types

Defect type	Code	Definition
Checking	CHK	Omission or incorrect validation of parameters or data in conditional statements
Assignment	ASN	Value incorrectly assigned or nor assigned at all
Algorithm	ALG	Efficiency or correctness issue in algorithm
Timing	TIM	Timing/serialization error between modules, shared resources
Interface	INT	Interface error (error in communications between modules, operating system, etc.)
Function	FUN	Omission of significant functionality
Documentation	DOC	Error in user guides, installation guides or code comments
Build/Merge	BLD	Error in build process/library system or version control
Miscellaneous	MIS	None of the above

The Orthogonal Defect Classification (ODC) scheme was developed at IBM [4], and a defect is classified according to three (orthogonal) viewpoints. Thee *defect trigger* is the catalyst that led the defect to manifest itself; the *defect type* indicates the change required for correction; and the *defect impact* indicates the impact of the defect at the phase in which it was identified. The ODC classification yields a rich pool of information about the defect, but requires effort to record this information. The defect type classification is described in Table 6.13.

The defect impact provides a mechanism to relate the impact of the software defect to customer satisfaction. The defect impact of a defect identified pre-release to the customer is viewed as the impact of the defect being detected by an end-user, and for a customer-reported defect, the impact is the actual information reported by the customer.

The inspection data is typically recorded in the inspection database; this will enable analysis to be performed on the most common types of defects, and enable actions to be identified to minimize reoccurrence. The data will enable the *phase containment effectiveness* (PCE) metric to be determined, and to determine if the software is ready for release to the customer.

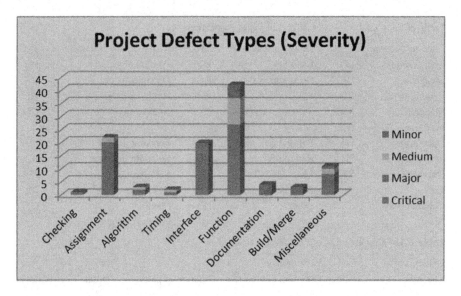

Fig. 6.4 Sample-defect types in a project (ODC)

The ODC classification scheme can give early warning on the quality and reliability of the software, as experience with the ODC classification scheme will enable an expected profile of defects to be predicted for the various phases. The expected profile may then be compared to the actual profile, and clearly it is reasonable to expect problems if the actual defect profile at the system test phase resembles the defect profile of the unit testing phase, as the unit testing phase is expected to identify a certain pool of defect types with system testing receiving higher-quality software with unit testing defects corrected. Consequently, ODC may be applied to make predictions of product quality and performance.

The project defects are classified according to some category scheme, for example, the defects may be categorized by the functional area in which they are identified, or via the ODC classification scheme as in Fig. 6.4. The frequency of defects per category is identified, and causal analysis employed to identify actions to prevent reoccurrence. Often the most problematic areas are targeted first (as in a pareto chart), and an investigation into the particular category is conducted. The action plans will identify and carry out improvements to existing processes.

6.7   Automated Software Inspections

Static code analysis is the analysis of software code without executing the code. It is usually performed with automated tools, and the actual analysis done depends on the sophistication of the tools. Some tools may analyze individual statements or declarations, whereas others may analyze the whole source code. The objective of the analysis is to highlight potential coding errors early in the development lifecycle.

These tools provide automated software inspections, and provide quality assessment reports on the extent to which the standards are satisfied. Many integrated development environments (IDEs) provide basic functionality for automated code reviews. These include Microsoft Visual Studio and Eclipse.

The LDRA Testbed Tool automatically determines the complexity of the source code, and it provides metrics that give an indication of the maintainability of the code. A useful feature of the LDRA tool is that it gives a visual picture of system complexity, and it has a re-factoring tool to assist with reducing complexity. It automatically generates code assessment reports listing all of the files examined, and provides metrics on the clarity, maintainability and testability of the code.

Compliance to coding standards is important in producing readable code and in preventing error-prone coding styles. There are several tools available to check conformance to coding standards including the LDRA TBvision tool, which has reporting capabilities to show code quality as well as fault detection and avoidance measures. It includes functionality to allow users to view the results presented intuitively in various graphs and reports.

6.8   Review Questions

1. What are software inspections?
2. Explain the difference between informal reviews, structured walkthroughs and formal inspections?
3. What are the benefits of software inspections?
4. Describe the seven steps in the Fagan Inspection process.
5. What is the purpose of entry and exit criteria?
6. What factors affect the effectiveness of a software inspection?
7. Describe the roles involved in a Fagan inspection.
8. Describe the benefits of automated inspections.

6.9   Summary

The objective of software inspections is to build quality into the software product, and there is clear evidence that the cost of correction of a defect increases the later in the development cycle in which it is detected. Consequently, there is an economic argument to employing software inspections, as it is more cost effective to build quality in rather than adding it later in the development cycle.

There are several approaches to software inspections, and these vary in the level of formality employed. A simple informal approach consists of a walkthrough of the document or code by an individual other than the author. The meeting is informal and usually takes place at the author's desk or in a meeting room, and the reviewer and author discuss the document or code informally.

There are formal software inspection methodologies such as the well-known *Fagan inspection* methodology. This approach includes pre-inspection activity, an inspection meeting, and post-inspection activity. Several inspection roles are typically employed, including an *author* role, an *inspector* role, a *tester* role, and a *moderator* role.

An organization will need to devise an inspection process which is suitable for its particular needs. The level of formality is influenced by its business, its culture, and the potential impact of a software defect on its customers. It may not be possible to have all of the participants present in a room, and participation by conference call or video link may be employed. A formal inspection process may not suit some organization cultures, and an informal approach such as a structured walkthrough may be the adopted approach.

Software inspections play an important role in building quality into each phase, and in ensuring that the quality of the delivered product is good. The quality of the delivered software product is only as good as the quality at the end each phase, and therefore a phase should be exited only when the desired quality has been achieved.

The effectiveness of an inspection is influenced by the expertise of the inspectors, adequate preparation, and speed of the inspection, and compliance to the inspection process. The inspection methodology provides guidelines on the inspection and preparation rates for an inspection, and guidelines on the entry and exit criteria for an inspection.

Software Testing

7

7.1   Introduction

Testing plays a key role in verifying the correctness of software, and confirming that the requirements are correctly implemented. It is a constructive and destructive activity in that while on the one hand it aims to verify correctness, on the other hand it aims to find as many defects as possible. In a mature software company the majority of defects (e.g., 80 %) will be detected by software inspections, with the remainder detected by the various forms of testing conducted in the organization. Software testing provides confidence that the product is ready for release to potential customers, and the recommendation of the testing department is crucial in the decision as to whether the software product is ready to be released. The advice of the test manager highlights any risks associated with the product, and these are considered prior to its release. The test manager and test department can

G. O'Regan, *Introduction to Software Quality*, Undergraduate Topics   119
in Computer Science, DOI 10.1007/978-3-319-06106-1_7,
© Springer International Publishing Switzerland 2014

be influential in an organization by providing strategic advice on product quality, and by encouraging organization change to improve the quality of the software product through the use of best practice in software engineering.

The testers need a detailed understanding of the software requirements to test the software effectively. Test planning commences at the early stages of the project, and testers play a role in building quality into the software product as well as verifying its correctness. The testers typically participate in the review of the requirements, and thus play an important role in ensuring that the requirements are correct and are testable. They develop an appropriate testing environment to enable effective testing to take place, and identify the resources, hardware, and test tools required. The test plan for the project is documented (this could be part of the project plan), and it includes the personnel involved, the resources required, the effort required, the definition of the test environment and the test tools, and the planned schedule. There is a separate plan for the actual test cases to verify that the requirements have been implemented correctly, and these test cases include the purpose of the test case, the inputs and expected outputs, and the test procedure for the particular test case.

The project testing performed includes unit testing, integration, system, regression, performance, and acceptance testing. The unit testing is performed by the software developers, and the objective is to verify the correctness of a module. This type of testing is termed *"white box"* testing, and is based on knowledge on the internals of the software module. White box testing involves checking that every path in a module has been tested, and it involves defining and executing test cases to ensure code and branch coverage. The objective of *"black box"* testing is to verify the functionality of a module or feature or the complete system itself.

Testing is both a constructive activity in that it is verifying the correctness of the functionality, and it also serves as a destructive activity in that another objective is to find defects in the software. Test reporting is a key part of the project, as this enables all project participants to understand the current quality of the software, and know what needs to be done to ensure that the product is meets the required quality criteria.

The test results are reported regularly throughout the project, and once the tester discovers a defect, a problem report is opened, and the problem is analysed and corrected by the software developers. The problem may indicate a genuine defect, a misunderstanding by the tester, or a request for an enhancement. An independent test group is more effective than a test group that is directly reporting to the development manager, as it helps to ensure that quality is not compromised during the inevitable pressures to make committed delivery dates. A good test group will play a proactive role in quality improvement, and this may involve participation in the analysis of the defects identified during testing phase at the end of the project, with the goal of prevention or minimization of reoccurrence of defects.

The test manager and test team write a test plan for the project, and the plan is reviewed by independent experts. This ensures that it is of a high quality and that the test cases are sufficient to confirm the correctness of the requirements. Effective testing requires sound test planning and execution, and a mature test process in the organization. Statistics are typically maintained to determine the effectiveness of the software testing.

The testing effort is often complicated by real world issues such as late delivery of the software from the developers. Software development is challenging, and deadline-driven, and missed deadlines potentially lead to the compression of the testing cycle, as the project manager may wish to stay with the original schedule. There are risks associated with shortening the test cycle as it may mean that the testers are unable to gather sufficient data to make an informed judgment as to whether the software is ready for release, with the obvious implication that a defect-laden product may be shipped. Test departments may be understaffed, as management may consider additional testers to be expensive and wish to minimize costs.

7.2   Test Process

The quality of the testing is dependent on the maturity of the test process, and a good test process will include test planning, test case analysis and design, test execution and test reporting. A simplified test process is sketched in Fig. 7.1 and the test process will include:
- Test planning and risk management
- Dedicated test environment and test tools
- Test case definition
- Test automation
- Formality in handover to test department
- Test execution
- Test result analysis
- Test reporting
- Measurements of test effectiveness
- Post mortem and test process improvement.

Test planning consists of a documented plan defining the scope of testing to be performed, the definition of the test environment, the sourcing of any required hardware or software for the test environment, the estimation of effort and resources for the various activities, risk management, the deliverables to be produced, the key milestones, the various types of testing to be performed, the schedule, etc. The test plan is generally reviewed by the affected parties to ensure its correctness, and that everyone understands and agrees to their responsibilities. The test plan may be revised in a controlled manner during the project. It will be described in detail in Sect. 7.3.

The test environment varies according to the type of business and project requirements. Large organizations may employ dedicated test laboratories, whereas a single workstation may be sufficient in a small organization. A dedicated test environment may require significant capital investment, but will pay for itself in reducing the cost of poor quality by verifying the quality of the software and in identifying defects.

The test environment includes the hardware and software needed to verify the correctness of the software. It needs to be defined early in the project so that any required hardware or software may be ordered in time. Tools for simulation of parts of the system may be required; automated regression and performance test tools may be required; as well as tools for defect reporting and tracking.

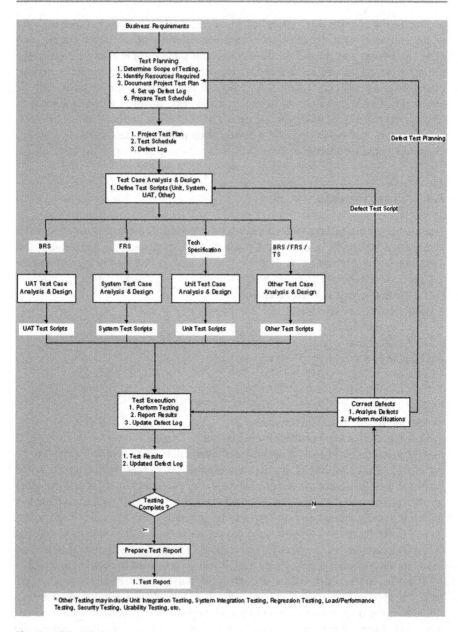

Fig. 7.1 Simplified test process

The software developers produce a software build under configuration management control, and the build is verified for integrity to ensure that testing may commence. There is generally a formal or informal handover of the software to the test department, and the formal handover generally includes documented criteria that must be satisfied

Table 7.1 Types of testing

Test type	Description
Unit testing	This testing is performed by the software developers, and it verifies the correctness of the software modules.
Component testing	This testing is used to verify the correctness of software components, to ensure that the component is correct and may be reused.
System testing	This type of testing is usually carried out by an independent test group to verify the correctness of the complete system.
Performance testing	This testing is typically carried out by an independent test group to ensure that the performance of the system is within the defined limits. It may require tools to simulate clients and heavy loads, and precise measurements of performance are made.
Load/stress testing	This testing is employed to verify that the system performance is within the defined limits for heavy system loads over long or short periods of time.
Browser compatibility	This testing is specific to web based applications and verifies that the web site functions correctly with the supported browsers.
Usability testing	This testing verifies that the software is easy to use, and that the look and feel of the application is good.
Security testing	This testing verifies that the confidentiality, integrity and availability requirements are satisfied
Regression testing	This testing verifies that the core functionality is preserved following changes or corrections to the software. Test tools may be employed to increase its productivity and efficiency.
Test simulation	This testing simulates part of the system where the real system currently does not exist, or where the real live situation is hard to replicate.
Acceptance testing	This testing carried out by the customer to verify that the software matches the customer's expectations prior to acceptance.

for the handover to take place. The test department must also be ready for testing with the test cases and test environment prepared.

The various types of testing employed to verify the correctness of the software are described in Table 7.1.

Good test cases are essential for effective testing, and the test cases need to be complete in the sense that their successful execution will provide confidence in the correctness of the software. Hence, the test cases must relate or cover the software requirements, and earlier in Chap. 4 (Table 4.4) we discussed the concept of a traceability matrix that maps the requirements to the design and test cases, and therefore provides confidence that each requirement has a corresponding test case for verification. The test cases will consist of a format similar to the following:

– Purpose of test case
– Setup required to execute the test case
– Inputs to the test case
– The test procedure
– Expected outputs or results

The test execution will follow the procedure outlined in the test cases, and the tester will compare the actual results obtained with the expected results. The test

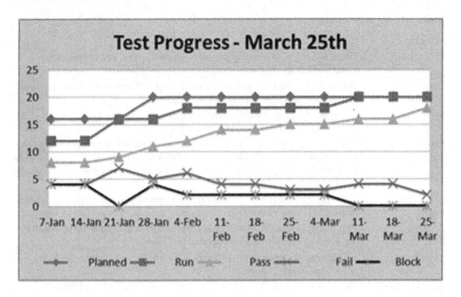

Fig. 7.2 Sample test status

completion status will be passed, failed or blocked (if unable to run at this time). The test results summary will indicate which test cases could be executed, which passed, which failed and which test cases could not be executed.

The tester records the test results including detailed information on the passed and failed tests. This will assist in identifying the precise causes of failure and the appropriate corrective actions. The developers and tester will agree to open a defect in the defect control system to track the successful correction of the defect.

The test status (Fig. 7.2) consists of the number of tests planned, the number of test cases run, the number that have passed, and the number of failed and blocked tests. The test status is reported regularly to management during the testing cycle. The test status and test results are analysed and extra resources provided where necessary to ensure that the product is of high quality with all defects corrected prior to the acceptance of the product.

Test tools and test automation are used to support the test process, and lead to improvements in quality, reduced cycle time, and productivity. Tool selection needs to be performed in a controlled manner, and it is best to identify the requirements for the tool first, and then to examine a selection of tools to determine which best meets the requirements for the tool. Tools may be applied to test management and reporting, test results management, defect management, and to the various types of testing.

A good test process will maintain measurements to determine its effectiveness, and an end of testing review is conducted at the end of testing to identify any lessons that need to be learned for continual improvement. The test metrics employed will answer questions such as:

- What is the current quality of the software?
- How stable is the product at this time?
- Is the product ready to be released at this time?
- How good was the quality of the software that was handed over?
- How does the product quality compare to other products?
- How effective was the testing performed on the software?
- How many open problems are there?
- How much testing remains to be done?

7.3   Test Planning

Testing requires good planning and execution to be effective. Testing is a sub-project of a project and needs to be managed as such, and the IEEE 829 standard includes a template for test planning. Test planning involves defining the scope of the testing to be performed; defining the test environment; estimating the effort required to define the test cases and to perform the testing; identifying the resources needed (including people, hardware, software, and tools); assigning the resources to the tasks; defining the schedule; identifying any risks to the schedule or quality and managing them; tracking progress and taking corrective action; re-planning as appropriate where the scope of the project has changed; providing test reports to give visibility of the test status to the full project team, including the number of test planned, executed, passed, blocked and failed; re-testing corrections to failed or blocked test cases; taking corrective action to ensure quality and schedule are achieved; and providing a final test report with a recommendation to go to acceptance testing. Test management involves:

- Identify the scope of testing to be done
- Determine types of testing to be performed
- Estimates of time, resources, people, hardware, software and tools
- Determine how test progress and results will be communicated
- Define how test defects will be logged and reported
- Provide resources needed
- Provision of test environment
- Assignment of people to tasks
- Define the schedule
- Identify and manage risks
- Track progress and take corrective action
- Provide regular test status of passed, blocked, failed tests
- Re-plan if scope of the project changes
- Conduct post mortem to learn any lessons

The scope of the testing is dependent on the requirements of the proposed system. The estimate for the various activities is determined and is used in the schedule. Table 7.2 shows a simple test schedule for a small project, and the test

Table 7.2 Sample test schedule

Activity	Resource name(s)	Start date	End/Re-plan date	Comments
Review requirements	Test team	15.02.2013	16.02.2013	Complete
Project test plan & review	Test manager	15.02.2013	28.02.2013	Complete
System test plan/review	Tester 1	01.03.2013	22.03.2013	Complete
Performance test plan/review	Tester 2	15.03.2013	31.03.2013	Complete
Regression plan/review	Tester 1	01.03.2013	15.03.2013	Complete
Set up test environment	Tester 1	15.03.2013	31.03.2013	Complete
System testing	Tester 1	01.04.2013	31.05.2013	In progress
Performance testing	Tester 2	15.04.2013	07.05.2013	In progress
Regression testing	Tester 2	07.05.2013	31.05.2013	In progress
Test reporting	Test manager	01.04.2013	31.05.2013	In progress

manager will often employ Microsoft Project for planning and tracking for larger projects (e.g., Fig. 3.2). The activities in the test plan are tracked and updated to record the tasks that have been completed, and dates are re-scheduled as appropriate. Testing is a key sub-project of the main project, and the project manager will track the key test milestones and will maintain close contact with the test manager.

It is essential to track the schedule, and to record the actual and estimated completion dates, and to reschedule accordingly. It is prudent to consider risk management early in test planning, and to identify risks that could potentially materialize during the testing project, estimate the probability and impact if a risk does materialize, and identify (as far as is practical) actions to mitigate the risk or a contingency plan to address the risk if it materialises.

7.4   Test Case Design and Definition

Several types of testing that may be performed were described in Table 7.2, and there is often a separate test plan for Unit, System and UAT testing. The unit tests are based on the software design; the system tests are based on the system requirements (or functional requirements specification); and the UAT tests are based on the business (or user) requirements.

Each of these test plans contains test scripts (e.g., the Unit Test Plan contains the Unit Test scripts and so on), and the test scripts are traceable to the design (for the Unit Tests), and for the system requirements (for the System Test scripts). The unit tests are more focused on white box testing whereas the system test and UAT tests are focused on black box testing.

Each test script contains the objective of the test script and the procedure by which the test is carried out. Each test script includes:

– Test Case ID
– Test Type (e.g., Unit, System, UAT)
– Objective/Description
– Test Script Steps
– Expected Results

– Actual Results
– Tested By

Regression testing involves carrying out a subset of the defined tests, and are carried out to verify that the core functionality remains in place following changes to the system.

7.5   Test Reporting and Project Sign-off

Testing is a sub-project of the project, and the test manager will report progress regularly during the project. The report provides the current status of testing for the project and includes:

• Quality Status (including tests run, passed and blocked).
• Risks and issues
• Status of Test Schedule
• Deliverables planned (next period)

The test manager discusses the test status with management, and highlights the key risks and issues to be dealt with. The test manager may require management support to deal with these.

The test status is important in judging whether the software is ready to be released to the customer. Various quality metrics may be employed to measure the quality of the software, and the key risks and issues are considered. The test manager will make a recommendation to release or not based on the actual test status. One useful metrics is the cumulative arrival rate (Fig. 7.3) which gives an indication of the stability of the product.

The slope of the curve is initially steep as defects are detected; as testing proceeds and defects are corrected and retested, the slope of the curves levels off, and indicates that the software has stabilized and is potentially ready to be released to the customer.

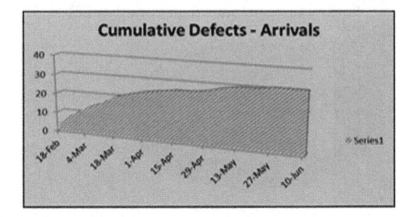

Fig. 7.3 Cumulative defects

However, it is important not to rush to conclusions based on an individual measurement. For example, the chart in Fig. 7.3 could possibly indicate that testing halted on May 13th with no testing since then, and that would explain why the defect arrival rate per week is zero. Careful investigation and analysis needs to be done before the interpretation of a measurement is made, and usually several measurements rather than one are employed in sound decision making.

7.6   Testing and Quality Improvement

Testing is an essential part of the software development process, and the recommendation of the test manager is considered in the decision to release the software product. Decision making is based on objective facts, and measurements are employed to assess the quality of the software. The cumulative test arrival rate (Fig. 7.3) gives an indication of the stability of the software product, and may be used in conjunction with other measures to decide on whether it is appropriate to release the software, or whether further testing should be performed.

Test defects are valuable in the sense that they enable an organization an opportunity to improve its software development process, to prevent them from reoccurring in the future. A mature development organization will perform internal reviews of requirements, design, and code prior to testing. The effectiveness of the internal review process and the test process may be seen in the phase containment metric (PCE).

Figure 7.4 indicates that the project had a phase containment effectiveness of approximately 54 %. That is, the developers identified 54 % of the defects, the system testing phase identified approximately 23 % of the defects, acceptance testing identified approximately 14 % of the defects, and the customer identified approximately 9 % of the defects. Many organizations set goals with respect to the

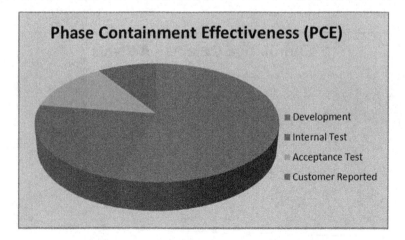

Fig. 7.4 Phase containment effectiveness metric

phase containment effectiveness of their software. For example, a mature organization might aim for their software development department to have a phase defect effectiveness goal of 80 %. This means that 80 % of the defects should be found by software inspections.

The PCE chart measures the current phase containment effectiveness, and improvement trends of the PCE may be tracked over time. There is no point in setting a goal for a particular group or area unless there is a clear mechanism to achieve the goal. Thus to achieve a goal of 80 % phase containment effectiveness the organization will need to implement a formal software inspection methodology as described in the previous chapter. Training on inspections will be required and the effectiveness of software inspections monitored and improved.

A mature organization will aim to have 0 % of defects reported by the customer, and this goal requires improvements in its software inspection methodology and its software testing methodology. Measurements provide a way to verify that the improvements have been successful. Each defect is potentially valuable as it, in effect, enables the organization to identify weaknesses in the software process and to target improvements.

Escaped customer defects offer an opportunity to improve the testing process, as an escaped customer defect indicates a weakness in the test process. These are categorized, causal analysis is performed, and corrective actions to improve the testing process are identified. This helps to prevent a reoccurrence of the defects. Thus software testing plays an important role is quality improvement.

7.7 Traceability of Requirements

The objective of requirement traceability is to verify and validate that all of the requirements for the project have been implemented and tested. One way to do this would be to examine each requirement number and to go through every part of the design document to find any reference to the particular requirement number, and similarly to go through the test plan and find any reference to the requirement number. This would demonstrate that the particular requirement number has been implemented and tested.

A more effective mechanism to do this was discussed in Chap. 4, and this involves using a trace matrix (Table 4.4) which may be a separate document or part of the design or test documents. The idea is that a mapping between the requirement numbers and sections of the design or test plan is defined, and this provides confidence that all of the requirements have been implemented and tested.

Requirements may be numbered or may be detailed in individual sections of the requirements document. A requirement number may map on to several sections of the design or to several test cases, i.e., the mapping may be one to many. Traceability provides confidence that each requirement number has been implemented in the software design and tested via the test plan.

- The trace matrix provides the mapping between each requirement number (or sections), and the associated test cases to verify that it has been correctly implemented.
- This mapping will typically be one to many (i.e., for a particular requirement, several test cases may be employed to demonstrate correctness).

7.8   Test Tools

Test tools are employed to support the test process, and are used to enhance quality, reduce cycle time, and increase productivity. Tool selection needs to be planned, and the evaluation plan includes the activities involved in the evaluation, the estimated and actual effort to complete, and the individual carrying out the activity. The evaluation and selection of a particular tool involves identifying the requirements for the proposed tool, and identifying tools to evaluate against the requirements. Each tool is then evaluated to yield a tool evaluation profile, and the results are analysed to enable an informed decision to be made. This is described in more detail in Chap. 16.

There are various tools to support testing such as test planning and management tools; defect tracking tools; regression test automation tools; performance tools; and so on. There are tools available from various vendors such as Compuware, Software Research, Inc., McCabe and Associates, and IBM Rational.

7.8.1   Test Management Tools

There are various test management tools available (e.g., the Quality Center tool from HP), and the main features of such a tool are:
- Management of entire testing process
- Test planning
- Support for building and recording test scripts
- Test status and reporting
- Graphs for presentation
- Defect control system
- Support for many testers
- Support for large volume of test data
- Audit trail proof that testing has been done
- Test automation
- Support for various types of testing

The Quality Center™ tool standardizes and manages the entire test and quality process, and is a web-based system for automated software quality management and testing. It employs dashboard technology to give visibility into the process.

It provides a consistent repeatable process for gathering requirements; planning and scheduling tests; analyzing results; and managing defects. It supports a high-level of collaboration and communication between the stakeholders. It allows the business analysts to define the application requirements and testing objectives.

The test managers and testers may then design test plans, test cases and automated scripts. The testers then run the manual and automated tests, report results and log the defects. The developers review and correct the logged defects. Project and test managers can create status reports and manage test resources. Test and product managers decide objectively whether the application is ready to be released.

7.8.2 Miscellaneous Testing Tools

There is a wide collection of test tools to support activities such as static testing, unit testing, system testing, performance testing, and regression testing.

Code coverage tools are useful for unit testing, and, for example, the LDRA Testbed is able to analyse source files to report on areas of code that were not executed at run time, thereby facilitating the identification of missing test data. Code coverage tools are useful in identifying the sources of errors as they will typically show the code areas that were executed through textual or graphic reports.

Regression testing involves re-running existing test cases to verify that the software remains correct following the changes made. It is often automated with capture and playback tools, and the Winrunner tool which was developed by Mercury (now part of HP) captures, verifies and replays user interactions, and allows regression testing to be automated. The Winrunner tool has been replaced by HP Unified Functional Testing Software. Effort is required to set up the tests for automation, but the payback is improvements in quality and productivity.

The purpose of performance testing is to verify that system performance is within the defined limits, and it requires measures on the server side, network side, and client side (e.g., processor speed, disk space used, memory used, etc.). It includes load testing and stress testing. . Mercury's LoadRunner tool allows the software application to be tested with hundreds or thousands of concurrent users to determine its performance under heavy loads. It allows the scaleability of the software system to be tested to determine if can support the predicted growth.

The decision on whether to automate and what to automate often involves a test process improvement team. It tends to be difficult for a small organization to make a major investment in test tools (especially if the projects are small). However, larger organizations will require a more sophisticated testing process to ensure that high-quality software is consistently produced.

7.9 E-commerce Testing

There has been an explosive growth in electronic commerce, and web site quality and performance is a key concern. A web site is a software application and so standard software engineering principles are employed to verify the quality of a web site. E-commerce applications are characterized by:
- Distributed system with millions of servers and billions of participants
- Often rapid application development is required
- Design a little, implement a little, and test a little

- Rapidly changing technologies
- Users may be unknown
- Browsers may be unknown
- High availability requirements (24 *7 * 365)
- Look and feel of the web site is highly important
- Performance may be un-predictable
- Security threats may be from anywhere

The standard waterfall lifecycle model is rarely employed for the front end of a web application, and instead RAD/JAD/Agile models are usually employed. The use of lightweight development methodologies does not mean that anything goes in software development, and similar project documentation is produced (except that the chrono-logical sequence of delivery of the documentation is more flexible). Joint application development allows early user feedback to be received on the look and feel and correctness of the application, and the method of design a little, implement a little, and test a little is valid for web development. The various types of web testing include:

- Static testing
- Unit testing
- Functional Testing
- Browser compatibility testing
- Usability testing
- Security testing
- Load/performance/stress testing
- Availability testing
- Post deployment testing

Static testing generally involves inspections and reviews of documentation. The purpose of static testing of web sites is to check the content of the web pages for accuracy, consistency, correctness, and usability, and also to identify any syntax errors or anomalies in the HTML. There are tools available (e.g., NetMechanic) for statically checking the HTML for syntax correctness.

The purpose of unit testing is to verify that the content of the web pages correspond to the design, that the content is correct, that all the links are valid, and that the web navigation operates correctly.

The purpose of functional testing is to verify that the functional requirements are satisfied. It may be quite complex as ecommerce applications may involve product catalogue searches, order processing, credit checking and payment processing, and the application may liaise with legacy systems. Also, testing of cookies, whether enabled or disabled, needs to be considered.

The purpose of browser compatibility testing is to verify that the web browsers that are to be supported are actually supported. The purpose of usability testing is to verify that the look and feel of the application is good, and that web performance (loading web pages, graphics, etc.) is good. There are automated browsing tools which go through all of the links on a page, attempt to load each link, and produce a report including the timing for loading an object or page. Usability needs to be considered early in design, and is important in GUI applications.

The purpose of security testing is to ensure that the web site is secure. The purpose of load, performance and stress testing is to ensure that the performance of the system is within the defined parameters.

The purpose of post-deployment testing is to ensure that web site performance remains good, and this may be done as part of a service level agreement (SLA). A SLA typically includes a penalty clause if the availability of the system or its performance falls below defined parameters. Consequently, it is important to identify performance and availability issues early before they become a problem. Thus post-deployment testing includes monitoring of web site availability, performance, and security, and taking corrective action. Ecommerce sites operate 24 h a day for 365 days a year, and major financial loss is incurred in the case of a major outage.

7.10   Review Questions

1. Describe the main activities in test planning.
2. What does the test environment consist of? When should it be set up?
3. What are the benefits of traceability of the requirements to the test cases?
4. Describe the various types of testing that may be performed.
5. Investigate available test tools to support testing? What areas of testing do they support and what are their benefits?
6. Describe an effective way to evaluate and select a test tool.
7. What are the characteristics of e-commerce testing that make it unique from other domains.

7.11   Summary

This chapter considered software testing in detail and discussed how testing may be used to verify that the software is of a high quality and fit to be released to potential customers. Testing is both a constructive and destructive activity, in that while on the one hand it aims to verify correctness, on the other hand it aims to find as many defects as possible.

Various test activities were discussed including test planning, the test environment setup, test case definition, test execution, defect reporting, and test management and reporting.

Various types of testing were discussed including black and white box testing, unit and integration testing, system testing, performance testing, security and usability testing. Testing in an e-commerce environment was considered. The unit testing is performed by the software developers, and the objective is to verify the correctness of a module.

Test reporting enables all project participants to understand the current quality of the software, and are aware of what needs to be done to ensure that the product is meets the required quality criteria.

Various tools to support the testing process were discussed, and a methodology to assist in the selection and evaluation of tools was considered.

Metrics to provide visibility into progress with the testing and the quality of the software were discussed, and also the role of testing in promoting quality improvement was discussed.

The testing effort is often complicated by real world issues such as late delivery of the software from the developers. This may lead to the compression of the testing cycle, as the project manager may wish to stay with the original schedule.

Supplier Selection and Management

8

Key Topics

Request for Proposal
Supplier Evaluation
Formal Agreement
Statement of Work
Service Level Agreement
Escrow

8.1 Introduction

Supplier selection and management is concerned with the selection and management of a third-party software supplier. Many large projects involve total or partial outsourcing of the software development, and it is therefore essential to select a supplier who is capable of delivering high-quality and reliable software on time and on budget.

This means that the process for the selection of the supplier needs to be rigorous, and that the capability of the supplier is clearly understood, as well as identifying any risks associated with the supplier. The selection is based on objective criteria such as the ability to deliver the required solution, and while cost is an important criterion it is just one among several other important factors.

Once the selection is finalised a legal agreement is drawn up which usually includes the terms and condition of the contract as well as a statement of work (which details the work to be carried out, the deliverables to be produced, when they will be produced, the personnel involved and their roles and responsibilities, and the standards to be followed). The supplier then commences the defined work, and is appropriately managed for the duration of the contract. The activities listed in Table 8.1 are generally employed in supplier selection and management.

G. O'Regan, *Introduction to Software Quality*, Undergraduate Topics
in Computer Science, DOI 10.1007/978-3-319-06106-1_8,
© Springer International Publishing Switzerland 2014

Table 8.1 Supplier selection and management

Activity	Description
Planning and requirements	This involves defining the approach to the procurement. It involves: Defining the procurement requirements Forming the evaluation team to rate each supplier against objective criteria.
Identify suppliers	This involves identifying suppliers and may involve research, recommendations from colleagues or previous working relations. Usually three to five potential suppliers will be identified.
Prepare and issue RFP	This involves the preparation and issuing of the Request for Proposal (RFP) to potential suppliers. The RFP may include the evaluation criteria and preliminary legal agreement.
Evaluate proposals	The received proposals are evaluated and a short-list of the suppliers invited to present.
Select supplier	Each supplier makes a presentation followed by a Q&A session. The evaluation criteria are completed for each supplier and reference sites checked (as appropriate). The decision on the preferred supplier is made.
Define supplier agreement	A formal agreement is made with the supplier. This may include Negotiations with the supplier/involvement with Legal Department. Agreement may vary (Statement of Work, Service Level Agreement, Escrow, etc.) Formal Agreement signed by both parties Unsuccessful parties informed Purchase Order raised
Project monitoring and control	This is concerned with monitoring and control of the supplier. It includes monitoring progress project risks, milestones and issues and change control management
Acceptance	This is concerned with the acceptance of the software and involves acceptance testing to ensure that the supplied software is fit for use.
Rollout	This is concerned with the deployment of the software and support/maintenance activities.

8.2 Planning and Requirements

The potential acquisition of software arises as part of a make-or-buy analysis at project initiation. The decision is whether the project team should (or has the competence to) develop a particular software system (or component of it), or whether there is a need to outsource (or purchase off-the-shelf) the required software. The supplied software may be the complete solution to the project's requirements, or it may need to be integrated with other software produced for the project. The following tasks are involved:

- The requirements are defined (these may be a subset of the overall business requirements)
- The solution may be an available in an off-the-shelf software package (with configuration needed to meet the requirements)

- The solution may be to outsource all or part of the software development
- The solution may be a combination of the above.

Once the decision has been made to outsource or purchase an off-the-shelf solution an evaluation team is formed to identify potential suppliers, and evaluation criteria is defined to enable each supplier's solution to be objectively rated. A plan will be prepared by the project manager detailing the approach to procurement, defining how the evaluation will be conducted, defining the members of the evaluation team and their roles and responsibilities, and preparing a schedule of the procurement activities to be carried out.

8.3 Identifying Suppliers

A list of potential suppliers may be determined in various ways including:
- Previous working relationship with suppliers
- Research via the Internet/Gartner
- Recommendations from colleagues or another company
- Advertisements/other

A previous working relationship with a supplier provides useful information on the capability of the supplier, and whether it would be a suitable candidate for the work to be done. Companies will often maintain a list of preferred suppliers, and these are the suppliers that have worked previously with the company, and whose capability is known. The risks with a supplier on the preferred supplier list are generally less than those of an unknown supplier. If the experience of working with the supplier is poor, then the supplier may be removed from the preferred supplier list.

For public procurement there may be additional requirements to ensure fairness in the procurement process, and often these public contracts need to be more widely advertised to allow all interested parties the opportunity to make a proposal to provide the product or service.

The list of candidate suppliers may potentially be quite large, and so shortlisting may be employed to reduce the list to a more manageable size of around five candidate suppliers.

8.4 Prepare and Issue RFP

The Request for Proposal (RFP) is prepared and issued to the short-listed suppliers, and the suppliers are required to complete a proposal detailing the solution that they will provide, as well as the associated costs, by the closing date. The proposal will need to detail the specifics of the supplier's solution, and it needs to show how the supplier plans to implement the requirements.

The RFP details the requirements for the software, and must contain sufficient detail to allow the candidate supplier to provide a complete and accurate response. The completed proposal will include technical and financial information, and this will allow a rigorous evaluation of each received proposal to be carried out.

The RFP may include the criteria defined to evaluate the supplier, and often weightings are employed to reflect the importance of individual criteria. The evaluation criteria may include several categories such as:

- Functional (related to business requirements)
- Technology (related to the technologies/non-functional requirements).
- Supplier capability and maturity
- Delivery approach
- Overall Cost

Once the proposals have been received further shortlisting may take place to limit the formal evaluation to around three suppliers.

8.5   Evaluate Proposals and Select Supplier

The evaluation team will evaluate all received proposals using an evaluation spread sheet, and the results are employed to produce a short list of around three suppliers.

The short-listed suppliers are then invited to make a presentation to the evaluation team, and this allows the team to question each supplier in detail to gain a better understanding of the solution that they are offering, and any risks associated with the supplier and their proposed solution.

Following the presentations and Q&A sessions the evaluation team will follow up with checks on reference sites for each supplier. The evaluation spread sheet is updated with all the information gained from the presentations, the reference site checks, and the risks associated with individual suppliers.

Finally, an evaluation report is prepared to give a summary of the evaluation, and this includes the recommendation of the preferred supplier. The project board then makes a decision to accept the recommendation, select an alternate supplier, or restart the procurement process.

8.6   Formal Agreement

The preferred supplier is informed on the outcome of the evaluation and negotiations on a formal legal agreement commences. The agreement will need to be signed by both parties, and may (depending on the type of agreement) include:

- Legal Contract
- Statement of Work
- Implementation Plan
- Training Plan
- User Guides and Manuals
- Customer Support to be provided
- Service Level Agreement
- Escrow Agreement
- Warranty Period

The *statement of work* (SOW) is employed in bespoke software development, and it details the work to be carried out, the activities involved, the deliverables to be produced, the personnel involved and their roles and responsibilities.

A *service level agreement* (SLA) is an agreement between the customer and service provider which specifies the service that the customer will receive as well as the response time to customer issues and problems. It will also detail the penalties should the service performance fall below the defined levels.

An *Escrow agreement* is an agreement made between two parties where an independent trusted third party acts as an intermediary between both parties, and receives money from one and sends it to the other party when contractual obligations are satisfied. Under an Escrow agreement documents and source code may also be held by the trusted third party.

8.7   Managing the Supplier

The activities involved in the management of the supplier are similar to the discussion on project management in Chap. 3. The supplier may be based in a different physical location (possibly in another country), and so regular communication is essential for the duration of the contract. The project manager is responsible for managing the supplier, and will typically communicate with the supplier on a daily basis. The supplier will send regular status reports detailing progress made as well as any risks and issues. The activities involved include:

– Managing schedule, effort and budget.
– Monitoring progress, project issues and risks
– Managing risks and issues
– Managing changes to the scope of the project
– Obtaining weekly progress reports from the supplier.
– Managing project milestones
– Managing quality
– Reviewing the supplier's work
– Performing audits of the project
– Monitoring test results and correction of defects.
– Acceptance testing of the delivered software
   The project manager needs to manage the risks associated with the supplier (e.g., supplier delivering late, supplier delivering poor quality, and so on).

8.8   Acceptance of Software

This activity is concerned with acceptance testing to ensure that the software developed by the supplier is fit for purpose. The supplier software may only be a part of the system and may need to be integrated with other software. The acceptance testing involves:

– Preparation of acceptance test cases (this is the acceptance criteria)
– Planning and scheduling acceptance testing

- Setting up the Test Environment
- Execution of test cases (UAT testing) to verify acceptance criteria is satisfied.
- Test Reporting
- Communication of Defects to Supplier
- Correction of the defects by Supplier
- Re-testing and Acceptance of Software

The project manager will communicate any defects with the software to the supplier, and the supplier makes the required corrections and modifications to the software. Re-testing then takes place and once all acceptance tests have successfully passed the software is accepted.

8.9 Rollout

This activity is concerned with the rollout of the software at the customer site, and the handover to the support and maintenance team. It involves:
- Deployment of the software at customer site.
- Provision of training to staff.
- Handover to the Support and Maintenance Team

8.10 Review Questions

1. What are the main activities in supplier selection and management?
2. What factors would lead an organization to seek a supplier rather than developing a software solution in-house?
3. What are the benefits of out-sourcing?
4. Describe how a supplier should be managed.
5. What is a service level agreement?
6. Describe the purpose of a statement of work?
7. What is an Escrow agreement?

8.11 Summary

Supplier selection and management is concerned with the selection and management of a third-party software supplier. Many large projects often involve total or partial outsourcing of the software development, and therefore it is essential to select a supplier who is capable of delivering high-quality and reliable software on time and on budget.

This means that the process for the selection of the supplier needs to be rigorous, and that the capability of the supplier is clearly understood, as well as any risks.

The selection is based on objective criteria, and cost is one important criterion but it is one among several other important factors.

Once the selection is finalised a legal agreement is drawn up (which usually includes the terms and condition of the contract as well as a statement of work which details the deliverables to be produced, when they will be produced, and the standards to be followed). The supplier then commences the defined work and is appropriately managed.

The project manager is responsible for managing the supplier and this involves communicating with the supplier on a daily basis and managing issues and risks. The software is subject to acceptance testing before it is accepted from the supplier.

Software Quality Assurance

9

Key Topics

Auditor
Audit Planning
Audit Meeting
Audit Reporting
Audit Actions
Tracking Actions
Audit Escalation
SQA Team
Independence of Auditor
Training

9.1 Introduction

The purpose of software quality assurance is to provide visibility to management on the processes being followed and the work products being produced in the organization. It is a systematic enquiry into the way that things are done in the organization, and involves conducting audits of projects, suppliers and departments. It provides:

- Visibility into the processes and standards in use in the organization.
- Visibility into the extent of compliance to the defined processes and standards.
- Visibility into the fitness for use of the work products produced
- Visibility into the effectiveness of the defined processes.

Software quality assurance involves planning and conducting audits; reporting the results to the affected groups; tracking the assigned audit actions to completion; and conducting follow up audits, as appropriate. It is generally conducted by the

G. O'Regan, *Introduction to Software Quality*, Undergraduate Topics
in Computer Science, DOI 10.1007/978-3-319-06106-1_9,
© Springer International Publishing Switzerland 2014

Table 9.1 Auditing activities

Activity	Description
Audit planning	Select projects/areas to be audited during period.
	Agree audit dates with affected groups
	Agree scope of Audit & advise what needs to be brought to the meeting.
	Book room & send invitation to the attendees.
	Prepare/update the Audit Schedule.
Audit meeting	Ask attendees as to their specific role in the project, the activities performed & determine the extent to which the process is followed.
	Employ an Audit Checklist as an aid
	Review agreed documentation.
	Determine if processes are appropriately followed
Audit reporting	Revise notes from the Audit Meeting and review any required additional documents.
	Prepare draft audit report, detail audit actions, and obtain feedback to ensure accuracy.
	Agree closure dates of the audit actions.
	Circulate approved report to attendees/management.
Track actions	Track audit actions to closure.
	Record the audit action status
	Escalation (as appropriate) to resolve open actions
Audit closure	Once all actions are resolved the audit is closed.

SQA group,[1] and this group is independent of the groups being audited. The activities involved are given in Table 9.1.

All involved in the audit process need to receive appropriate training. This includes the participants in the audit who receive appropriate orientation; the auditor needs to be trained in interview techniques including asking open and closed questions; effective documentation skills to record the results; and to deal with any conflicts that might arise during an audit.[2]

The flow of activities in a typical audit process is sketched in Fig. 9.1, and they are described in more detail in the following sections.

---

[1] This group may vary from a team of auditors in a large organization to a part-time role in a small organization.

[2] The auditor may face a situation where one or more individuals become defensive, and will need to reassure individuals that the objective of the audit is not to find fault with individuals, rather the objective is to fix a defective process. The culture of an organization has an influence on how open individuals will be during an audit (for example if there is a blame culture in the organization rather than an emphasis on fixing the process).

Fig. 9.1 Sample audit
process

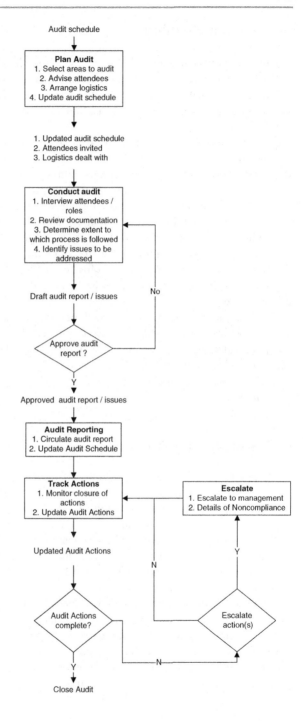

9.2   Audit Planning

Organizations vary in size and complexity and so the planning required for audits will vary. In a large organization the quality manager or auditor is responsible for planning and scheduling the audits. In a small organization the quality assurance activities may be performed by a part time auditor who has to plan and schedule the audits.

A representative sample of projects/areas in the organization will be audited, and the number and types of audits employed will depend on the current maturity of the organization. Mature organizations with a strong process culture will require fewer audits, whereas immature organizations may need a larger number of audits to ensure that the process is ingrained in the way that work is done.

It is essential that the *auditor is independent of the area being audited*. That is, the auditor should not be reporting to the manager whose area is being audited, as otherwise important findings in the audit may be omitted from the report. The independence of the auditor helps to ensure that the findings are fair and objective, as the auditor may state the facts as they are without fear of negative consequences.

The auditor needs to be familiar with the process, and in a position to judge the extent to which the standards have been followed. The audit needs to be factual, as incorrect statements will lead to a loss of credibility. The planning and scheduling activities will determine:

– Project/Area to be audited
– Planned Date of Audit
– Scope of Audit
– Checklist to be used
– Documentation required
– Auditor
– Attendees

The auditor may receive orientation on the project/area to be audited prior to the meeting, and may review any relevant documentation in advance. A checklist may be employed by the auditor as an aid to structure the interview.

The role requires good verbal and documentation skills as well as the ability to deal with any conflicts that may arise during the audit. The auditor needs to be fair and objective, and audit criteria will be employed to establish the facts in a non-judgmental manner.

Software quality assurance requires that an independent group (e.g., the SQA group) be set up. This may be a part time group of one person in a small organization or a team of auditors in a large organization. The auditor role requires good verbal and documentation skills, and auditors must be appropriately trained to carry out their roles. The individuals being audited need to receive orientation on the purpose of audits and their role in the audit.

9.3   Audit Meeting

An audit consists of interviews and document reviews, and involves a structured interview of the various team members. The goal is to give the auditor an understanding of the work done, the processes employed, and the extent to which they are followed and effective. A checklist tailored to the particular type of audit being conducted is often employed. This will assist in determining relevant facts to judge whether the process is followed and effective (Table 9.2).

The audit is an enquiry into to the particular role of each attendee, the activities performed, the output produced, the standards followed, and so on. The interviews allow the auditor to determine the extent to which the processes and standards are followed and whether they are effective. The auditor needs to be familiar with the process and in a position to judge the extent to which it has been followed.

Table 9.2 Sample auditing checklist

Item to check
Project Management
Has the project planning process been consistently followed?
Is the project plan complete and approved?
Are the Risk Log, Issue Log and Lessons Learned Log set up?
Is the Microsoft Schedule (or equivalent) available and up to date?
Are the weekly reports available?
Configuration Management
Are the appropriate people involved in defining, assessing the impact, and approving the change request?
Are the affected deliverables (with the CR) identified and updated?
Are all documents and source code in the repository?
Are checking in/checking out procedures followed?
Supplier Management
Is the Statement of Work complete?
Have the PM skills of the supplier been considered in the evaluation?
Does the formal agreement include strict change control?
Requirements, Design and Testing
Are the Business Requirements complete and is the Sign-off available?
Is Requirements Traceability addressed?
Are the System Requirements complete and approved?
Is the Technical and Database design complete and approved?
Are the Unit Test scripts available with the results recorded?
Are the System Test Cases available with results recorded?
Are UAT Test Cases available with results recorded?
Deployment and Support
Are the User Manuals complete and available?
Are all open problems documented?

The auditor opens the meeting with an explanation of the purpose and scope of the audit, and usually starts with one or more open questions to get the participants to describe their particular role. Each attendee is asked to describe their specific role, the activities performed, the deliverables produced and the standards followed. Closed questions are employed to obtain specific information when required.

The auditor will take notes during the meeting and these are reviewed and revised after the audit. There may be a need to review additional documentation after the meeting or to schedule follow up meetings.

9.4   Audit Reporting

Once the audit meeting and follow up activities are completed, the auditor will need to prepare an audit report to communicate the findings from the audit. A draft audit report is prepared and circulated to the attendees, and the auditor reviews any comments received, and makes final changes to address any valid feedback.[3] The approved audit report is then circulated to the attendees and management.

The audit report will include audit actions that need to be addressed by groups and individuals, and the auditor will track these actions to completion. In rare cases the auditor may need to escalate the audit actions to management to ensure resolution.

The audit report may include three parts such as the overview, the detailed findings and an action plan. This is described in Table 9.3.

Table 9.3 Sample audit report

Area	Description
Overview of audit	This gives an overview of the audit including the area audited, the date of the audit, its scope, the auditor and attendees and the number of audit actions raised.
Audit findings	These will vary depending on the type of audit but it may include findings from project management, requirements, design, coding, configuration management, testing and peer reviews, customer support, etc.
Action plan	This will include an action plan to address the findings.

---

[3] The approach depends on how the SQA function is implemented. In other implementations the audit report may be issued directly to the attendees without the step to request comments.

9.5   Follow Up Activity

Once the auditor has circulated the audit report to the affected groups, the focus then moves to closure of the assigned audit actions. The auditor will follow up with the affected individuals to monitor closure of the actions by the agreed date, and where appropriate a time extension may be granted. The auditor will update the status of an audit action to closed once it has been completed correctly. In rare cases the auditor may need to escalate the audit action to management for resolution. This may happen when an assigned action has not been dealt with despite one or more time extensions. Once all audit actions have been closed the audit is closed.

9.6   Audit Escalation

In rare cases the auditor may encounter resistance from one or more individuals in completing the agreed audit actions. The auditor will remind the individual(s) of the audit process and their responsibilities in the process. In rare cases, where the individual(s) fail to address their assigned action(s) in a reasonable time frame, the auditor will escalate the non-compliance to management. The escalation may involve:
• Escalation of actions to Middle Management
• Escalation to Senior Management
   Escalation is generally a rare occurrence, especially if good software engineering practices are embedded in the organization.

9.7   Review of Audit Activities

The results of the audit activities will be reviewed with management on a periodic basis. Audits provide important information to management on the processes being used in the organization; the extent to which they are followed; and the extent to which they are effective.
   An independent audit (usually a third party or separate internal audit function) of SQA activities may be conducted to ensure that the SQA function is effective. Any non-compliance issues identified and assigned to the auditor and quality manager for resolution.

9.8   Review Questions

1. What is the purpose of an audit?
2. What planning is done prior to the audit?
3. Explain why the auditor needs to be independent?
4. Describe the activities in the audit process.

(continued)

5. What happens at an audit meeting?
6. What happens after an audit meeting?
7. How will the auditor deal with a situation where the audit actions are still open after the due date?

9.9   Summary

The purpose of software quality assurance is to provide visibility to management on the processes being followed and the work products being produced in the organization. It is a systematic enquiry into the way that things are done in the organization, and involves conducting audits of projects, suppliers and departments. It provides:

- Visibility into the processes and standards in use in the organization.
- Visibility into the compliance to the defined processes and standards.
- Visibility into the effectiveness of the defined processes.

It involves planning and conducting audits; reporting the results to the affected groups; tracking the assigned audit actions to completion; and conducting follow up audits, as appropriate. It is generally conducted by the SQA group, and this group is independent of the groups being audited.

The audit planning is concerned with selecting projects/areas to be audited, determining who needs to be involved and dealing with the logistics. The audit meeting is concerned with a formal meeting with the audit participants to discuss their specific responsibilities in the project, the processes followed, and so on. The audit report details the findings from the audit, and includes audit actions that need to be resolved. Once the audit report has been published the auditor will track the assigned audit actions to completion, and once all actions have been addressed the audit may then be closed.

Software Metrics

10

Key Topics

Measurement
Goal, Question, Metric
Balanced Scorecard
Problem Solving
Data Gathering
Fishbone Diagram
Histogram
Pareto Chart
Trend Graph
Statistical Process Control

10.1 Introduction

Measurement is an essential part of mathematics and the physical sciences, and in recent years it has been successfully applied to the software engineering discipline. The purpose of a measurement program is to establish and use quantitative measurements to manage the software development environment in the organization, to assist the organization in understanding its current software capability, and to provide an objective indication that improvements have been successful. Measurements provide visibility into the various functional areas in the organization, and the actual quantitative data allow trends to be seen over time. The analysis of the trends and quantitative data allow action plans to be derived for continuous improvement. Measurements may

G. O'Regan, *Introduction to Software Quality*, Undergraduate Topics
in Computer Science, DOI 10.1007/978-3-319-06106-1_10,
© Springer International Publishing Switzerland 2014

be employed to track the quality, timeliness, cost, schedule, and effort of software projects. The term "*metric*" and "*measurement*" are used interchangeably in this book. The formal definition of measurement given by Fenton [21] is:

> Measurement is the process by which numbers or symbols are assigned to attributes or entities in the real world in such a way as to describe them according to clearly defined rules.

Measurement plays a key role in the physical sciences and everyday life, for example, the distance to the planets and stars, the mass of objects, the speed of mechanical vehicles, the electric current flowing through a wire, the rate of inflation, the unemployment rate, and so on. Measurement provides a more precise understanding of the entity under study. Often several measurements are used to provide a detailed understanding of the entity, for example, the cockpit of an airplane contains measurements of altitude, speed, temperature, fuel, latitude, longitude, and various devices essential to modern navigation and flight, and clearly an airline offering to fly passengers using just the altitude measurement would not be taken seriously.

Metrics play a key role in problem solving, and Chap. 1 discussed various problem-solving techniques. Good data is essential for obtaining a precise objective understanding of the extent of a particular problem.

For example, an outage is measured as the elapsed time between down-time and subsequent up-time. For many organizations, e.g., telecommunications companies it is essential to minimize outages and their impact should one occur. Measurements provide this data, and the measurement data is used to enable effective analysis to take place to enable the root cause of a particular problem, e.g., an outage, to be identified, and to verify that the actions taken to correct the problem have been effective.

Metrics provide an internal view of the quality of the software product, and care is needed before deducing the behaviour that a product will exhibit externally from the various internal measurements of the product. A leading measure is a software measure that usually precedes the attribute that is under examination; for example, the arrival rate of software problems is a leading indicator of the maintenance effort. Leading measures provide an indication of the likely behaviour of the product in the field and need to be examined closely. A lagging indicator is a software measure that is likely to follow the attribute being studied; for example, escaped customer defects are an indicator of the quality and reliability of the software. It is important to learn from lagging indicators even if the data can have little impact on the current project.

10.2   The Goal Question Metric Paradigm

The *Goal Question Metric* (GQM) paradigm was developed by Victor Basili of the University of Maryland, and it is described in detail in [2]. It is a rigorous goal oriented approach to measurement, in which goals, questions, and measurements are closely integrated. The business goals are first defined, and then questions that relate to the achievement of the goal are identified, and for each question a metric

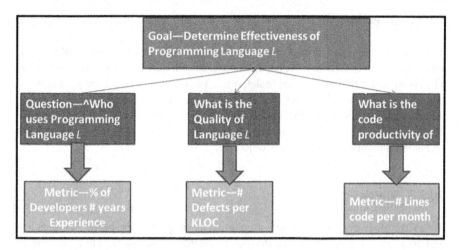

Fig. 10.1 GQM example

that gives an objective answer to the particular question is defined. The statement of the business goal is precise, and it is related to individuals or groups. Many software metrics programs have failed because they had poorly defined, or even non-existent goals and objectives. The GQM concept is a simple one, and managers and engineers proceed according to the following three stages:

- Set goals specific to needs in terms of purpose, perspective and environment
- Refine the goals into quantifiable questions
- Deduce the metrics and data to be collected (and the means for collecting them) to answer the questions

GQM has been applied to several domains, and so we consider an example from the software field. Consider the goal of determining the effectiveness of a new programming language L. There are several valid questions which may be asked at this stage, including who are the programmers that use L and what is their level of experience? What is the quality of software code produced with language L? What is the productivity of language L? This leads naturally to the quality and productivity metrics as detailed in Fig. 10.1.

10.2.1 Goal

The focus on improvements in an organization should be closely related to the business goals, and the first step is to identify the business goals that the improvement program is to address. The business goals are related to the strategic direction of the organization and the problems that it is currently facing. There is little sense in directing improvement activities to areas which do not require improvement, or for which there is no business need to improve, or from which there will be a minimal return to the organization.

10.2.2 Question

These are the key questions that determine the extent to which the goal is being satisfied, and for each business goal the set of pertinent questions need to be identified. The information that is required to determine the current status of the goal is determined, and this naturally leads to the set of questions that must be answered to provide this information. Each question is analysed to determine the best approach to obtain an objective answer, and to define the metrics which are needed, and the data that needs to be gathered to answer the question objectively.

10.2.3 Metrics

These are measurements that give a quantitative answer to the particular question, and they are closely related to the achievement of the goals. They provide an objective picture of the extent to which the goal is currently satisfied. Measurement improves the understanding of a specific process or product, and the GQM approach leads to focused measurements which are closely related to the goal, *rather than measurement for the sake of measurement*.

GQM helps to ensure that the measurements will be used by the organizations to improve and to satisfy the business goals more effectively. The successful improvement of software development is impossible without knowing what the improvement goals are and how they are related with the business goals. GQM is a rigorous approach to software measurement, and the measures may be from various viewpoints, e.g., manager viewpoint, project team viewpoint, etc. The idea is always first to identify the goals, and once the goals have been decided common-sense questions and measurement are employed.

There are two key approaches to software process improvement: i.e., *top-down* or *bottom-up* improvement. Top-down approaches are based on process improvement models and appraisals: e.g., models such as the CMMI, 15504, and ISO 9000, whereas GQM is a bottom-up approach to software process improvement, and is focused on improvements related to certain specific goals. The top down and bottom up approaches are often combined in practice.

10.3   The Balanced Scorecard

The balanced scorecard (BSC) (Fig. 10.2) is a management tool to clarify and translate the organization vision and strategy into action. It was developed by Kaplan and Norton [34], and has been applied to many organizations.

The BSC assists in selecting appropriate measurements to indicate the success or failure of the organization's strategy. There are four perspectives in the scorecard: *customer, financial, internal process*, and *learning and growth*. Each perspective includes objectives to be accomplished for the strategy to succeed, measures to indicate the extent to which the objectives are being met, targets to be achieved in

Fig. 10.2 The balanced scorecard

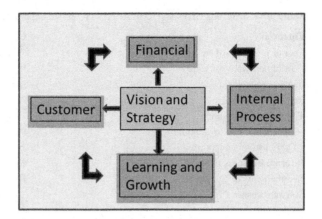

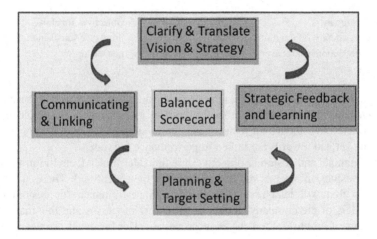

Fig. 10.3 Balanced score card and implementing strategy

the perspective, and initiatives to achieve the targets. The balanced scorecard includes financial and non-financial measures.

The BSC is useful in selecting the key processes which the organization should focus its process improvement efforts on in order to achieve its strategy (Fig. 10.3). Traditional improvement is based on improving quality, reducing costs and improving productivity, whereas the balanced scorecard takes the future needs of the organization into account, and identifies the processes that the organization needs to excel at in the future to achieve its strategy. This results in focused process improvement, and the intention is to yield the greatest business benefit from the improvement program.

The starting point is for the organization to define its *vision* and *strategy* for the future. This often involves clarifying the vision and gaining consensus among the senior management team. The vision and strategy are then translated into *objectives* for the organization or business unit. The next step is communication, and the

Table 10.1 BSC objectives and measures for IT service organization

Financial	Customer
Cost of provision of services	Quality service
Cost of hardware/software	Reliability of solution
Increase revenue	Rapid response time
Reduce costs	Accurate information
Timeliness of solution	Timeliness of solution
99.999 % network availability	99.999 % network availability
24 × 7 customer support	24 × 7 customer support
Internal business process	**Learning and growth**
Requirements elicitation	Expertise of staff
Software design	Software development capability
Implementation	Project management
Testing	Customer support
Maintenance	Staff development career structure
Customer support	Objectives for staff
Security/proprietary information	Employee satisfaction
Disaster prevention and recovery	Leadership

vision and strategy and objectives are communicated to all employees. These critical objectives must be achieved in order for the strategy to succeed. All employees will need to determine their own local objectives to support the organization strategy. Goals are set and rewards are linked to performance measures.

The financial and customer objectives are first determined from the strategy, and the key business processes to be improved are then identified. These are the key processes that will lead to a breakthrough in performance for customers and shareholders of the company. It may require new processes and this may require re-training of employees on the new processes. The balanced scorecard is very effective in driving organization change. The financial objectives require targets to be set for customer, internal business process, and the learning and growth perspective. The learning and growth perspective will examine competencies and capabilities of employees and the level of employee satisfaction. Figure 10.3 describes how the balanced scorecard may be used for implementing the organization vision and strategy.

Table 10.1 presents sample objectives and measures for the four perspectives in the BSC for an IT service organization.

10.4   Metrics for an Organization

The objective of this section is to define a set of metrics to provide visibility into various areas in the organization, and to show how metrics can facilitate improvements. Several examples of metrics that may assist an organization are presented, and these may be applied or tailored to an individual organization.

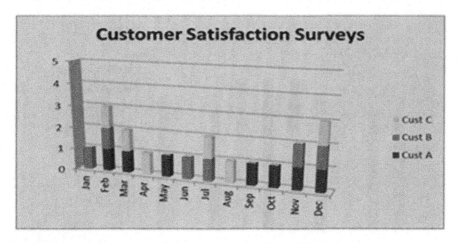

Fig. 10.4 Customer survey arrivals

The objective is to give an overview of how metrics may be employed for effective management, and many organizations have monthly quality or operation reviews in which the presentation of metrics play a key part.

This section includes sample metrics for the various functional areas in a software organization, including human resources, customer satisfaction, supplier quality, internal audit, project management, requirements and development, testing, and process improvement. These metrics are typically presented at a monthly management review, and performance trends observed. The main output from a management review is a series of actions to be completed by the following review.

10.4.1 Customer Satisfaction Metrics

Figure 10.4 shows the survey arrival rate per customer per month, and it indicates that there is a customer satisfaction process in place in the organization, that the customers are surveyed, and the extent to which they are surveyed. It does not provide any information as to whether the customers are satisfied, whether any follow-up activity from the survey is required, or whether the frequency of surveys is sufficient for the organization.

Figure 10.5 gives the customer satisfaction measurements in several categories including quality, the ability of the company to meet the committed dates and to deliver the agreed content, the ease of use of the software, the expertise of the staff and the value for money. Figure 10.5 is interpreted as follows:

7–10	Exceeds expectations
6–7	Meets expectations
5	Fair
0–4	Below expectations

Fig. 10.5 Customer satisfaction measurements

Another words, a score of 8 for quality indicates that the customers considers the software to be of high quality, and a score of 9 for value for money indicates that the customers considers the solution to be excellent value.

10.4.2 Process Improvement Metrics

The objective of process improvement metrics is to provide visibility into the improvement program in the organization.

Figure 10.6 shows the arrival rate of improvement suggestions from the software community. The chart indicates that initially the arrival rate is high and the closure rate low, which is consistent with the commencement of a process improvement program. The closure rate then improves which indicates that the improvement team is active and acting upon the improvement suggestions. The closure rate is low during July and August, which may be explained by the traditional holiday period.

The chart does not indicate the effectiveness of the process improvement suggestions and the overall impact the particular suggestion has on quality, cycle time, or productivity. There are no measurements included of the cost of performing improvements, and this is important as the organization will need to be able to compare the benefits of the improvement activities with the cost of the improvements.

Figure 10.7 provides visibility into the status of the improvement suggestions, and the number of raised, open, and closed suggestions per month. The chart indicates that gradual progress has been made in the improvement program with a gradual increase in the number of suggestions that are closed.

Figure 10.8 provides visibility into the age of the improvement suggestions, and indicates the effectiveness of the organization in acting on the them. It is a measure of the productivity of the improvement team and its ability to do its assigned work.

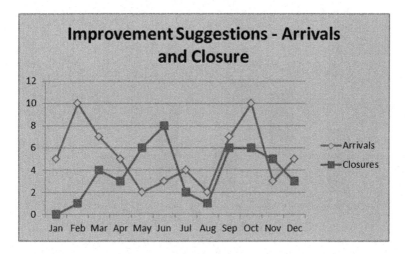

Fig. 10.6 Process improvement measurements

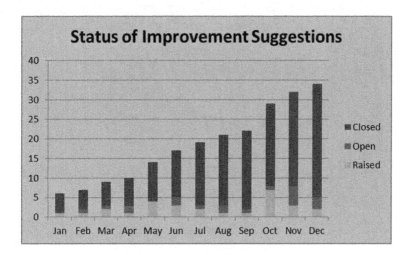

Fig. 10.7 Status of process improvement suggestions

Figure 10.9 gives an indication of the productivity of the improvement programme, and shows how often the team meets to discuss the improvement suggestions and to act upon them. This chart is slightly naive as it just tracks the number of improvement meetings which have taken place during the year, and contains no information on the actual productivity of the meeting. The chart could be considered with Fig. 10.6 to get a more accurate idea of productivity as the number of closed improvement suggestions per month. There will usually be other charts associated with an improvement program, for example, a metric to indicate the status of the CMMI program is provided in Fig. 10.26. Similarly, a measure of

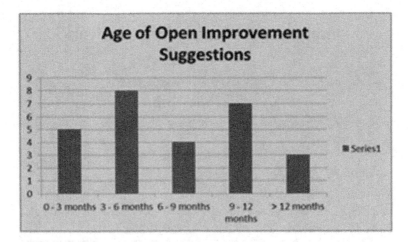

Fig. 10.8 Age of open process improvement suggestions

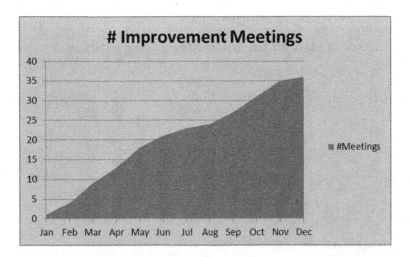

Fig. 10.9 Process improvement productivity

the current status of an ISO 9000 implementation could be derived from the number of actions which are required to implement ISO 9000, the number implemented, and the number outstanding.

10.4.3 Human Resources and Training Metrics

These metrics give visibility into the human resources and training areas of a company. They provide visibility into the current headcount (Fig. 10.10) of the

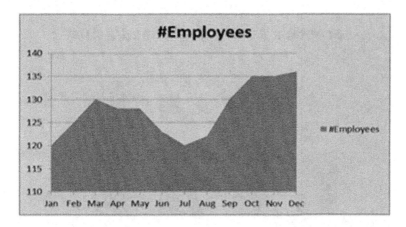

Fig. 10.10 Employee headcount in current year

Fig. 10.11 Employee turnover in current year

organization per calendar month and the turnover of staff in the organization (Fig. 10.11). The human resources department will typically maintain measurements of the number of job openings to be filled per month, the arrival rate of resumes per month, the average number of interviews to fill one position, the percentage of employees that have received their annual appraisal, etc.

The key goals of the HR department are defined and the questions and metrics are associated with the key goals. For example, one of the key goals of the HR department is to attract and retain the best employees, and this breaks down into the two obvious sub-goals of attracting the best employees and retaining them.

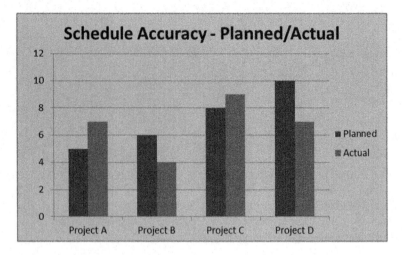

Fig. 10.12 Schedule timeliness metric

The next chart gives visibility into the turnover of staff during the calendar year. It indicates the effectiveness of staff retention in the organization.

10.4.4 Project Management Metrics

The goal of project management is to deliver a high-quality product that is fit for purpose on time and on budget. The project management metrics provide visibility into the effectiveness of the project manager in delivering the project on time, on budget, and with the right quality.

The timeliness metric provides visibility into the extent to which the project has been delivered on time (Fig. 10.12), and the number of months over or under schedule per project in the organization is shown. The schedule timeliness metric is a lagging measure, as it indicates that the project has been delivered within schedule or not after the event.

The on-time delivery of a project requires that the various milestones in the project be carefully tracked and corrective actions taken to address slippage in milestones during the project.

The second metric provides visibility into the effort estimation accuracy of a project (Fig. 10.13). Effort estimation is a key component in calculating the cost of a project, and in preparing the schedule, and its accuracy is essential. We mentioned the Standish Research data on projects in an earlier chapter, and this report showed that accurate project estimation is difficult.

The effort estimation chart is similar to the schedule estimation chart, except that the schedule metric is referring to time as recorded in elapsed calendar months, whereas the effort estimation chart refers to the planned number of person months required to carry out the work, and the actual number of person months that it took.

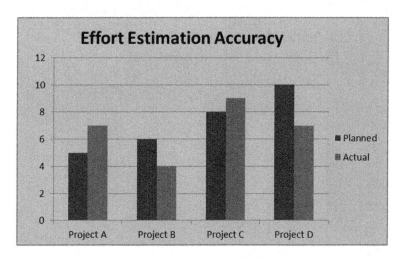

Fig. 10.13   Effort timeliness metric

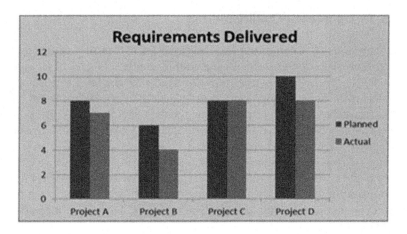

Fig. 10.14   Requirements delivered

Projects need an estimation methodology to enable them to be successful in project management, and the project manager will use historical data and metrics to determine how accurate the estimation has actually been.

The next metric is related to the commitments which are made to the customer with respect to the content of a particular release, and it indicates the effectiveness of the projects in delivering the agreed requirements to the customer (Fig. 10.14). This chart could be adapted to include enhancements or fixes promised to a customer for a particular release of a software product.

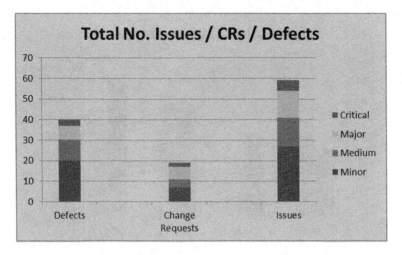

Fig. 10.15 Total number of issues in project

10.4.5 Development Quality Metrics

These metrics give visibility into the development and testing of the software product, and Chap. 7 presented several testing metrics. Figure 10.15 gives an indication of the quality of the software produced and the stability of the requirements. It shows the total number of defects and the total number of change requests raised during the project, as well as details on their severities. The presence of a large number of change requests suggests that there is room for improvement in the requirements management process.

Figure 10.16 gives the status of open issues with the project which gives an indication of the current quality of the project, and the effort required to achieve the desired quality in the software. This chart is not used in isolation, as the project manager will need to know the arrival rate of problems to determine the stability of the software product.

The organization may decide to release a software product with open problems provided that the associated risks can be managed. It is therefore important to perform a risk assessment of the known problems to ensure that the product may operate effectively. A work-around for each problem is typically included in a set of release notes for the product.

The project manager will also need to know the age of the open problems, as this will indicate the effectiveness of the team in resolving problems in a timely manner. Figure 10.17 presents the age of the open defects and it highlights the fact that there is one major problem that has been open for over 1 year. The project manager needs to prevent this situation from arising, as critical and major problems need to be addressed in a prompt and efficient manner.

The problem arrival rate (Fig. 10.18) is a key metric, and it enables the project manager to judge the stability of the software, and this helps in judging whether the

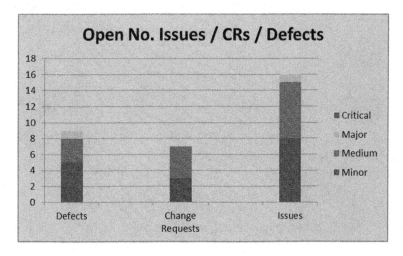

Fig. 10.16 Open issues in project

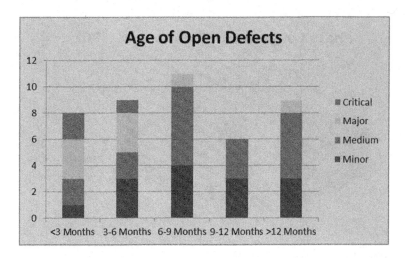

Fig. 10.17 Age of open defects in project

software is fit for purpose and ready for release to potential customers. A sample problem arrival chart is included here, and a preliminary analysis of the chart indicates that the trend is positive, with the arrival rate of problems falling. The project manager will need to do analysis to determine if there are other causes that could contribute to the fall in the arrival rate; for example, it may be the case that testing was completed in September, which would mean, in effect, that no testing has been performed since then, with an inevitable fall in the number of problems reported. The important point is not to jump to a conclusion based on a particular

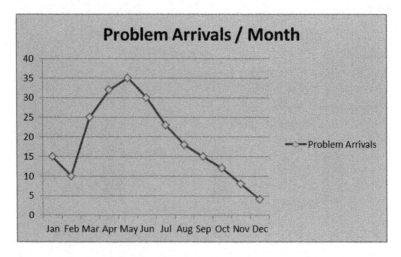

Fig. 10.18 Problem arrivals per month

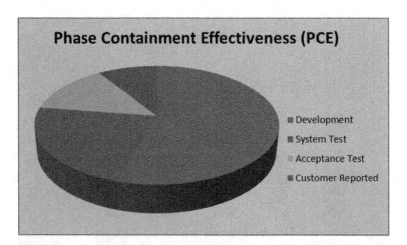

Fig. 10.19 Phase containment effectiveness

chart, as the circumstances behind the chart must be fully known and taken into account in order to draw valid inferences.

The next metric measures the effectiveness of the project in identifying defects in the development phase (Fig. 10.19), and the effectiveness of the test groups in detecting defects that are present in the software. The development portion typically includes defects reported on inspection forms and in unit testing.

The system testing is usually performed by an independent test group, and it may include usability and performance testing. Acceptance testing is performed at the customer site. The objective is that the number of defects reported at acceptance test and after the product is officially released to customer should be minimal.

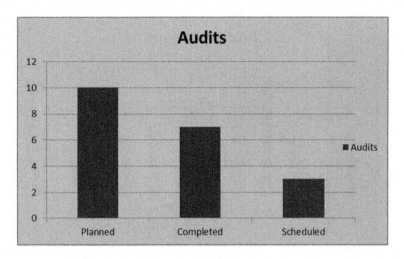

Fig. 10.20   Annual audit schedule

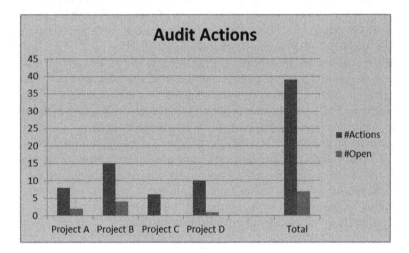

Fig. 10.21   Status of audit actions

10.4.6 Quality Audit Metrics

These metrics provide visibility into the audit program in an organization, and include metrics for the number of audits planned and performed (Fig. 10.20), and the status of the audit actions (Fig. 10.21). The first chart presents visibility into the number of audits carried out in the organization, and the number of audits which remain to be done. It shows that the organization has an audit program, and gives

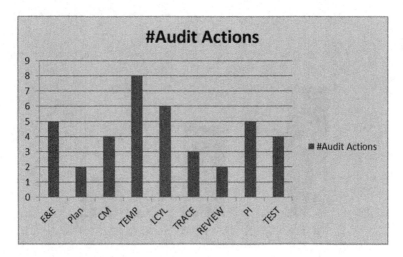

Fig. 10.22 Audit action types

information on the number of audits performed during a particular time period. The chart does not give a breakdown into the type of audits performed, e.g., supplier audits, project audits, and audits of particular departments in the organization, but it could be adapted to provide this information.

The next chart gives an indication of the status of the various audits performed. An audit is performed by an auditor, and the results are documented in an audit report, and the audit actions need to be completed by the affected individuals and groups. Figure 10.21 presents the status of the audit actions assigned to the affected groups, and the actions need to be resolved in a timely manner.

Figure 10.22 gives visibility into the type of actions raised during the quality audit of a particular area. The audit categories need to be defined by the organization but could potentially include entry and exit criteria, planning issues, configuration management issues, issues with compliance to the lifecycle or templates, traceability to the requirements, issues with the review of various deliverables, issues with testing, or process improvement suggestions.

10.4.7 Customer Care Metrics

The goals of the customer care group in an organization are to respond efficiently and effectively to customer problems, to ensure that their customers receive the highest standards of service from the company, and to ensure that its products function reliably at the customer's site. The organization will need to know its efficiency in resolving customer queries, the number of customer queries, the availability of its software systems at the customer site, and the age of open queries. A customer query may result in a defect report in the case of a problem with the software.

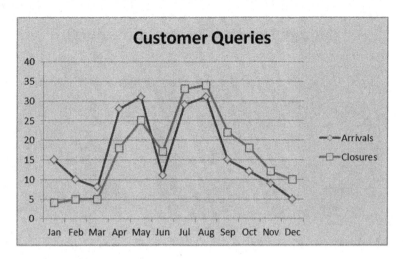

Fig. 10.23 Customer queries (arrivals/closures)

Figure 10.23 could be developed further to include a severity attribute for the query, and quantitative goals may be set for the resolution of queries (especially in the case of service level agreements). The organization will often maintain a chart for the age of open queries (similar to the chart in Fig. 10.17 presented earlier). The organization will need to know the status of the backlog of open queries per month, and a simple trend graph would provide this. Figure 10.23 shows the arrivals and closures of queries: in the early part of the year the arrival rate exceeds the closure rate of queries per month. This indicates an increasing backlog which needs to be addressed.

The customer care department responds to any outages and ensures that the outage time is kept to a minimum. Many companies set ambitious goals for network availability: e.g., the "*five nines initiative*" has the objective of developing systems which are available 99.999 % of the time, i.e., approximately 5 min of down time per year. The calculation of availability is from the formula:

$$\text{Availability} = \frac{\text{MTBF}}{\text{MTBF} + \text{MTTR}}$$

where the mean time between failure (MTBF) is the average length of time between outages.

$$\text{MTBF} = \frac{\text{Sample Interval Time}}{\#\text{Outages}}$$

The formula for MTBF above is for a single system only, and the formula is adjusted when there are multiple systems.

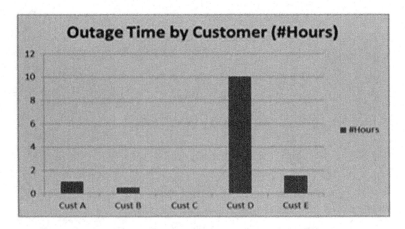

Fig. 10.24 Outage time per customer

$$\text{MTBF} = \frac{\text{Sample Interval Time}}{\#\text{Outages}} * \#\text{Systems}$$

The mean time to repair (MTTR) is the average length of time that it takes to correct the outage, i.e., the average duration of the outages that have occurred, and it is calculated from the following formula:

$$\text{MTTR} = \frac{\text{Total Outage Time}}{\#\text{Outages}}$$

Figure 10.24 presents outage information on the customers impacted by the outage during the particular month, and the extent of the impact on the customer.

An effective customer care department will ensure that a post-mortem of the outages is performed to ensure that lessons are learned to prevent a reoccurrence. This causal analysis details the root causes of the outages and the actions to be taken to prevent a reoccurrence. Metrics to record the amount of outage time per month will typically be maintained by the customer care group in the form of a trend graph.

Figure 10.25 provides visibility on the availability of the system at the customer sites (as per the availability formula described earlier). Ambitious organizations are designing systems to be available 99.999 % of the time.

10.4.8 Miscellaneous Metrics

Metrics may be applied to many other areas in the organization. This section includes metrics on CMMI maturity in the organization and configuration management. Figure 10.26 gives visibility into the time to create a software release from the configuration management system.

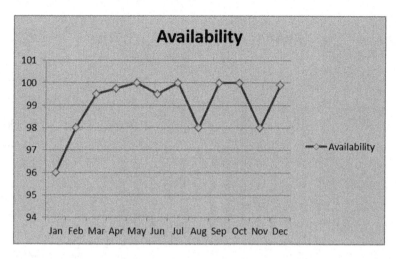

Fig. 10.25   Availability of system per month

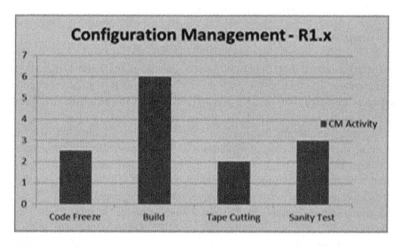

Fig. 10.26   Configuration management

The internal CMMI maturity of the organization is given by Fig. 10.27, and its current state of readiness for a formal CMMI assessment may be determined. A numeric score of 1 to 10 is used to rate each process area and a score of 7 or above indicates that the process area is satisfied.

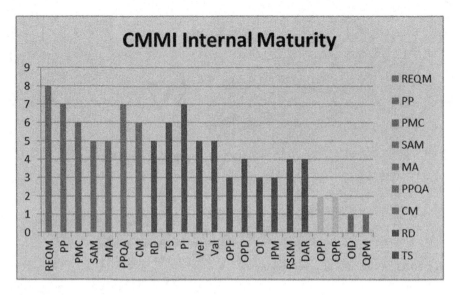

Fig. 10.27 CMMI maturity in current year

10.5   Implementing a Metrics Program

The metrics discussed in this chapter may be adapted and tailored to meet the needs of organizations. The metrics are only as good as the underlying data, and good data gathering is essential. Table 10.2 gives typical steps in the implementation of a metrics program.

The business goals are the starting point in the implementation of a metrics program, as there is no sense in measurement for the sake of measurement, and so metrics must be closely related to the business goals. It is important to identify the relevant questions to determine the extent to which the business goal is being achieved, and metrics provide an objective answer to the questions.

The organization defines its business goals, and each department develops specific goals to meet the organization's goals. Measurement will indicate the extent to which specific goals are being achieved, and good data gathering and recording are essential. First, the organization will need to determine which data need to be gathered, and to determine methods by which the data may be recorded. The information that is needed to answer the questions related to the goals will determine the precise data to be recorded. A small organization may decide to record the data manually, but often automated or semi-automated tools will be employed. It is essential that the data collection and extraction is efficient, as otherwise the metrics program is likely to fail. The data gathering is described in more detail in the next section.

Table 10.2 Implementing
metrics

Implementing metrics in organization
Define the business goals
Identify the pertinent questions
Define metrics
Identify tools to (semi-) automate metrics
Identify data that needs to be gathered.
Provide resources
Gather data and prepare metrics
Communicate the metrics and review monthly
Provide training

Table 10.3 Identifying data to be gathered

Goal	Reduce escaped defects from each lifecycle phases by 10 %.
Questions	How many faults are identified within each lifecycle phase?
	How many defects are identified after each lifecycle phase is exited?
	What % of defects escaped from each lifecycle phase?

The roles and responsibilities of staff will need to be defined with respect to the implementation and day-to-day operation of the metrics program. Training is needed to enable staff to perform their roles effectively. Finally, a regular management review is needed, where the metrics and trends are presented, and actions identified and carried out to ensure that the business goals are achieved.

10.5.1 Data Gathering for Metrics

Metrics are only as good as the underlying data, and so data gathering is a key activity in a metrics program. The data to be recorded will be closely related to the questions, and the data are used to give an objective answer to the question. The starting point is the business goal (often quantitative for extra precision). Table 10.3 illustrates how the data to be gathered are identified in a top-down manner.

Table 10.4 is an approach to determine the effectiveness of the software development process, and to enable the above questions to be answered. It includes a column for inspection data which records the number of *faults* recorded at the various inspections. The *defects* include the phase where the defect originated; for example, a defect identified in the coding phase may have originated in the requirements phase. The data is typically maintained in a spreadsheet, e.g., Excel, and it needs to be kept up to date. It enables the phase containment effectiveness (PCE) to be calculated for the various phases.

We will distinguish between a fault and a defect. *A fault is a problem which is usually detected by a software inspection*, and it is detected in the phase in which it is created. *A defect is a problem which is detected out of phase*, for example,

Table 10.4 Phase containment effectiveness

Phase of origin							
Phase	Inspect faults	Reqs	Design	Code	Accept test	Total faults	Total defects	% PCE
Reqs	4		1	1		4	6	40 %
Design	3					3	4	42 %
Code	20					20	15	57 %
Unit test		2	2	10				
System test		2	2	5				
Accept test								

a problem with the requirements may be discovered in the design phase, which is out of the phase in which it was created.

For the example Table 10.4, the effectiveness of the requirements phase is judged by its success in identifying defects as early as possible, as the cost of correction of a requirements defect increases the later in the cycle that it is identified. The requirements PCE is calculated to be 40 %, i.e., the total number of faults identified in phase divided by the total number of faults and defects identified. There were four faults identified at the inspection of the requirements, and six defects were identified: one at the design phase, one at the coding phase, two at the unit testing phase, and two at the system testing phase: i.e., $4/10 = 40$ %. Similarly, the code PCE is calculated to be 57 %.

The overall PCE for the project is calculated to be the total number of faults detected in phase in the project divided by the total number of faults and defects, i.e., $27/52 = 52$ %. Table 10.4 is a summary of the collected data and consists of:
- Maintain inspection data of requirements, design and code inspections
- Identify defects in each phase and determine their phase of origin
- Record the number of defects in each phase per phase of origin.

The staff who perform inspections need to record the problems identified, whether it is a fault or a defect, and its phase of origin. Staff will need to be appropriately trained to do this consistently.

Table 10.4 is just one example of data gathering, and in practice the organization will need to collect various data to enable it to give an objective answer to the extent that the particular goal is being satisfied.

10.6   Problem-Solving Techniques

Problem solving is a key part of quality improvement, and a *quality circle* (or problem-solving team) is a group of employees who do similar work and volunteer to come together on company time to identify and analyse work-related problems. Quality circles were first proposed by Ishikawa in Japan in the 1960s. Various tools that assist problem solving include *process mapping*, *trend charts*, *bar charts*, *scatter*

diagrams, fishbone diagrams, histograms, control charts, and *pareto charts* [9]. These provide visibility into the problem and help to quantify the extent of the problem. The main features of a problem-solving team include:
- Group of employees who do similar work
- Voluntarily meet regularly on company time
- Supervisor as leader
- Identify and analyse work-related problems
- Recommend solutions to management
- Implement solution where possible

The facilitator of the quality circle coordinates the activities, ensures that the team leaders and teams members receive sufficient training, and obtains specialist help where required. The quality circle facilitator has the following responsibilities:
- Focal point of quality circle activities
- Train circle leaders/members
- Coordinate activities of all the circle groups
- Assist in inter-circle investigations
- Obtain specialist help when required

The circle leaders receive training in problem-solving techniques, and are responsible for training the team members. The leader needs to keep the meeting focused and requires skills in team building. The steps in problem solving include:
- Select the problem
- State and restate the problem
- Collect the facts
- Brainstorm
- Choose course of action
- Present to management
- Measurement of success

The benefits of a successful problem solving culture in the organization include:
- Savings of time and money
- Increased productivity
- Reduced defects
- Fire prevention culture

Various problem-solving tools are discussed in the following sections.

10.6.1 Fishbone Diagram

This well-known problem-solving tool consists of a cause and effect diagram that is in the shape of the backbone of a fish. The objective is to identify the various causes of some particular effect, and then these various causes are broken down into a number of sub-causes. The various causes and sub-causes are analysed to determine the root cause of the particular effect, and actions to address the root cause are then defined to prevent a reoccurrence of the manifested effect. There are various categories of causes and these may include people, methods and tools, and training.

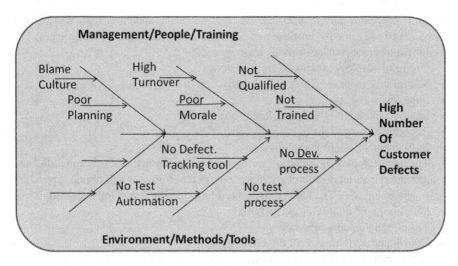

Fig. 10.28 Fishbone cause-and-effect diagram

The great advantage of the fishbone diagram is that it offers a crisp mechanism to summarize the collective knowledge that a team has about a particular problem, as it focuses on the causes of the problem, and facilitates the detailed exploration of the causes.

The construction of a fishbone diagram involves a clear statement of the particular effect, and the effect is placed at the right-hand side of the diagram. The major categories of cause are drawn on the backbone of the fishbone diagram; brainstorming is used to identify causes; and these are then placed in the appropriate category. For each cause identified the various sub-causes may be identified by asking the question *"Why does this happen?"* This leads to a more detailed understanding of the causes for a particular effect.

Example 10.1

An organization wishes to determine the causes of a high number of customer reported defects. There are various categories which may be employed such as people, training, methods, tools, and environment. In practice, the fishbone diagram in Fig. 10.28 would be more detailed than that presented, as sub-causes would also be identified by a detailed examination of the identified causes. The root cause(s) are determined from detailed analysis.

This example suggests that the organization has significant work to do in several areas, and that an improvement program is required. The improvements needed include the implementation of a software development process and a software test process; the provision of training to enable staff to do their jobs more effectively; and the implementation of better management practices to motivate staff and to provide a supportive environment for software development.

The causes identified may be symptoms rather than actual root causes: for example, high staff turnover may be the result of poor morale and a "blame culture", rather than a cause in itself of poor quality software. The fishbone diagram gives a better understanding of the possible causes of the high number of customer defects. A small subset of these causes is then identified as the root cause(s) of the problem following further discussion and analysis.

The root causes are then addressed (e.g., an appropriate software development process and test process are defined and providing training to all development staff on the new processes). The management attitude and organization culture will need to be corrected to enable a supportive software development environment to be put in place.

10.6.2 Histograms

A histogram is a way of representing data in bar chart format, and it shows the relative frequency of various data values or ranges of data values. It is typically employed when there are a large number of data values, and it gives a very crisp picture of the spread of the data values, and the centring and variance from the mean.

The histogram has an associated shape; e.g., it may be a *normal distribution*, a *bimodal* or *multi-modal distribution*, or be positively or negatively skewed. The variation and centring refer to the spread of data, and the relation of the centre of the histogram to the customer requirements. The spread of the data is important as it indicates whether the process is variable or whether it is performing within the requirements. The histogram is termed process centred if its centre coincides with the customer requirements; otherwise the process is too high or too low. A histogram enables predictions of future performance to be made, assuming that the future will reflect the past.

The construction of a histogram first requires that a frequency table be constructed, and this requires that the range of data values be determined. The data are divided into a number of data buckets, where a bucket is a particular range of data values, and the relative frequency of each bucket is displayed in bar format. The number of class intervals or buckets is determined, and the class intervals are defined. The class intervals are mutually disjoint and span the range of the data values. Each data value belongs to exactly one class interval and the frequency of each class interval is determined.

The histogram is a well-known statistical tool and its construction is made more concrete with the following example.

Example 10.2

An organization wishes to characterize the behaviour of the process for the resolution of customer queries in order to achieve its customer satisfaction goal.

Goal

Resolve all customer queries within 24 h.

Question

How effective is the current customer query resolution process?
What action is required (if any) to achieve this goal?

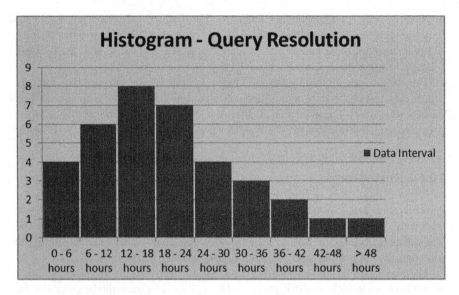

Fig. 10.29 Histogram

The data class size for the histogram in Fig. 10.29 is 6 h, and data class sizes are the same for standard histograms, whereas the size may be different for non-standard histograms. The sample mean is 19 h in this example.

This histogram (Fig. 10.29) is based on query resolution data from 36 samples. The organization goal of customer resolution of all queries within 24 h is not met, and the goal is satisfied in (25/36 = 70 % for this particular sample).

Further analysis is needed to determine the reasons why 30 % of the goals are outside the target 24-h time period. It may prove to be impossible to meet the goal for all queries, and the organization may need to refine the goal to state that instead all critical and major queries will be resolved within 24 h.

10.6.3 Pareto Chart

The objective of a pareto chart is to identify and focus on the resolution of problems that have the greatest impact, as *often 20 % of the causes are responsible for 80 % of the problems*. The problems are classified into various categories, and the frequency of each category of problem is determined. The chart is displayed in a descending sequence of frequency, with the most significant cause presented first, and the least significant cause presented last.

It is a key problem-solving tool, and a properly constructed pareto chart will allow the organization to resolve the key causes of problems, and to verify their resolution. The success of the improvements may be determined at a later stage from an analysis of the new problems and creating a new pareto chart. The result should show tangible improvements.

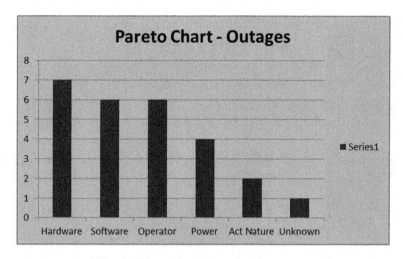

Fig. 10.30 Pareto chart outages

The construction of a pareto chart requires the organization to decide on the problem to be investigated; to identify the causes of the problem via brainstorming; to analyse the historical or real time data; to compute the frequency of each cause; and finally display the frequency in descending order of each cause category.

Example 10.3

An organization wishes to understand the various causes of outages, and to minimize their occurrence.

The pareto chart in Fig. 10.30 includes data from an analysis of outages, where each outage is classified into a particular causes. The six causal categories identified are: hardware, software, operator error, power failure, an act of nature, and unknown. The three key causes of outages are hardware, software, and operator error, and analysis is needed to identify to address these. The hardware category may indicate that problems the reliability of the system hardware, and that existing systems may need improvement or replacement. There may be a need to address availability and reliability concerns.

The software category may be due to the release of poor-quality software, or to usability issues in the software, and this requires further investigation. Finally, operator issues may be due to lack of knowledge or inadequate training of the operators.

10.6.4 Trend Graphs

A trend graph monitors the performance of a variable over time, allows trends in performance to be identified, and enables predictions of future trends to be made. Its construction involves deciding on the variable to measure and to gather the data points to plot the data.

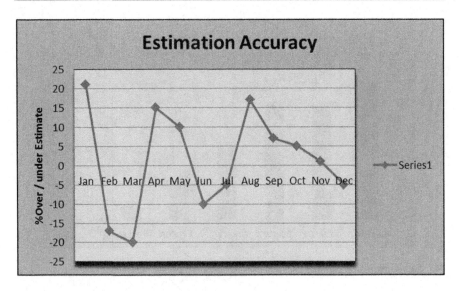

Fig. 10.31 Trend chart estimation accuracy

Example 10.4

An organization plans to deploy an enhanced estimation process, and wishes to determine if estimation is actually improving.

The estimation accuracy determines the extent to which the actual effort differs from the estimated effort. A reading of 25 % indicates that the project effort was 25 % more than estimated, whereas a reading of −10 % indicates that the actual effort was 10 % less than estimated. The trend chart (Fig. 10.31) indicates that initially that estimation accuracy is very poor, but then there is a gradual improvement coinciding with the implementation of the new estimation process.

It is important to analyse the performance trends in the chart. For example, the estimation accuracy for August (17 % in the chart) needs to be investigated to determine the reasons why it occurred. It could potentially indicate that a project is using the old estimation process or that a new project manager received no training. A trend graph is useful for noting positive or negative trends in performance; negative trends are analysed and actions identified to correct performance.

10.6.5 Scatter Graphs

The scatter diagram is used to measure the relationship between two variables, and to determine whether there is a relationship or correlation between the variables. The results may be a positive correlation, negative correlation, or no correlation. Correlation has a precise statistical definition, and it provides a precise mathematical understanding of the extent to which the two variables are related or unrelated.

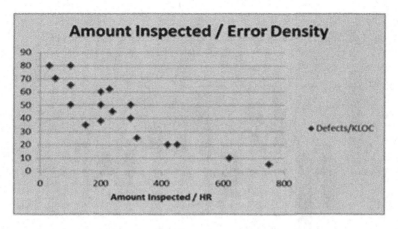

Fig. 10.32 Scatter graph amount inspected rate/error density

The scatter graph provides a graphical way to determine the extent that two particular variables are related, and it may be used to determine if there a connection between an identified causes and the effect.

The construction of a scatter diagram requires the collection of paired samples of data, and the drawing of one variable as the *x*-axis, and the other as the *y*-axis. The data are then plotted and interpreted.

Example 10.5

An organization wishes to determine if there is a relationship between the inspection rate and the error density of defects identified.

The scatter graph (Fig. 10.32) provides evidence for the hypothesis that there is a relationship between the lines of code inspected and the error density recorded (per KLOC). The graph suggests that the error density of defects identified during inspections is low if the speed of inspection is too fast, and the error density is high if the speed of inspection is below 300 lines of code per hour. A line can be drawn through the data which indicates a linear relationship.

10.6.6 Metrics and Statistical Process Control

The principles of statistical process control were described in an earlier chapter, and process performance is measured and controlled within upper and lower control limits. Figure 10.33 presents an example on breakthrough in performance of an estimation process, and is adapted from [35].

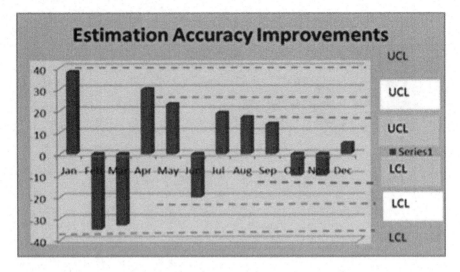

Fig. 10.33 Estimation accuracy and control charts

The initial upper and lower control limits for estimation accuracy are set at ±40 %, and the performance of the process is within the defined upper and control limits. However, the organization will wish to improve its estimation accuracy and this leads to the organization's revising the upper and lower control limits to ±25 %. The organization will need to analyse the slippage data to determine the reasons for the wide variance in the estimation, and part of the solution will be the use of enhanced estimation methods in the organization. In this chart, the organization succeeds in performing within the revised control limit of ±25 %, and the limit is revised again to ±15 %. This requires further analysis to determine the causes for slippage and further improvement actions are needed to ensure that the organization performs within the ±15 % control limit.

10.7   Review Questions

1. Describe the Goal, Question, Metric model.
2. Explain how the Balanced Scorecard may be used in the implementation of organization strategy.
3. Describe various problem solving techniques.
4. What is a fishbone diagram?
5. What is a histogram? A Pareto Chart?
6. What is a scatter graph?
7. Discuss how a metrics programme may be implemented.
8. What is statistical process control?

10.8   Summary

Measurement is an essential part of mathematics and the physical sciences, and has been successfully applied in recent years to the software engineering discipline. The purpose of a measurement program is to establish and use quantitative measurements to manage software development environment in the organization, to assist the organization in understanding its current software capability, and to provide an objective indication that improvements have been successful. This chapter included a collection of sample metrics to give visibility into the various functional areas in the organization, including customer satisfaction metrics, process improvement metrics, project management metrics, HR metrics, development and quality metrics, and customer care metrics.

The balanced scorecard assists the organization in selecting appropriate measurements to indicate the success or failure of the organization's strategy. Each of the four scorecard perspectives includes objectives that need to be achieved for the strategy to succeed, and measurements indicate the extent to which the objectives are being met.

The Goal, Question, Metric paradigm is a rigorous, goal-oriented approach to measurement in which goals, questions, and measurements are closely integrated. The business goals are first defined, and then questions that relate to the achievement of the goal are identified, and for each question a metric that gives an objective answer to the particular question is defined.

Metrics play a key role in problem solving, and various problem solving techniques were discussed. These include histograms, pareto charts, trend charts and scatter graphs. The measurement data are used to assist the analysis and to determine the root cause of a particular problem, and to verify that the actions taken to correct the problem have been effective. They allow trends to be seen over time, and the analysis of the trends allows action plans to be prepared and implemented for continuous improvement.

Metrics may be employed to track the quality, timeliness, cost, schedule, and effort of software projects. They provide an internal view of the quality of the software product, but care is needed before deducing the behaviour that a product will exhibit externally.

ISO 9000

11

Key Topics

Quality Management System
ISO 9001 and ISO 9004
Customer Satisfaction
Customer Requirements
Implementing ISO 9000
Continuous Improvement
Measurement and Analysis
Self-Assessment Methodology

11.1 Introduction

ISO 9000 is a widely employed quality management standard, and it was developed by the International Standards Organization (ISO). The standard was influenced by the British quality standard (BS 5750), and it was originally published as a standard in 1987, and revised in 1994, 2000 and in 2008.

The ISO 9000 family of standards may be applied to various types of organizations, including manufacturing, software and service organizations. The achievement of ISO 9001 by a company typically indicates that the company has a sound quality system in place, and that quality and customer satisfaction are core values of the company. ISO 9001 is regarded as a minimal standard that an organization which takes quality seriously should satisfy, and many organizations require their subcontractors to be ISO 9001 certified.

G. O'Regan, *Introduction to Software Quality*, Undergraduate Topics
in Computer Science, DOI 10.1007/978-3-319-06106-1_11,
© Springer International Publishing Switzerland 2014

It arose due to the need by organizations to know the capability or maturity of their subcontractors prior to selection. The existing approach was to assess the capability of a potential supplier prior to its selection. This generally involved a quality representative from the organization visited the proposed subcontractor, and assessing its process maturity. This was expensive and time consuming, especially if the organization had many subcontractors. Once the international standard became available, it allowed the organization to place ISO 9001 certification as a minimum requirement on the subcontractor, and thereby to expect certain minimal quality standards from the subcontractor. ISO 9001 became a discriminator in the selection of a contractor, and the certification provided confidence in the contractor to deliver a high-quality solution.

The standard places requirements on the quality management system of the company, but it allows the company to choose how it may satisfy the requirements. The ISO requirements include controls, processes and procedures, and the maintenance of quality records as evidence.

11.2   Motivation for ISO 9000

The ISO 9000 family of standards offers a structured way for a company to improve, and the company can focus its initial improvements to those clauses that will yield the greatest business benefit. Then as the company increases in maturity, the other clauses in the standard may be implemented. A standard is a useful way to show the organization how good it actually is, and to prioritize further improvements. Table 11.1 provides some reasons for the company to embark on an ISO 9000 initiative.

Table 11.1 Motivation for ISO 9000 implementation

Enhances credibility of the company
Marketing benefit of ISO 9000
Shows commitment to quality and customer satisfaction
Shows commitment to continuous improvement
Provides a framework for improvement
Shows that a fire prevention culture is in place
Less rework of defective products
Reduced cost of poor quality
Improved productivity due to less rework
Improved morale
A more effective organization

11.3   ISO 9000

The ISO 9000 family of standards consists of three standards: namely ISO 9000, ISO 9001, and ISO 9004. The ISO 9000 standard covers the fundamentals and vocabulary of quality management systems.

The ISO 9001 standard specifies the requirements of a quality management system, and applies to manufacturing, software, and service organizations. It details the requirements which the quality management system of the organization must satisfy to be ISO 9001 compliant. There is a simple process model defined in the standard, and there is an emphasis on measurement, continual improvement, and customer satisfaction. There are five clauses in the new standard, and the standard is customer focused.

The ISO 9004 standard (Managing for the Sustained Success of the Organization) provides guidance for performance improvement, and it is helpful in assisting organizations in the implementation of ISO 9001. It includes a simple self-assessment methodology to allow the organization to determine its current maturity with respect to ISO 9001. There are five main clauses in ISO 9001 standard (Table 11.2), with each clause having several sub-clauses.

The objective is to determine the customer requirements; to develop a product which satisfies the requirements, and which matches or exceeds customer expectations; and to continually improve to serve the customer better. Figure 11.1 describes the interaction between the various ISO 9001 clauses.

11.3.1 Quality Management System

This clause is concerned with documenting and implementing the quality management system (Fig. 11.1), and defining the procedures required by the standard. The procedures required include the quality manual, and procedures for the control of documents and the control of quality records.

Table 11.2 ISO 9001 clauses

Clause	Description
Quality Management System	This clause refers to the documentation and implementation of the Quality Management System (QMS)
Resource Management	This is concerned with the provision of the resources required to implement the QMS.
Product or Service Realisation	This is concerned with the provision of processes to implement the product or service.
Management Responsibility	This is concerned with defining the responsibilities of management in implementing the quality system.
Measurement, Analysis and Improvement	This is concerned with the establishment of a measurement programme, and using measures for continuous improvement.

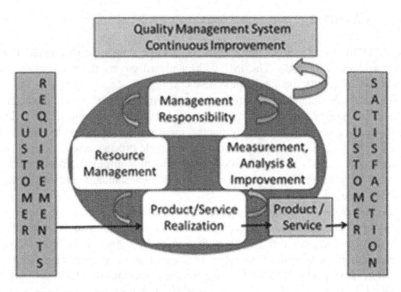

Fig. 11.1   ISO 9000 quality management system

The clause is also concerned with the control of quality records, as these are used to provide evidence of conformity to the quality system. The sub-clauses include general requirements of the quality management system, documentation requirements and the use of quality management principles in the organization. The procedures required include:

– Quality Manual
– Control of Documents
– Control of records
– Internal Audit
– Control of Non-conforming product
– Corrective Action Procedure
– Preventive Action Procedure.

There is more than one way to implement the specified ISO 9001 requirements, and the organization needs to choose an implementation which is tailored to its own needs.

The quality manual is a key document in the QMS, and it will provide details of the quality policy, the key goals and initiatives of the organization to achieve customer satisfaction, an organization chart to show where quality fits into the organization, and so on. The quality manual is one of the first things that an ISO 9001 auditor will examine, as it shows how the quality management system has been implemented.

The control of documents requires the definition of a document control procedure, which specifies the layout of a document, including its version number, revision history, its current status, and so on. Quality records provide evidence that the quality system and associated processes are being consistently performed, and the control of records procedure defines the records that will be maintained, the length of time that they will be maintained for, the means by which they are maintained, and so on. The records may include minutes and actions from management reviews, training records, records from the reviews of project deliverables, records from testing, records from audits, and so on.

11.3.2 Management Responsibility

The commitment of management is fundamental to the success of the QMS, and management play a key role in creating an environment in which the quality management system can operate effectively in the organization. Management need to promote quality, customer satisfaction and continuous improvement, and this clause defines the responsibilities of management in the quality system. It includes defining and communicating the quality policy, planning for quality, setting quality objectives, defining a quality policy, and participating in reviews of the quality management system. It consists of the following sub-clauses:
– Management Commitment
– Customer Focus
– Defining Quality Policy and Quality Manual
– Planning and setting quality objectives
– Responsibility, Authority and Communication
– Management Review
Management and staff need to focus on the customers and on customer satisfaction. They need to identify customers' needs and expectations, and to make customer satisfaction a core value of the organization.

The quality policy expresses the core values of the company on quality, customer satisfaction and continuous improvement. Management needs to communicate the quality policy and quality expectations, and all employees need to actively implement the policy. The quality policy needs to be reviewed periodically to ensure that it continues to meet the needs of the organization.

Management is responsible for quality planning in the organization, and the quality policy is employed to set the quality objectives (usually quantitative) for the organization. For example, the objectives may be to deliver 100 % of the projects on time and on budget; achieve a customer satisfaction measure in excess of 8.1; and resolve 100 % of critical problems within 24 h. The quality planning may also involve defining several high-quality processes such as a software development process and a project management process. These processes will allow high-quality software to be delivered on time and on budget.

Management needs to assign responsibility and authority to people to implement and maintain the quality system. Management is responsible for approving the quality system, monitoring it for effectiveness, and improving it. The responsibility of the different roles in the process is defined, and management will monitor process performance, and take corrective action when performance deviates from expectations. The organization will have a quality manager (this may be a part time role for smaller organizations).

Management will review the quality system at regular intervals to ensure its effectiveness. The quality review will examine the various parts of the quality system such as customer satisfaction, human resources and training, project management, development and test, customer support, process improvement, quality audits, and so on. Each group has an allocated period of time to provide visibility into their area, and this enables management to examine trends in the performance of the quality system, and to identify improvements. Actions to resolve any identified issues are assigned to groups and individuals. The management review is often metrics driven as this provides objective facts, and the review is often chaired by the quality manager, and attended by management in the organization.

11.3.3 Resource Management

Resource management is concerned with ensuring that the appropriate resources are in place to deliver high quality software, and this includes the human resources, training, the work environment and the physical infrastructure. It consists of the following sub-clauses:
- Provision of Resources
- Human Resources
- Infrastructure
- Work Environment

The provision of resources is the process concerned with determining the resources needed to implement the quality management system, and providing them. The resources include people, buildings, computers, and so on, and the organization needs to plan for future resource needs, as well as its current needs. The organization needs to enhance the knowledge and competence of people by education and training, and to develop leadership skills for future managers.

The human resource function plays a strategic role in the organization. It is responsible for staff recruitment and retention, career planning for employees, employee appraisals, health and safety, training in the organization, and providing a pleasant working environment. It facilitates communication between management and staff.

The responsibilities and skills required for the various roles in the organization need to be defined, and training identified to address any gaps in the current qualification, skills and experience of the employees and the roles which they are performing. An annual organization training plan is often prepared, and the plan is updated throughout the year. There may be mandatory training for employees on key areas, e.g., on quality. The training needs of the organization may change during the year due to changes in the technologies and processes employed, or due to a change in the strategic direction of the organization.

The organization needs to have a process for defining the appropriate infrastructure for efficient product realization, and this includes buildings, furniture, office equipment, computer hardware and software, technologies, and tools. The infrastructure plan is prepared well in advance, and is updated in a controlled manner in response to medium and short-term needs. It supports the organization in achieving its strategic goals and customer satisfaction. The infrastructure needs to be maintained to ensure that it continues to meet the needs of the organization.

The organization needs a disaster management plan to identify preventive measures to prevent disasters from happening, and a disaster recovery procedure to minimize disruption following an actual disaster. The actual recovery steps depend on the scale of damage, and it is essential that the recovery is planned with clearly defined roles and responsibilities. The individuals with responsibility for disaster prevention and recovery need to be trained in their roles, and the plan needs to be tested to ensure its effectiveness in the case of a real disaster. The damage assessment team assesses the actual damage, and the damage recovery team is responsible for responding to the disaster.

The organization needs to develop a work environment that will promote employee satisfaction, motivation and performance.

11.3.4 Product or Service Realization

This is concerned with the provision of efficient processes for product or service realization to ensure that the organization has the capability to develop products or services that will meet customer expectations. It may involve developing processes for defining and managing the requirements; processes for design and development; processes for testing; a process for project management; a change management process; and so on. It involves the following sub-clauses:

- Planning of product realization
- Customer related processes
- Customer requirements
- Customer communication
- Design and development
- Control of changes
- Purchasing process (information and verification)
- Production and service provision
- Validation of processes
- Identification and traceability
- Customer property
- Preservation of product
- Control of measuring and monitoring devices

The planning of product realization requires the organization to plan and define the processes needed for product realization. This requires a sound project management process as well as an effective software development process to identify the customer requirements and to design and develop an appropriate solution that will satisfy the customer's expectations. It will require other processes such as a change management process and a testing process.

The customer related processes are concerned with processes for defining customer requirements; managing customer requirements; and verifying and validating customer requirements to ensure customer satisfaction. There is also a need for an effective communication mechanism where customer feedback (enquiries and complaints) may be made and a process to determine the level of customer satisfaction.

The customer requirements are the foundation for the product, and these need to be correct before design and development commences. The requirements are documented, and reviewed by all stakeholders to ensure that they are correct and reflect the customer's needs.

The design and development process needs to be defined and capable of delivering high-quality software on time to the customer. It involves design and development planning, the design of the solution, a review of the design and development, verification and validation of design and development, and control of changes during design and development. There will be controls in the process to ensure that the defined deliverable are produced, reviewed and approved at key milestones, and to ensure that the requirements have been properly implemented.

The importance of reviews of design and development activities is evident from Chap. 6 on software inspections, and reviews enable defects to be identified earlier and help to reduce the cost of poor quality. The verification and validation activities are concerned with *"building it right"* and *"building the right product"* as discussed in Chap. 4. A traceability matrix may also be employed for verification and validation, as well as reviews and the various types of testing as discussed previously. There is a need for a change control process to manage changes to the requirements, and to keep all the deliverables consistent with the requirements. This has been described in Chap. 5 on configuration management.

The purchasing process is important as a product often is built from components that are procured from one or more suppliers. Therefore, the purchased products or components need to be fit for purpose, and this involves verification (by testing or inspections) that the purchased products satisfy the purchase requirements. The capability of the supplier needs to be clearly understood, and this may involve a formal evaluation of the supplier capability as discussed in Chap. 8. Outsourcing is often employed in the software sector, and it is important to select a supplier with the capability to deliver a high-quality solution on time and on budget.

There are ISO 9001 requirements for planning and carrying out production and service provision under controlled conditions; validating production and service provision processes; establishing a process for identification and traceability; handling customer property correctly; and preserving the product. These need to be interpreted to a software organization, and efficient and reliable processes are essential to producing high-quality software. The production of software involves the definition of the content of a release, performing a release build to produce the executable files, and the storage of the released software on electronic media such as a CD or floppy disk.

Identification and traceability requires a sound configuration management system which includes document change control, software source code control management, change control management, and release builds. The released software is usually accompanied by release notes and an installation guide. The validation of processes for production and service is addressed by audits of processes and products, and quantitative measurement of processes.

The contents of a release and the versions of the source files which make up the release should be known, as well as notes to specify the defects corrected and enhancements implemented. A product in the manufacturing field is composed of many components, which are provided by various suppliers. It is important that the constituents of each product be fully known and traceable, as if it is discovered that a batch of components which has been used in the manufacture of a product contains defective items, it may be necessary to recall all products which have been manufactured with components from this particular batch. Consequently, the product must be clearly identified and traceable.

The customer property sub-clause requires the organization to exercise care with customer property while it is under the organization's control. This requires the organization to identify all customer property and to verify and protect it. This could potentially include confidential information, intellectual property, and test data. The software organization may have access to the customer computer network, and must handle the network with the utmost care and confidentiality.

The preservation of product clause requires the organization to have implemented processes for handling, storage, packaging, and delivery of the product. The implementation for a software organization usually requires that the software be stored on electronic media and packaged and delivered to the customer.

The control of measuring and monitoring devices is important in the manufacturing sector, and regular calibration of the machines is required to ensure correct performance. For a software organization this is interpreted to the testing environment, the test tools and test scripts, and automated testing.

11.3.5 Measuring, Analysis, and Improvement

This clause is concerned with the measurement of processes to improve the performance of the quality management system. It involves the analysis of data to plan improvement actions, and to verify that the improvements have been effective. Measurement provides objective data on the effectiveness of the quality system, and detailed analysis using problem-solving techniques is done to identify the key issues, and to define improvement actions. It includes the following sub-clauses:

- Measurement of customer satisfaction
- Internal audits
- Measurement and monitoring of processes
- Measurement and monitoring of product
- Control of nonconformity
- Analysis of data
- Continual improvement
- Corrective action
- Preventative action

The measurement of customer satisfaction is important, as the goal is to develop a high-quality product that will satisfy the customer. A customer satisfaction survey (as discussed in an earlier chapter) is often employed to measure the level of satisfaction, as well as monitoring customer problems and complaints. The feedback from the survey is discussed with the customer, and an action plan is prepared to address any issues. The monitoring of customer satisfaction will indicate the success of the organization in satisfying its customers.

The organization needs to establish an internal audit process, and the objective of an audit is to provide visibility to management on the processes being used and the product being built. The audit is an independent examination, and is typically carried out by a trained auditor. The level of compliance to the defined process is considered, as is the effectiveness of the defined process. Improvement opportunities are identified and tracked to completion. The output from the audit is an audit report, and the audit report includes the findings of the audit and recommendations. Audits were discussed in Chap. 9.

The measurement and monitoring of processes requires the organization to implement measurements to evaluate process performance. Process measurement is essential in a manufacturing environment, and process measurement in a software organization is focused on measuring key software processes. Quantitative goals are set for the performance of key processes, and actual results compared against the objectives. There is more information for software organizations in the discussion of CMMI level 4 discussed in Chap. 13. The idea is that if process performance falls outside the control limits, then this will trigger corrective actions to adjust the performance of the process to ensure that it performs within the upper and lower control limits. This is best seen with a process performance diagram (e.g., Fig. 1.2).

The measurement and monitoring of a product is performed to verify that the product requirements are fulfilled. This enables an objective decision to be made on whether it is appropriate to release the software to potential customers. It may involve specifying various quantitative goals to be satisfied prior to release.

The control of nonconformity is concerned with the procedure for reporting defects, and taking action to correct the defect. The defects are often recorded with a defect reporting tool or a spreadsheet, and relevant information recorded. This includes the severity of the defect, its description, the date that it occurred, the technical person responsible for its correction, the type of defect, and so on. The quality status of the project includes the open defects, and the most serious defects need to be resolved prior to release of the software.

The analysis of data is used in decision making, and the organization needs to analyse the data to determine the appropriate actions for improvement. The objective of continual improvement is to improve the effectiveness of the quality management system through the use of the quality policy, quality objectives, audit results, customer satisfaction measurements, management review, analysis of data, and corrective and preventive actions.

Corrective action is taken on customer complaints, defect reports, audit reports, etc., and the results lead to a more effective QMS. It involves analysis of the identified issues or defects, with actions defined to address, and the effectiveness of the actions periodically reviewed. The objective of preventive action is to identify actions to prevent potential defects from occurring. This requires analysis to determine the causes of defects, identifying actions to be taken, implementing the actions, and periodically reviewing the effectiveness of the actions.

11.4   Implementing ISO 9001

The implementation of ISO 9001 in an organization is closely related to the activities described in Sects. 11.3.1, 11.3.2, 11.3.3, 11.3.4, and 11.3.5. ISO 9001 is implemented to improve quality and customer satisfaction, and a certified ISO 9001 organization has demonstrated to the satisfaction of the ISO 9001 auditors that a sound quality system is in place in the organization. ISO 9001 implementation consists of the steps listed in Table 11.3.

11.5   ISO 9000 and Improvement

Many organizations aspire to excellence, and superior results may be achieved by continuous improvement of the underlying processes and standards. An organization may assess its current level of excellence with respect to some international quality standard or model, and use the assessment results to improve its capability.

The ISO 9000 standard may be used by an organization to assess its current level of maturity. The findings from the assessment will indicate the areas which the organization needs to work on to improve. This section describes a simple self-assessment process, which has been adapted from ISO 9004.

11.5.1 Self-Assessment Process

Table 11.4 is a self-assessment of an imaginary organization with respect to the ISO 9001 standard. The self-assessment yields a maturity profile, and it indicates the extent to which the various ISO 9001 clauses are implemented in the organization. It is typically carried out internally by one or more people from the organization.

The example presented here includes a small selection of the ISO 9001 clauses, and they are rated as either "*not implemented*", "*partially implemented*", "*largely implemented*", or "*fully implemented*".

The results of the self-assessment are analysed and used to prepare an action plan for improvement.

11.5.2 ISO 9001 Certification Process

The steps required to implement ISO 9001 were described in Sect. 11.4 (Table 11.3). The activities involved in the certification process involve determining if the organization is ready for an ISO 9001 assessment; contacting the certification body; preparing the participants; agreeing a date for the assessment;

Table 11.3 ISO 9001 implementation

Step	Description
Awareness training	This involves briefing management on ISO 9000 and the steps involved in its implementation.
Establish a team	Management sets up a team with responsibility for ISO 9000 implementation. The team will consist of management and employees, and the team chairperson will provide regular progress reports to management. The team members will champion ISO 9000 in the organization, and will receive more detailed training on ISO 9000.
Establish ISO 9000 status	The current ISO 9001 status of the organization is determined. This may be done by a consultant, or if the team has sufficient expertise it may perform a self-assessment of the organization as described in ISO 9004. The areas that need to be addressed to satisfy the standards are identified.
Prepare action plan	The actual ISO 9001 status is used to prepare the action plan for implementation, and the resources needed for implementation are identified and provided. The action plan defines the activities to be performed, the resources required, and the estimated completion date of each activity.
Track action plan	The action plan is the project plan for ISO 9001 implementation, and the plan is tracked and updated to reflect the progress made, and the work that needs to be done.
Present status of action plan	The status of the action plan is presented regularly to management. The chairperson presents the status of the action plan, and will re-plan as appropriate.
ISO 9000 readiness assessment	It is useful to determine if the organization is ready for a formal ISO 9001 assessment. This optional step may be done with a readiness review, and this is carried out by an independent body or consultant. This review identifies any serious issues that need to be resolved prior to the official assessment.
Contact registrar (certification body)	Once the organization is confident that it has implemented an ISO 9001 quality system (Fig. 11.1), it may then apply to the certification body for an ISO 9001 audit of its quality system. This involves
	Contact the certification body.
	Furnish relevant details about the company.
	Supply the quality manual and any requested processes or procedures to the certification body.
	Arrange a date for when the auditors will visit the company.
	Brief participants in the company on the visit and the expected behaviour during the visit.
	Arrange logistics for the visit.
	Arrange interview rooms.
	Facilitate interview schedule.
	Supply any requested documentation.
Official ISO 9000 Audit	The auditor(s) compare the quality system against the ISO 9001 requirements, and they interview individuals and groups.
	The participants answer all questions openly and honestly.
	The auditor(s) will stay on site for 1–2 days

(continued)

Table 11.3 (continued)

Step	Description
	The standard requires certain processes and procedures, records, and controls to be in place.
	The auditors will examine evidence of compliance and records
	The auditors will determine the extent to which the written procedures correspond to the actual observed behaviour.
	The auditors will publish an evaluation report which will detail the findings of the audit.
	The auditors may identify corrective actions to be carried out prior to the granting of ISO 9001 certification.
	The company is required to carry out the corrective actions, and these are then verified.
	The ISO 9001 registration is then granted.
	The registration is valid for approximately 2 years, and follow-up audits are conducted to ensure that the quality system remains ISO 9001 compliant.
Continuous improvement	The organization will use the feedback from the formal assessment to continuously improve.
Celebrate	The award of ISO 9001 certification is a major achievement for the organization and merits a celebration. The celebration demonstrates the importance attached to quality and customer satisfaction

Table 11.4 Simple ISO 9000 self-assessment

ISO 9000 clause	Not implemented	Partially implemented	Largely implemented	Fully implemented
4.2.4 Control of records				
5.3 Quality policy				
5.6 Management review				
6.2.2 Competence				
7.2.3 Customer reqs				

arranging the logistics; providing all required documentation and records to the assessors; and acting on any feedback provided by the assessors.

11.6 Review Questions

1. What is ISO 9000?
2. Explain the differences between ISO 9000, ISO 9001 and ISO 9004.
3. What are the advantages of achieving ISO 9001 certification?
4. Describe the ISO 9001 clauses.
5. Describe the steps involved in implementing ISO 9001.
6. Describe the steps involved in applying for ISO 9001 certification.
7. Describe how ISO 9000 may be used for improvement.

11.7   Summary

ISO 9000 is an international quality standard which enables an organization to implement a sound quality system that is dedicated to customer satisfaction and continuous improvement. The independent certification of ISO 9001 indicates that the company has a sound quality management system in place, and that the company is committed to the core values of quality, customer satisfaction, and continuous improvement.

The ISO 9000 standards may be applied to various types of organizations, including manufacturing, software, and service organizations. It is regarded as a minimal quality standard that an organization committed to quality should satisfy. Many organizations require their subcontractors to be ISO 9001 certified, as this provides confidence in the subcontractor's quality system, and in the ability of the subcontractor to produce high-quality software.

The latest revision of ISO 9000 is termed ISO 9000:2008, and it places emphasis on customer satisfaction and continuous improvement. It includes a process model and the emphasis in the standard is on processes, and in improvement to the processes. It is a family of standards and includes ISO 9000, ISO 9001, and ISO 9004. The ISO 9004 standard provides practical guidance on the implementation of ISO 9001, and guidelines for performance improvement of the quality system.

The implementation of ISO 9001 involves setting up a team to manage the implementation, and in providing the required resources for implementation. A self-assessment may be performed to indicate the current ISO 9001 status, and an action plan prepared to address the weaker areas. The implementation is managed and tracked like a normal project, and it involves defining processes and procedures, maintaining records, and training. The quality group in the organization will play a key role in the implementation of the standard and in ensuring compliance with the ISO 9001 requirements. The award of ISO 9001 certification provides an indication that the company is focused on quality, customer satisfaction and continuous improvement.

Software Process Improvement

12

12.1 Introduction

The success of business today is highly influenced by the functionality and quality of the software that it uses. It is essential that the software is safe, reliable, of a high quality and fit for purpose. Companies may develop their own software internally, or they may acquire software solutions off-the-shelf or from bespoke software development. Software development companies need to deliver high-quality and reliable software consistently on time to their customers.

Cost is a key driver in most organizations and it is essential that software is produced as cheaply and efficiently as possible, and that waste is reduced or eliminated in the software development process. In a nutshell, companies need to produce software that is *better, faster and cheaper* than their competitors in order to survive in the market place. That is, companies need to continuously work smarter to improve their businesses and to deliver superior solutions to their customers.

G. O'Regan, *Introduction to Software Quality*, Undergraduate Topics
in Computer Science, DOI 10.1007/978-3-319-06106-1_12,
© Springer International Publishing Switzerland 2014

Software process improvement initiatives are aligned to business goals and play a key role in helping companies achieve their strategic goals. It is invaluable in the implementation of best practice in organizations, and allows companies to focus on fire prevention rather than firefighting. It allows companies to problem solve key issues to eliminate quality problems, and to critically examine their current processes to determine the extent to which they meets its needs, as well as identifying how the processes can be improved, and where waste can be minimized or eliminated.

It allows companies to identify the root causes of problems (e.g., using the *five why tool*), and to determine appropriate solutions to the problems. The benefits of successful process improvement include the consistent delivery of high-quality software, improved financial results and increased customer satisfaction.

Software process improvement initiatives lead to a focus on the process and on ways to improve it. Many problems are caused by defective processes rather than people, and a focus on the process helps to avoid a blame culture that occurs when blame is apportioned to individuals rather than the process. The focus on the process leads to a culture of openness in discussing problems and their solutions, and in instilling process ownership in the process practitioners.

Software process improvement allows companies to mature their software engineering processes, and to achieve their business goals more effectively. It helps software companies to deliver high-quality software on-time and on-budget, as well, reducing the cost of development, and improving customer satisfaction. It has become an indispensable tool for software engineers and managers to achieve their goals, and provides a return on investment to the organization.

12.2 What Is a Software Process?

A software development process is the process used by software engineers to design and develop computer software. It may be an undocumented ad hoc process as devised by the team for a particular project, or it may be a standardized and documented process used by various teams on similar projects. The process is seen as the glue that ties people, technology and procedures coherently together.

The processes employed in software development include processes to determine the requirements; processes to design and development software; processes to verify that the software is fit for purpose; and processes to maintain the software.

A software process is a set of activities, methods, practices and transformations that people use to develop and maintain software and the associated work products.

DEFINITION 12.1 (SOFTWARE PROCESS) A *process* is a set of practices or tasks performed to achieve a given purpose. It may include tools, methods, material and people.

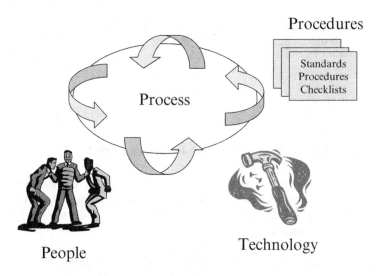

Fig. 12.1 Process as glue for people, procedures and tools

An organization will typically have many processes in place for doing its work, and the object of process improvement is to improve these to meet business goals more effectively.

The Software Engineering Institute (SEI) believes that there is a close relationship between the quality of the delivered software and the quality and maturity of the underlying processes employed to create the software. The SEI adopted and applied the principles of process improvement employed in the manufacturing field to develop process maturity models such as the CMM and its successor the CMMI. These maturity models are invaluable in maturing software processes in software intensive organizations.

The process is an abstraction of the way in which work is done in the organization, and is seen as the glue that ties people, procedures and tools together (Fig. 12.1).

A process is often represented by a process map which details the flow of activities and tasks. The process map will typically include the inputs to each activity as well as the output from an activity. Often, the output from one activity will become an input to the next activity. A simple example of a process map for creating the system requirements specification is described in Fig. 12.2. The input to the activity to create the systems requirements specification will typically be the business requirements, whereas the output is the systems requirements specification document itself.

As a process matures it is defined in more detail and documented. It will have clearly defined entry and exit criteria, inputs and outputs, an explicit description of the tasks, verification of the process and consistent implementation throughout the organization.

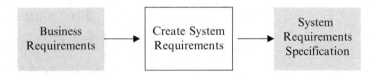

Fig. 12.2 Sample process map

12.3   What Is Software Process Improvement?

The origins of the software process improvement field go back to Walter Shewhart's work on statistical process control in the 1930s. Software process improvement is concerned with practical action to improve the processes in the organization to ensure that they meet business goals more effectively. For example, the goal may be to deliver projects faster and with higher quality.

Shewhart's work was later refined by Deming and Juran, and they argued that high-quality processes are essential to the delivery of a high-quality product. They argued that the quality of the end product is largely determined by the processes used to produce and support it, and that therefore needs to be an emphasis on the process as well as the product.

These quality gurus argued that product quality will improve as variability in process performance is reduced [15], and their approach was effective in transforming manufacturing companies with quality problems to companies that could consistently deliver high-quality products. Further, the improvements to quality led to cost reductions and higher productivity, as less time was spent in reworking defective products.

The work of Deming and Juran was later applied to the software quality field by Watt Humphries and others at the SEI leading to the birth of the software process improvement field.

DEFINITION 12.2 (SOFTWARE PROCESS IMPROVEMENT) A program of activities designed to improve the performance and maturity of the organization's software processes and the results of such a program.

Software process improvement initiatives support the organization in achieving its key business goals such as delivering software faster to the market, improving quality, reducing or eliminating waste. The objective is to work smarter and to build software better, faster, and cheaper than competitors. Software process improvement makes business sense and provides a return on investment.

There are international standards and models available to support software process improvement. These include the CMMI Model, the ISO 90001 standard, and ISO 15504 (popularly known as SPICE). The CMMI model was developed by the Software Engineering Institute (SEI), and includes best practice for processes in software and systems engineering. The ISO 9001 standard is a quality management system that may be employed in hardware or software development companies. The ISO 15504 standard is an international standard for software process improvement and process assessment.

Software process improvement is concerned with defining the right processes and following them consistently. It involves training all staff on the new processes, refining the processes, and continuously improving the processes.

12.4   What Are the Benefits of Software Process Improvement?

It is a challenge to deliver high-quality software consistently on time. There are problems with budget and schedule overruns, late delivery of the software, spiralling costs, quality problems with the delivered software, customer complaints, and staff morale.

Software process improvement can assist in dealing with these problems. There are costs involved but it provides a return on the investment made. Specifically, the benefits from software process improvement include:
- Improvements to quality
- Reductions in the cost of poor quality
- Improvements in productivity
- Reductions to the cost of software development
- Improvements in on-time delivery
- Improved consistency in budget and schedule delivery
- Improvements to customer satisfaction
- Improvements to employee morale

The Software Engineering Institute maintains data on the benefits that organizations have achieved from using the CMMI. These include improvements in several categories such as cost, schedule, productivity, quality, customer satisfaction, and the return on investment.

Table 12.1 presents the results from 25 organizations. These results are from conference presentations, published papers and individual collaborations [59].

For example, *Northrop Grumman Defense Systems* met every milestone (25 in a row) with high-quality and customer satisfaction; *Lockheed Martin* reported an 80 % increase in software productivity over a 5 year period when it achieved CMM level 5 and obtained further increases in productivity as it moved to CMMI level 5. *Siemens (India)* reported an improved defect removal rate from over 50 % before testing to over 70 % before testing, and a post- release defect rate of 0.35 defects per KLOC. *Accenture* reported a 5:1 return on investment from software process improvement activities.

Table 12.1 Benefits of software process improvement (CMMI)

Improvements	Median (%)	#Data points (%)	Low (%)	High (%)
Cost	20	21	3	87
Schedule	37	19	2	90
Productivity	62	17	9	255
Quality	50	20	7	132
Customer satisfaction	14	6	−4	55
ROI	4.7:1	16	2:1	27:1

12.5   What Models Are Used in Software Process Improvement?

A process model[1] such as the CMMI defines best practice for software processes in an organization. It describes what the processes should do rather than how they should be done, and this allows the organization to use its professional judgment in the implementation of processes to meet its needs. The process model will need to be interpreted and tailored to the particular organization.

A process model provides a place to start an improvement initiative and it provides a common language and shared vision for improvement. It provides a framework to prioritize actions and allows the benefits of the experience of other organizations to be shared. The popular process models used in software process improvement include:

- Capability Maturity Model Integration (CMMI)
- ISO 9001 Standard
- ISO 15504
- PSP and TSP
- Six Sigma
- IEEE standards
- Root Cause Analysis (RCA)
- Balanced Scorecard

The CMMI was developed by the Software Engineering Institute, and is the successor to the older software CMM which was released in the early 1990s. The latter was specific to the software field it was influenced by Watt Humphrey's work at IBM [29]. The CMMI is a suite of products used for improving processes, and it includes models, appraisal methods and training material. The CMMI models address three areas of interest:

- CMMI for Development (CMMI-DEV)
- CMMI for Services (CMMI-SVC)
- CMMI for Acquisition (CMMI-ACQ)

The CMMI Development Model is discussed in the next chapter. It is a framework that allows organizations to improve their maturity by improvements to their

---

[1] There is the well-known adage "All models are wrong, some are useful".

underlying processes. It provides a structured approach and allows the organization to set improvement goals and priorities. It provides a clearly defined roadmap for improvement and it allows the organization to improve at its own pace. Its approach is evolutionary rather than revolutionary, and it recognizes that a balance is required between project needs and process improvement needs. It allows the processes to evolve from ad hoc immature activities to disciplined mature processes.

The CMMI practices may be used for the development, acquisition and maintenance of products and services. A SCAMPI appraisal determines the process maturity of an organization and allows it to benchmark itself against other organizations.

ISO 9001 is an internationally recognized quality management standard and is customer and process focused. It applies to the processes that an organization uses to create and control products and services, and it emphasizes continuous improvement.[2] The standard is designed to apply to any product or service that an organization supplies.

The implementation of ISO 9001 involves understanding the requirements of the standard and how the standard applies to the organization. It requires the organization to identify its quality objectives, define a quality policy, produce documented procedures, and carry out independent audits to ensure that the processes and procedures are followed. An organization may be certified against the ISO 9001 standard to gain recognition to its commitment to quality and continuous improvement. The certification involves an independent assessment of the organization to verify that it has implemented the ISO 9001 requirements properly, and that the quality management system is effective. It will also verify that the processes and procedures defined are consistently followed and that appropriate records are maintained. The ISO 9004 standard provides guidance for continuous improvement.

The ISO/IEC 15504 standard (popularly known as ISO SPICE) is an international standard for process assessment. It includes guidance for process improvement and for process capability determination, as well as guidance for performing an assessment. It includes an exemplar process model for software and systems lifecycle processes. There is a version of SPICE termed *"Automotive SPICE"* that is used in the automotive sector.

ISO/IEC 15504 can be used in a similar way to the CMMI and its exemplar models (for either software or systems lifecycles) may be employed to implement best practice in process definition. Assessments may be performed to identify strengths and opportunities for improvement.

The Personal Software Process (PSP) is a disciplined data driven software development process that is designed to help software engineers understand and to improve their personal software process performance. It was developed by Watt Humphrey at the SEI, and it helps engineers to improve their estimation and planning skills and to and to reduce the number of defects in their work. This enables them to make commitments that they can keep and to manage the quality of their projects.

---

[2] The ISO 9004 standard provides guidance on continuous improvement.

The Team Software Process (TSP) was developed by Watt Humphries at the SEI, and is a structured approach designed to help software teams understand and improve their quality and productivity. Its focus is on building an effective software development team, and it involves establishing team goals, assigning team roles as well as other teamwork activities. Team members must already be familiar with the PSP.

Six Sigma (6σ) was developed by Motorola as a way to improve quality and reduce waste. Its approach is to identify and remove the causes of defects in processes by reducing process variability. It uses quality management techniques and tools such as the five whys, business process mapping, statistical techniques, and the DMAIC and DMADV methodologies. There are several roles involved in six sigma initiatives such as Champions, Black Belts and Green Belts, and each role requires knowledge and experience and is awarded on merit subject to training and certification. Sponsorship and leadership is required from top management to ensure the success of a Six Sigma initiative. Six Sigma was influenced by earlier quality management techniques developed by Shewhart, Deming and Juran.

A Six Sigma project follows a defined sequence of steps and has quantified targets. These targets may be financial, quality, customer satisfaction, and cycle time reduction.

12.6   Process Mapping

The starting point for improving a process is first to understand the process as it is currently performed. The process stakeholders reach a common understanding of how the process is actually performed, and to identify how it may be improved. The process as currently performed is then sketched pictorially, with the activities and their inputs and outputs recorded graphically. This graphical representation is termed a "*process map*" and is an abstract description of the process "*as is*".

The process map is an abstraction of the way that work is done, and it may be critically examined to determine how effective it really is, and to identify weaknesses. This critical examination of the process by the process practitioners leads to modifications to its definition, and the proposed definition is sketched in a new process map to yield the process "*to be*". Once the team has agreed the new process the templates required to support the process become clear from an examination of the input and output of the various activities. Procedures or guidelines will be documented to provide the details on how the process is to be carried out.

12.7   Process Improvement Initiatives

The need for a software process improvement initiative often arises from the realization that the organization is weak in some areas in software engineering, and that it needs to improve to achieve its business goals more effectively.

The starting point of any improvement initiative is an examination of the business goals of the organization and these may include:
- Delivering high-quality products on time
- Delivering products faster to the market
- Reducing the cost of software development
- Improving software quality

There is more than one approach to the implementation of the CMMI. A small organization has fewer resources available and team members involved in the initiative will typically be working part time. Larger organizations may be able to assign people full time on the improvement activities. The software process improvement initiative should be designed to enable the organization achieve its business goals more effectively.

Once the organization goals have been defined the improvement initiative commences. This involves conducting an appraisal to determine the current strengths and weaknesses of the processes; analysing the results to formulate a process improvement plan; implementing the plan; piloting the improved processes and verifying that they are effective; rolling out the new processes. The improvements are monitored for effectiveness and the cycle repeats. The philosophy is:
- The improvement initiative is based on business needs
- Improvements should be planned based on an objective understanding of the strengths and weaknesses of the current processes in the organization
- The CMMI Model or an alternate model is the vehicle for improvement.
- The improvements are prioritized (it is not possible to do everything at once).
- The improvement initiative needs to be planned and managed as a project.
- The results achieved need to be reviewed at the end of the period, and a new improvement cycle started for continuous improvement
- Software process improvement requires people to change their behaviour, and so organization culture needs to be considered.
- There needs to be a Process Champion to drive the process improvement initiative in the organization.
- Senior management need to be 100 % committed to the success of the initiative.
- Staff need to be involved in the improvement initiative, and there needs to be a balance between project needs and the improvement activities

The continuous improvement cycle is influenced by the IDEAL[SM] model and by Deming's Plan-Do-Check-Act (PDCA) process improvement cycle. It is described in Chap. 14.

12.8 Barriers to Success

Software process improvement initiatives are not always successful, and occasionally an improvement initiative is abandoned. Some of the reasons for failure are:
- Unrealistic expectations
- Trying to do too much at once
- Lack of Senior Management Sponsorship

- Focusing on a Maturity Level
- Poor Project Management of the initiative
- Not run as a standard project
- Insufficient involvement of staff
- Insufficient time to work on improvements
- Inadequate training on Software Process Improvement
- Lack of pilots to validate new processes
- Inadequate rollout of new processes

It is essential that a software process improvement initiative is treated as a standard project with a project manager assigned to manage the initiative. Senior management need to be 100 % committed to the success of the initiative, and they need to make staff available to work on the improvement activities. It needs to be clear to all staff that the improvement initiative is a priority to the organization. All employees need to receive appropriate training on software process improvement and on the process maturity model.

The CMMI project manager needs to consider the risks of failure of the initiative and to manage them accordingly.

12.9 Review Questions

1. What is a software process?
2. What is software process improvement?
3. What are the benefits of software process improvement?
4. Describe the various models available for software process improvement?
5. Draw the process map for the process of cooking your favourite meal.
6. Describe how a process improvement initiative may be run?
7. What are the main barriers to successful software process improvement initiatives and how can they be overcome?

12.10 Summary

The success of business is highly influenced by software, and companies may develop their own software internally, or they may acquire software solutions off-the-shelf or from bespoke software development. Companies need to produce software that is *better, faster and cheaper* than their competitors in order to survive in the market place.

Software process improvement plays a key role in helping companies to achieve their strategic goals, and is invaluable in the implementation of best practice in organizations. It allows companies to focus on fire prevention rather than firefighting, and to critically examine their processes to determine the extent to which they meet their needs. It enables them to identify how the process may be improved and how waste can be minimized or eliminated.

Software process improvement initiatives lead to a focus on the process, and a focus on process thinking is important since many problems are caused by defective processes rather than by people. A focus on the process rather than people leads to a culture of openness in discussing problems, and instils process ownership in the process practitioners.

Software process improvement allows companies to mature their software engineering processes, and to achieve their business goals more effectively. It helps software companies to deliver the agreed software on-time and on-budget, as well as improving the quality of the delivered software, reducing the cost of development, and improving customer satisfaction. It has become an indispensable tool for software engineers and managers to achieve their goals, and provides a return on investment to the organization.

The next chapter gives an introduction to the Capability Maturity Model Integration.

Capability Maturity Model Integration

13

Key Topics

CMMI Maturity Levels
CMMI Capability Levels
CMMI Staged Representation
CMMI Continuous Representation
CMMI Process Areas
Appraisals

13.1 Introduction

The Software Engineering Institute[1] developed the Capability Maturity Model
(CMM) in the early 1990s as a framework to help software organizations improve
their software process maturity. The CMMI is the successor to the older CMM, and
its implementation brings best practice in software and systems engineering into the
organization. The SEI and many other quality experts believe that there is a close
relationship between the maturity of software processes and the quality of the
delivered software product.

---

[1] The SEI was founded by the US Congress in 1984 and has worked successfully in advancing
software engineering practices in the US and worldwide. It performs research to find solutions to
key software engineering problems, and its proposed solutions are validated through pilots. These
solutions are then disseminated to the wider software engineering community through its training
programme. The SEI's research and maturity models have played an important role in helping
companies to deliver high-quality software consistently on time and on budget. The SEI opened a
European office in Frankfurt, Germany in 2004.

G. O'Regan, *Introduction to Software Quality*, Undergraduate Topics
in Computer Science, DOI 10.1007/978-3-319-06106-1_13,
© Springer International Publishing Switzerland 2014

Fig. 13.1 Process as glue for
people, procedures and tools

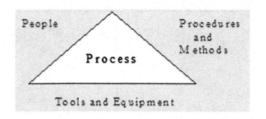

The CMM built upon the work of quality gurus such as Deming [15], Juran [33] and Crosby [14]. These quality gurus were effective in transforming struggling manufacturing companies with quality problem to companies that could consistently produce high quality products. Their success was due to the focus on improving the manufacturing process and in reducing variability in the process. The work of these quality experts was discussed in Chap. 1

Similarly, software companies need to have quality software processes to deliver high-quality software to their customers. The SEI has collected empirical data to suggest that there is a close relationship between software process maturity and the quality of the delivered software. Therefore there is a need to focus on the software process as well as on the product.

The CMM was released in 1991 and its successor, the CMMI® model, was released in 2002 [13]. The CMMI is a framework to assist an organization in the implementation of best practice in software and systems engineering. It is an internationally recognized model for process improvement and is used worldwide by thousands of organizations.

The focus of the CMMI is on improvements to the software process to ensure that they meet business needs more effectively. A *process* is a set of practices or tasks performed to achieve a given purpose. It may include tools, methods, material and people. An organization will typically have many processes in place for doing its work, and the object of process improvement is to improve these to meet business goals more effectively.

The process is an abstraction of the way in which work is done in the organization, and is seen as the glue (Fig. 13.1) that ties people, procedures and tools together.

It may be described by a process map which details the flow of activities and tasks. The process map will include the input to each activity and the output from each activity. Often, the output from one activity will become the input to the next activity. A simple example of a process map for creating the system requirements specification was described in the previous chapter (Fig. 12.2).

The ISO/IEC 12207 standard for software processes distinguishes between several categories of software processes including the primary life cycle processes for developing and maintaining software; supporting processes to support the software development lifecycle; and organization life cycle processes. These are summarized in Fig. 13.2.

Watt Humphries began applying the ideas of Deming, Juran and Crosby to software development, and he published the book *"Managing the Software*

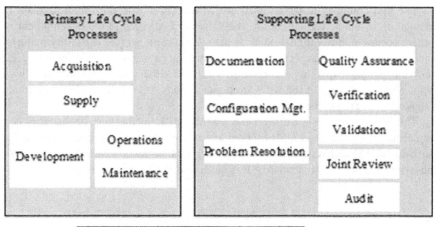

Fig. 13.2 ISO/IEC 12207 standard for software engineering processes

Process" [29] after he moved to the SEI to work on software process maturity models with the other SEI experts. The SEI released the Capability Maturity Model in the early 1990s, and this process model has proved to be effective in assisting companies in improving their software engineering practices and in achieving consistent results and high-quality software.

The CMM is a process model and it defines the characteristics or best practices of good processes. It does not prescribe how the processes should be done and allows the organization the freedom to interpret the model to suit its particular context and business needs. It also provides a roadmap for an organization to get from where it is today to a higher level of maturity. The advantage of model-based improvement is that it provides a place to start process improvement, as well as a common language and a shared vision.

The CMM consists of five maturity levels with the higher maturity levels representing advanced software engineering capability. The lowest maturity level is level 1 and the highest is level 5. The SEI developed an assessment methodology (CBA IPI) to determine the maturity of software organizations, and initially most organizations were assessed at level 1 maturity. However, over time companies embarked on improvement initiatives, and matured their software processes, and today many companies are performing at the higher maturity levels.

214 13 Capability Maturity Model Integration

The first company to be assessed at CMM level 5^2 was the Motorola plant in Bangalore in India. The success of the software CMM led to the development of other process maturity models such as the systems engineering capability maturity mode (CMM/SE) which is concerned with maturing systems engineering practices, and the people capability maturity model (P-CMM) which is concerned with improving the ability of the software organizations to attract, develop, and retain talented software engineering professionals.

The SEI commenced work on the CMMI® [13] in the late 1990s. This is a replacement for the older CMM model and its development included merging the software CMM and systems CMM, and ensuring that the new model was compatible with the ISO 15504 standard.[3] It is described in the next Section.

13.2 The CMMI

The CMMI consists of five maturity levels with each maturity level (except level 1) consisting of a number of process areas. Each process area consists of a set of goals, and these must be implemented by a set of related practices in order for the process area to be satisfied. The practices specify what is to be done rather than how it should be done. Processes are activities associated with carrying out certain tasks, and they need to be defined and documented. The users of the process need to receive appropriate training to enable them to carry out the process, and process discipline need to be enforced by independent audits. Process performance needs to be monitored and improvements made to ineffective processes.

The emphasis for level 2 of the CMMI is on maturing management practices such as project management, requirements management, configuration management, and so on. The emphasis on level 3 of the CMMI is on maturing engineering and organization practices. Maturity level 3 is concerned with defining standard organization processes, and it also includes process areas for the various engineering activities needed to design and develop the software. Level 4 is concerned with ensuring that key processes are performing within strict quantitative limits, and adjusting processes, where necessary, to perform within these limits. Level 5 is concerned with continuous process improvement. Maturity levels may not be skipped in the staged implementation of the CMMI, as each maturity level is the foundation for work on the next level.

---

[2] Of course, the fact that a company has been appraised at a certain CMM or CMMI rating is no guarantee that it is performing effectively as a commercial organization. For example, the Motorola plant in India was appraised at CMM level 5 in the late 1990s while Motorola lost business opportunities in the GSM market.

[3] ISO 15504 (popularly known as SPICE) is an international standard for software process assessment.

Table 13.1 Motivation for CMMI implementation

Motivation for CMMI implementation
Enhances the credibility of the company
Marketing benefit of CMMI maturity level
Implementation of best practice in software and systems engineering
Logical path to improvement
It increases the capability and maturity of an organization
It improves the management of subcontractors
It provides improved technical and management practices
It leads to higher quality of software
It leads to increased timeliness of projects
It reduces the cost of maintenance and incidence of defects
It allows the measurement of processes and products
It allows projects/products to be quantitatively managed
It allows innovative technologies to be rigorously evaluated to enhance process performance
It improves customer satisfaction
It changes the culture from firefighting to fire prevention
It leads to a culture of improvement
It leads to higher morale in company

There is also a continuous representation[4] of the CMMI that allows the organization to focus its improvements on key processes that are closely related to its business goals. This allows it the freedom to choose an approach that should result in the greatest business benefit rather than proceeding on the standard improvement roadmap. However, in practice it is often necessary to implement several of the level 2 process areas before serious work can be done on maturing a process to a higher capability level. Table 13.1 presents the motivation for the implementation of the CMMI.

The CMMI model covers both the software engineering and systems engineering disciplines. Systems engineering is concerned with the development of systems that may or may not include software, whereas software engineering is concerned with the development of software systems. The model contains extra information relevant to a particular discipline, and this is done by discipline amplification.[5]

---

[4] Our focus is on the implementation of the staged representation of the CMMI rather than the continuous representation. This is my preferred approach to process improvement as it provides a clearly defined roadmap, and also allows benchmarking of organizations. Appraisals against the staged representation are useful since a CMMI maturity level rating is awarded to the organization, and the company may use this to publicise its software engineering capability.

[5] Discipline amplification is a specialised piece of information that is relevant to a particular discipline. It is introduced in the model by text such as "For Systems Engineering"

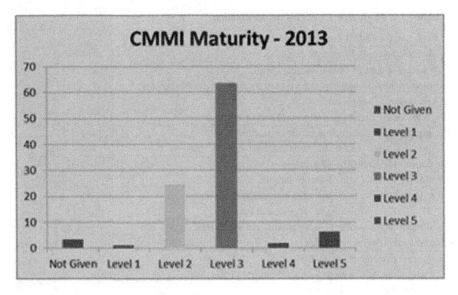

Fig. 13.3 CMMI Worldwide maturity 2013

The CMMI allows organizations to benchmark themselves against similar organizations. This is generally done by a formal SEI SCAMPI Class A appraisal[6] conducted by an authorized SCAMPI lead appraiser (Fig. 13.3). The results will generally be reported back to the SEI, and there is a strict qualification process to become an authorised lead appraiser. The qualification process helps to ensure that the appraisals are conducted fairly and objectively and that the results are consistent. An appraisal is verifies that an organization has improved, and it enables the organization to prioritize improvements for the next improvement cycle. Small organizations will often prefer a SCAMPI Class B or C appraisal as these are less expensive and time consuming.[7]

The time required to implement the CMMI in an organization depends on its size and current maturity. It generally takes 1–2 years to implement maturity level 2, and a further one to two years to implement level 3. The implementation of the CMMI

---

[6] A SCAMPI appraisal is a systematic examination of the processes in an organization to determine the maturity of the organization with respect to the CMMI. An appraisal team consists of a SCAMPI lead appraiser, one or more external appraisers, and usually one internal appraiser. It consists of interviews with senior and middle management and reviews with project managers and project teams. The appraisers will review documentation and determine the extent to which the processes defined are effective as well as the extent to which they are institutionalized in the organization. Data will be gathered and reviewed by the appraisers, ratings produced and the findings presented to the organization.

[7] Small organizations may not have the budget for a formal SCAMPI Class A appraisal. They may be more interested in an independent SCAMPI Class B or C appraisal, which is used to provide feedback on their strengths and opportunities for improvement. Feedback allows the organization to focus its improvement efforts for the next improvement cycle.

Table 13.2 Benefits of
CMMI implementation

Benefit	Actual saving
Cost	34 %
Schedule	50 %
Productivity	61 %
Quality	48 %
Customer satisfaction	14 %
Return on investment	4:1

needs to be balanced against the day-to-day needs of the organization in delivering products and services to its customers.

The SEI has gathered empirical data (Table 13.2) on the benefits gained from the implementation of the CMMI [60]. The table shows the median results reported to the SEI.

The processes implemented during a CMMI initiative will generally include:
- Developing and Managing Requirements
- Design and Development
- Project Management
- Selecting and managing Subcontractors
- Managing change and Configurations
- Peer reviews
- Risk Management and Decision Analysis
- Testing
- Audits

13.3   CMMI Maturity Levels

The CMMI is divided into five maturity levels (Fig. 13.4) with each maturity level (except level 1) consisting of several process areas. The maturity level is a predictor of the results that will be obtained from following the software processes in the organization. The higher the maturity level of the organization, the more capable it is and the more predictable its results. The current maturity level acts as the foundation for the improvements to be made in the move to the next level.

The maturity levels provide a roadmap for improvements in the organization, and maturity levels are not skipped in the staged implementation. A particular maturity level is achieved only when all process areas belonging to that maturity level (and all process areas belonging to lower maturity levels) have been successfully implemented and institutionalized[8] in the organization (Table 13.3).

---

[8] Institutionalization is a technical term and means that the process is ingrained in the way in which work is performed in the organization. An institutionalised process is defined, documented and followed in the organization. All employees have been appropriately trained in its use and process discipline is enforced via audits. It is illustrated by the phrase *"That's the way we do things around here"*.

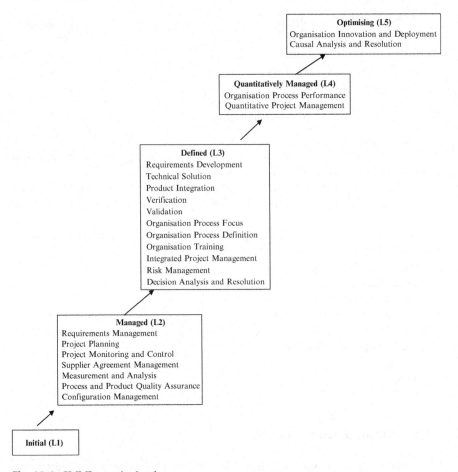

Fig. 13.4 CMMI maturity levels

The implementation of the CMMI generally starts with improvements to processes at the project level. The focus at level 2 is on improvements to managing projects and suppliers, and improving project management, supplier selection and management practices, and so on.

The improvements at level 3 involve a shift from the focus on projects to the organization. It involves defining standard processes for the organization, and projects may then tailor the standard process (using tailoring guidelines) to produce the project's software process. Projects are not required to do everything in the same way as the tailoring of the process allows the project's defined software process to reflect the unique characteristics of the project: i.e., a degree of variation is allowed as per the tailoring guidelines.

The implementation of level 3 requires defining procedures and standards for engineering activities such as design, coding and testing. Procedures are defined for peer reviews, testing, risk management and decision analysis.

Table 13.3 CMMI maturity levels

Maturity level	Description
Initial	Processes are often ad hoc or chaotic with performance often unpredictable. Success is often due to the heroics of people rather than having high-quality processes in place. The defined process is often abandoned in times of crisis, and there are no audits to enforce the process.
	It is difficult to repeat previous success, since success is due to heroic efforts of its people rather than processes. These organizations often over-commit, as they often lack an appropriate estimation process on which to base project commitments.
	Firefighting is a way of life in these organizations. High-quality software might be produced but at a cost including long hours, high level of rework, over budget and schedule and unhappy customers. Projects do not perform consistently as their success is dependent on the people involved.
	They may have few processes defined and poor change control, poor estimation and project planning, and weak enforcement of standards.
Managed	A level 2 organization has good project management practices in place, and planning and managing new projects is based on experience with similar previous projects.
	The process is planned, performed and controlled. A level 2 organization is disciplined in following processes, and the process is enforced with independent audits.
	The status of the work products produced by the process is visible to management at major milestones, and changes to work products are controlled. The work products are placed under appropriate configuration management control.
	The requirements for a project are managed and changes to the requirements are controlled. Project management practices are in place to manage the project, and a set of measures are defined for budget, schedule and effort variance. Subcontractors are managed.
	Independent audits are conducted to enforce the process. The processes in a level 2 organization are defined at the project level.
Defined	A maturity level 3 organization has standard processes defined that support the whole organization.
	These standard processes ensure consistency in the way that projects are conducted across the organization. There are guidelines defined that allow the organization process to be tailored and applied to each project.
	There are standards in place for design and development and procedures defined for effective risk management and decision analysis.
	Level 3 processes are generally defined more rigorously than level 2 processes, and the definition includes the purpose of the process, inputs, entry criteria, activities, roles, measures, verification steps, exit criteria and output. There is also an organization wide training program.
Quantitatively Managed	A level 4 organization sets quantitative goals for the performance of key processes, and these processes are controlled using statistical techniques.
	Processes are stable and perform within narrowly defined limits. Software process and product quality goals are set and managed.
	A level 4 organization has predictable process performance, with variation in process performance identified and the causes of variation corrected.

(continued)

Table 13.3 (continued)

Maturity level	Description
Optimizing	A level 5 organization has a continuous process improvement culture in place, and processes are improved based on a quantitative understanding of variation.
	Defect prevention activities are an integral part of the development lifecycle. New technologies are evaluated and introduced (where appropriate) into the organization. Processes may be improved incrementally or through innovative process and technology improvements.

The implementation of level 4 involves achieving process performance within defined quantitative limits. This involves the use of metrics and setting quantitative goals for project and process performance, and managing process performance. The implementation of level 5 is concerned with achieving a culture of continuous improvement in the company. The causes of defects are identified and resolution actions implemented to prevent a reoccurrence.

13.3.1 CMMI Representations

The CMMI is available in the staged and continuous representations. Both representations use the same process areas as well as the same specific and generic goals and practices.

The staged representation was described in Fig. 13.4 and is the approach followed here. It follows the well-known improvement roadmap from maturity level 1 through improvement cycles until the organization has achieved its desired level of maturity. The staged approach is concerned with organization maturity and allows statements of organization maturity to be made, whereas the continuous representation is concerned with individual process capability.

The continuous representation is illustrated in Fig. 13.5, and it has been influenced by the ISO 15504 standard for process assessment. It is concerned with improving the capability of those selected processes, and gives the organization the freedom to choose the order of improvements that best meet their business needs. The continuous representation allows statements of individual process capability to be made. It employs six capability levels and a process is rated at a particular capability level.

Each capability level consists of a set of specific and generic goals and practices, and the capability levels provide a path for process improvement within the process area. Process improvement is achieved by the evolution of a process from its current capability level to a higher capability level. For example, a company may wish to mature its project planning process from its current process rating of capability level 2 to a rating of capability level 3. This requires the implementation of practices to define a standard project planning process as well as collecting improvement data. The capability levels are listed in Table 13.4.

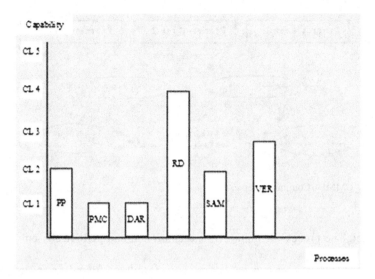

Fig. 13.5 CMMI capability levels

Table 13.4 CMMI capability levels for continuous representation

Capability level	Description
Incomplete (0)	The process does not implement all of the capability level 1 generic and specific practices. The process is either not performed or partially performed.
Performed (1)	A process that performs all of the specific practices and satisfies its specific goals. Performance may not be stable.
Managed (2)	A process at this level has infrastructure to support the process. It is managed: i.e., planned and executed in accordance with policy, its users are trained; it is monitored and controlled and audited for adherence to its process description.
Defined (3)	A process at this level has a defined process: i.e., a managed process that is tailored from the organization's set of standard processes. It contributes work products, measures and other process improvement information to the organization's process assets.
Quantitatively managed (4)	A process at this level is a quantitatively managed process: i.e., a defined process that is controlled by statistical techniques. Quantitative objectives for quality and process performance are established and used to control the process.
Optimizing (5)	A process at this level is an optimizing process: i.e., a quantitatively managed process that is continually improved through incremental and innovative improvements.

An incomplete process is a process that is either partially performed or not performed at all. A performed process carries out the expected practices and work products. However, such a process may not be adequately planned or enforced. A managed process is planned and executed with appropriately skilled and trained

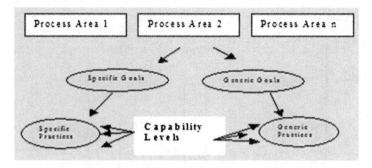

Fig. 13.6 CMMI – Continuous representation

personnel. The process is monitored and controlled and periodically enforced via audits.

A defined process is a managed process that is tailored from the standard process in the organization using tailoring guidelines. A quantitatively managed process is a defined process that is controlled using quantitative techniques. An optimizing process is a quantitatively managed process that is continuously improved through incremental and innovative improvements.

The process is rated at a particular capability level provided it satisfies all of the specific and generic goals of that capability level, and it also satisfies the specific and generic goals of all lower capability levels (Fig. 13.6).

We shall be concerned with the implementation of the staged representation of the CMMI rather than the continuous representation. The reader is referred to [13] for more information on both representations.

13.4 Categories of CMMI Processes

The process areas on the CMMI can be divided into four categories, as given in Table 13.5.

13.5 CMMI Process Areas

This section provides an overview of the process areas of the CMMI model. All maturity levels with the exception of level 1 contain several process areas. The process areas are described in more detail in [13] (Table 13.6).

Table 13.5 CMMI process categories

Maturity level	Description
Process management	The process areas in this category are concerned with activities to define, plan, implement, deploy, monitor, control, appraise, measure and improve the processes in the organization: They include:
	Organization Process Focus
	Organization Process Definition
	Organization Training
	Organization Process Performance
	Organization Innovation and Deployment
Project management	These process areas are concerned with activities to create and maintain a project plan, tailoring the standard process to produce the project's defined process, monitoring progress with respect to the plan, taking corrective action, the selection and management of suppliers, and the management of risk. They include:
	Project Planning
	Project Monitoring and Control
	Risk Management
	Integrated Project Management
	Supplier Agreement Management
	Quantitative Project Management
Engineering	These process areas are concerned with engineering activities such as determining and managing requirements, designing and development the software, testing and maintenance of the product. They include:
	Requirements Development
	Requirements Management
	Technical Solution
	Product Integration
	Verification
	Validation
Support	These process areas include activities that support product development and maintenance. They include:
	Configuration Management
	Process and Product Quality Assurance
	Measurement and Analysis
	Decision Analysis and Resolution

13.6 Components of CMMI Process Areas

The maturity level of an organization indicates the expected results that its projects will achieve, and is a predictor of future project performance. Each maturity level consists of a number of process areas, and each process area consists of specific and generic goals, and specific and generic practices. Each maturity level is the foundation for improvements for the next level.

The specific goals and practices are listed first and then followed by the generic goals and practices. The specific goals and practices are unique to the process area

Table 13.6 CMMI process areas

Maturity level	Process area	Description of process area
Level 2	REQM	**Requirements Management**
		This process area is concerned with managing the requirements for the project and ensuring that the requirements, project plan(s) and work products are kept consistent with the requirements.
	PP	**Project Planning**
		This process area is concerned with estimation for the project, developing and obtaining commitment to the project plan and maintaining the plan.
	PMC	**Project Monitoring and Control**
		This process area is concerned with monitoring progress with the project and taking corrective action when project performance deviates from the plan.
	SAM	**Supplier Agreement Management**
		This process area is concerned with the selection of suppliers, documenting the (legal) agreement/statement of work with the supplier and managing the supplier during the execution of the agreement.
	MA	**Measurement and Analysis**
		This process area is concerned with determining management information needs and measurement objectives. Measures are then specified to meet these objectives, and data collection and analysis procedures are defined. Data is collected and measurements analyzed and communicated.
	PPQA	**Process and Product Quality Assurance**
		This process area is concerned with providing objective visibility to management on the extent of process compliance. Non-compliance issues are documented and resolved by the project team.
	CM	**Configuration Management**
		This process area is concerned with the management of change. It involves setting up a configuration management system; identifying the items that will be subject to change control and controlling changes to them. Configuration audits are conducted.
Level 3	RD	**Requirements Development**
		This process area is concerned with eliciting and defining customer, product and product-component requirements and analyzing and validating the requirements.
	TS	**Technical Solution**
		This process area is concerned with the design, development and implementation of an appropriate solution to the customer requirements.
	PI	**Product Integration**
		This process area is concerned with the assembly of the product components to deliver the product, and verifying that the assembled components function correctly together.
	VER	**Verification**
		This process area is concerned with ensuring that selected work products satisfy their specified requirements. This is achieved by peer reviews and testing.

(continued)

Table 13.6 (continued)

Maturity level	Process area	Description of process area
	VAL	**Validation**
		This process area is concerned with demonstrating that the product or product component is fit for purpose and satisfies its intended use.
	OPF	**Organization Process Focus**
		This process area is concerned with planning and implementing process improvements based on a clear understanding of the current strengths and weakness of the organization's processes.
	OPD	**Organization Process Definition**
		This process area is concerned with creating and maintaining a usable set of organization processes. This allows consistent process performance across the organization.
	OT	**Organization Training**
		This process area is concerned with developing the skills and knowledge of people to enable them to perform their roles effectively.
	IPM	**Integrated Project Management**
		This process area is concerned with tailoring the organization set of standard processes to define the project's defined process. The project is managed according to the project's defined process.
	RSKM	**Risk Management**
		This process area is concerned with identifying risks and determining their probability of occurrence and impact should they occur. Risks are identified and managed throughout the project.
	DAR	**Decision Analysis and Resolution**
		This process area is concerned with formal decision making. It involves identifying options, specifying evaluation criteria and method, performing the evaluation, and recommending a solution.
Level 4	**OPP**	**Organization Process Performance**
		This process area is concerned with obtaining a quantitative understanding of the performance of selected organization processes in order to quantitatively manage projects in the organization.
	QPM	**Quantitative Project Management**
		This process area is concerned with quantitatively managing the project's defined process to achieve the project's quality and performance objectives.
Level 5	**OID**	**Organization Innovation and Deployment**
		This process area is concerned with incremental and innovative process improvements.
	QPM	**Causal Analysis and Resolution**
		This process area is concerned with identifying causes of defects and taking corrective action to prevent a re-occurrence in the future.

being implemented, and are concerned with what needs to be done to perform the process. The specific practices are linked to a particular specific goal, and they describe activities that when performed achieve the associated specific goal for the process area (Fig. 13.7).

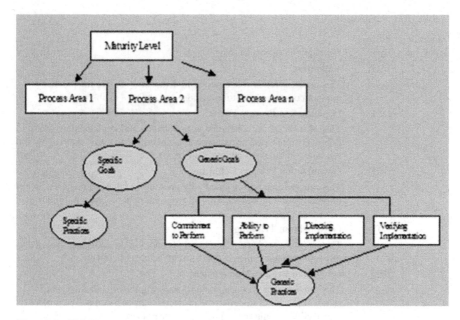

Fig. 13.7 CMMI staged model

The generic goals and practices are common to all process areas for that maturity level, and are concerned with process institutionalization at that level. Four common features organize the generic practices and these are:
- Commitment to perform
- Ability to perform
- Directing implementation
- Verifying implementation

They describe activities that when implemented achieve the associated generic goal(s) for the process area. The commitment to perform practices relate to the creation of policies and sponsorship of process improvement; the ability to perform practices are related to the provision of appropriate resources and training to perform the process; the directing implementation practices relate to activities to control and manage the process; and verifying practices relate to activities to verify adherence to the process.

The implementation of the generic practices institutionalizes the process and makes it ingrained in the way that work is done. Institutionalization means that the process is defined, documented and understood. Process users are appropriately trained and the process is enforced by independent audits. Institutionalization helps to ensure that the process is performed consistently and is more likely to be retained during times of stress. The degree of institutionalization is reflected in the extent to which the generic goals and practices are satisfied. The generic practices ensure the sustainability of the specific practices over time.

There is one specific goal associated with the Requirements Management process area and it has five associated specific practices (Fig. 13.8):

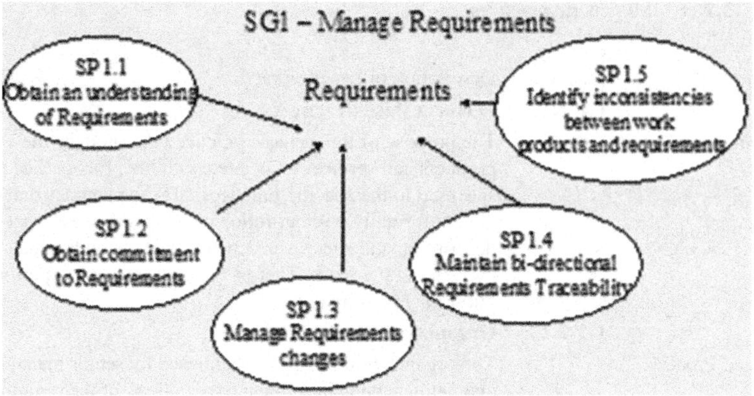

Fig. 13.8 Specific practices for SG1 – manage requirements

13.6.1 SG 1 – Manage Requirements

Requirements are managed and inconsistencies with project plans and work products are identified.

The components of the CMMI model are grouped into three categories: namely, required, expected, and informative components. The *required category* is essential to achieving goals in a particular area and includes the *specific* and *generic goals* that must be implemented and institutionalized for the process area to be satisfied. The *expected category* includes the *specific and generic practices* that an organization will typically implement to perform the process effectively. These are intended to guide individuals or groups who are implementing improvements, or who are performing appraisals to determine the current maturity of the organization. They state what needs to be done rather than how it should be done thereby giving freedom on the most appropriate implementation for the organization.

The informative category includes information to guide the implementer on how best to approach the implementation of the specific and generic goals and practices. These include *sub-practices, typical work products, discipline amplifications,* and so on. This information assists with the implementation of the process area.

The implementation and institutionalization of a process area involves the implementation of the specific and generic practices. The specific practices are concerned with process implementation and are described in detail in [49]. The generic practices are concerned with process institutionalization and are summarized in Table 13.7.

The generic goals support an evolution of process maturity, and the implementation of each generic goal provides a foundation for further process improvements. That is, a process rated at a particular maturity level has all of the maturity of a process at the lower levels and the additional maturity of its rated level. In other words, a defined process is a managed process; a quantitatively managed process is a defined process, and so on.

Table 13.7 CMMI generic practices

Generic goal	Generic practice	Description of generic practice
GG 1 Performed Process	**GP 1.1**	**Perform Base Practices**
		The purpose of this generic practice is to produce the work products and services associated with the process (i.e., as specified in the specific practices). These practices may be done informally without following a documented process description and success is dependent on the individuals performing the work. That is, the basic process is performed but it may be immature.
GG 2 Managed Process	**GP 2.1**	**Organization Policy**
		The organization policy is established by senior management, and defines the management expectations of the organization.
	GP 2.2	**Plan the Process**
		This generic practice is concerned with preparing a plan to perform the process. The plan will assign responsibilities and document the resources needed to perform the process as well as any training requirements. The plan/schedule are revised as appropriate.
	GP 2.3	**Provide Resources**
		The purpose of this generic practice is to ensure that the resources required to perform the process (as specified in the plan) are available when required.
	GP 2.4	**Assign Responsibility**
		The purpose of this generic practice is to assign responsibility for performing the process and developing the work products.
	GP 2.5	**Train People**
		This generic practice is concerned with ensuring that people receive the appropriate training to enable them to perform and support the process.
	GP 2.6	**Manage Configurations**
		This generic practice is concerned with identifying the work products created by the process that will be subject to configuration management control. These are documented in the plan for the process.
	GP 2.7	**Identify and Involve Relevant Stakeholders**
		This is concerned with ensuring that the stakeholders are identified (as described in the plan for the process) and involved appropriately during the execution of the process.
	GP 2.8	**Monitor and Control the Process**
		This generic practice is concerned with monitoring process performance and taking corrective action when necessary.
	GP 2.9	**Objectively Evaluate Adherence**
		This generic practice is concerned with conducting audits to verify that process execution adheres to the process description.
	GP 2.10	**Review Status with Higher Level Management**
		This generic practice is concerned with providing higher level management with appropriate visibility into the process.

(continued)

Table 13.7 (continued)

Generic goal	Generic practice	Description of generic practice
GG 3 Defined Process	**GP 3.1**	**Establish a Defined Process** This generic practice is concerned with tailoring the organization set of standard processes to produce the project's defined process.
	GP 3.2	**Collect Improvement Information** This generic practice is concerned with collecting improvement information and work products to support future improvement of the processes.
GG 4 Quantitatively Managed Process	**GP 4.1**	**Establish Quantitative Objectives** This is concerned with agreeing quantitative objectives (e.g., quality/performance) for the process with the stakeholders.
	GP 4.2	**Stabilize Sub-process Performance** This generic practice is concerned with stabilizing the performance of one or more key sub-processes of the process using statistical techniques. This enables the process to achieve its objectives.
GG 5 Optimizing Process	**GP 5.1**	**Ensure Continuous Process Improvement** This generic practice is concerned with systematically improving selected processes to meet quality and process-performance targets.
	GP 5.2	**Correct Root Cause of Problems** This generic practice is concerned with analyzing defects encountered to correct the root cause of these problems and to prevent re-occurrence.

Several of the CMMI process areas support the implementation of the generic goals and practices. These process areas contain one or more specific practices that when implemented may either fully implement a generic practice, or generate a work product that is used in the implementation of the generic practice. The implementation of the generic practices is supported by the process areas mentioned in Table 13.8.

13.7 SCAMPI Appraisals

An appraisal is conducted to enable an organization to understand its current software process maturity, and to prioritize future improvements. The appraisal is an independent examination of the processes used in the organization against the CMMI standard. Its objective is to identify strengths and weaknesses in the processes, and it is used to prioritize improvements in the next improvement cycle.

The SCAMPI methodology is the appraisal methodology used with the CMMI, and it comes in three distinct flavours (SCAMPI Class A, B, and C). These classes

Table 13.8 Implementation of generic practices

Generic goal	Generic practice	Process area supporting implementation of generic practice
GG 2	**GP 2.2**	Project Planning
Managed Process	Plan the Process	
	GP 2.5	Organization Training
	Train the people	Project Planning
	GP 2.6	Configuration Management
	Manage Configurations	
	GP 2.7	Project Planning
	Identify/involve relevant stakeholders	
	GP 2.8	Project Monitoring and Control
	Monitor and Control the process	
	GP 2.9	Process and Product Quality Assurance
	Objectively evaluate adherence	
GG 3	**GP 3.1**	Integrated Project Management
Defined Process	Establish defined process	Organization Process Definition
	GP 3.2	Integrated Project Management
	Improvement Information	Organization Process Focus
		Organization Process Definition
GG 4	**GP4.1**	Quantitative Project Management
Quantitatively Managed Process	Establish quantitative objectives for process	Organization Process Performance
	GP 4.2	Quantitative Project Management
	Stabilize sub-process performance	Organization Process Performance
GG 5	**GP5.1**	Organization Innovation and Deployment
Optimizing Process	Ensure Continuous Process Improvement	
	GP 5.2	Causal Analysis and Resolution
	Correct root cause of problems	

vary in formality, the cost, effort and timescales involved, the rating of the processes, and the reporting of results.

The scope of the appraisal includes the process areas to be examined, and the projects and organization unit to be examined. It may be limited to the level 2 process areas, or the level 2 and level 3 process areas, and so on. The scope depends on how active the organization has been in process improvement.

The appraisal will identify any gaps that exist with respect to the implementation of the CMMI practices for each process area within the scope of the appraisal. The appraisal team will conduct interviews and review project documentation, and they will examine the extent to which the practices are implemented. The appraisal findings are presented and are used to plan and prioritize the next improvement cycle. Chapter 15 discusses SCAMPI appraisals in more detail.

13.8 Review Questions

1. Describe the CMMI Model.
2. Describe the staged and continuous representations of the CMMI. What are the advantages and disadvantages of each representation?
3. Describe the CMMI maturity levels and the process areas in each level.
4. What is the purpose of the CMMI generic practices? How are they implemented?
5. What is the difference between implementation and institutionalization?
6. What is the purpose of CMMI appraisals and how do they fit into the software process improvement cycle?

13.9 Summary

The Capability Maturity Model Integration is a framework to assist an organization in the implementation of best practice in software and systems engineering. It was developed at the Software Engineering Institute and is used by many organizations around the world.

The SEI and other quality experts believe that there is a close relationship between the quality of the delivered software, and the maturity of the processes used to create the software. Therefore, there needs to be a focus on the process as well as on the product, and the CMMI contains best practice in software and systems engineering to assist in the creation of high-quality processes.

The process is seen as the glue that ties people, technology and procedures coherently together. Processes are activities associated with carrying out certain tasks, and they need to be defined and documented. The users of the process need to receive appropriate training on their use, and process discipline need to be enforced with independent audits. Process performance needs to be monitored and improvements made to ineffective processes.

The CMMI consists of five maturity levels with each maturity level (except level one) consisting of several process areas. Each maturity level acts as a foundation for improvement for the next improvement level, and each increase in maturity level represents more advanced software engineering capability. The higher the maturity level of the organization, the more capable it is, and the more predictable its results. The lowest level of maturity is maturity level 1 and the highest level is maturity level 5.

Each process area consists of a set of specific and generic goals, and these must be implemented by an associated set of specific and generic practices. The practices specify what is to be done rather than how it should be done, and the organization is given freedom in choosing the most appropriate implementation to meet its needs.

The SCAMPI appraisal methodology is used to determine the maturity of software organizations. It is a systematic examination of the processes used in the organization against the CMMI model, and it includes interviews and reviews of documentation. A successful SCAMPI Class A appraisal allows the organization to report its maturity rating to the SEI and to benchmark itself against other companies. Appraisals are a part of the improvement cycle, and improvement plans are prepared after the appraisal to address the findings and to prioritize improvements.

The next chapter is concerned with setting up a CMMI improvement initiative, and it discusses the activities involved, the teams that need to be set up, the roles involved and their responsibilities.

Setting Up a CMMI Initiative

14

Key Topics

Continuous Improvement Cycle
CMMI Improvement Teams
CMMI Project Plan and Schedule
CMMI Kick-off Session
Process Mapping
Piloting a New Process
Deploying a New Process
CMMI Appraisals

14.1 Introduction

The implementation of the CMMI is a project, and as with any project it needs good planning and management to ensure its success. Once an organization makes a decision to embark on a CMMI initiative, a project manager needs to be appointed to manage the project. The CMMI project manager will treat the implementation as a standard project, and plans are made to implement the CMMI within the approved schedule and budget. The improvement initiative will often consist of several improvement cycles, with each improvement cycle implementing one or more process areas. Small improvement cycles may be employed to implement findings from an appraisal or improvement suggestions from staff.

G. O'Regan, *Introduction to Software Quality*, Undergraduate Topics
in Computer Science, DOI 10.1007/978-3-319-06106-1_14,
© Springer International Publishing Switzerland 2014

One of the earliest activities carried out on any improvement initiative is to determine the current maturity of the organization with respect to the CMMI model. This will usually involve a SCAMPI[1] Class B or C appraisal conducted by one or more experienced appraisers. The findings will indicate the current strengths and weaknesses of the processes as well as gaps with respect to the practices in the CMMI. This initial appraisal is important, as it allows management in the organization to understand its current maturity with respect to the model, and to communicate where it wants to be, as well as how it plans to get there. The initial appraisal assists in prioritising improvements for the first improvement cycle, which is usually to implement the CMMI level 2 process areas. These include

- Project Planning and Monitoring and Control
- Requirements Management
- Configuration Management.
- Process and Product Quality Assurance.
- Measurement and Analysis.
- Selection and Management of Suppliers

The project manager will then prepare a project plan and schedule. The plan will detail the scope of the initiative, the budget, the process areas to be implemented, the teams and resources required, the initial risks identified, the key milestones, the quality and communication plan, and so on.

The project schedule will detail the deliverables to be produced, the resources required and the associated timeline for delivery.

14.2   Approach to Continuous Improvement

The need for a process improvement initiative often arises due to the realization that the organization is weak in some areas in software engineering, and that it needs to improve to achieve its business goals more effectively. The starting point of any improvement initiative is an examination of the business needs of the organization, and these may include goals such as delivering high-quality products on time or delivering products faster to the market.

The software process improvement initiative is designed to support the organization in achieving its business goals more effectively. The steps include examining organization needs; conducting an appraisal to determine the current strengths and weaknesses; and analysing the results to formulate an improvement plan. The improvement plan is then implemented; the improvements monitored and confirmed as being effective; and the improvement cycle repeats. These steps are described in Fig. 14.1.

---

[1] There are three types of SCAMPI Appraisals (Class A, B, and C) which may be carried out in an organization, and they vary in formality and expense. A SCAMPI Class A appraisal has strict requirements and the appraisal team consists of 4–9 members. It is conducted when an organization wants its processes rated against the CMMI standard to benchmark itself against other organizations. The appraisal results including the maturity rating are reported back to the SEI. A SCAMPI Class C appraisal is the least formal and costly appraisal type and is often sufficient at the start of an improvement initiative.

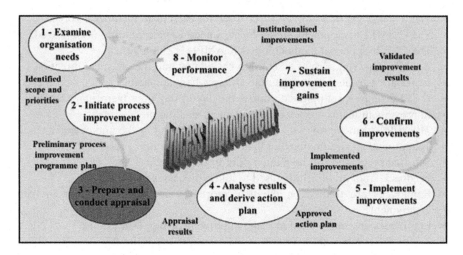

Fig. 14.1 Steps in process improvement

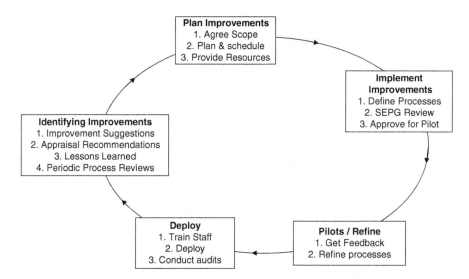

Fig. 14.2 Continuous improvement cycle

There is more than one approach to implement the CMMI. A small organization has fewer resources available, and team members will typically be working part time. Larger organizations may be able to assign people full time to the improvement project. The improvement cycle suggested here is influenced by the IDEAL model and is described in Fig. 14.2. The following is a suggested approach to implementing the CMMI:

- The CMMI initiative is run as a project with a CMMI project manager.
- There is a project plan and schedule for the initiative.

- There is a target of 3–4 h work per week for each team member involved.
- The CMMI Development Model V1.3 (Staged Representation) is employed.
- The CMMI appraisal methodology (SCAMPI) is employed
- A CMMI Steering Group is set up to provide overall management direction.
- Issues are escalated to the Steering Group where applicable
- A SEPG team is set up to coordinate the day-to-day improvement activities
- Improvement teams are setup to implement specific process areas
- The SEPG team approves the new processes produced by the improvement teams
- Team members are involved in the definition of the new processes.
- Selected processes will be piloted prior to deployment
- Feedback from pilots will be used to refine processes and standards
- Employees are trained on the new processes and standards prior to their deployment.
- Employees are encouraged to make improvement suggestions.
- Audits are conducted to verify that the processes are followed.
- Lessons learned will feed into improvement cycles.
- Periodic process reviews are conducted to determine which processes are working well and which need to be adjusted.
- Independent appraisals are carried out at the end of an improvement cycle.
- Feedback from appraisals will be acted upon in next improvement cycle.
- Appropriate training and consultancy are provided during the initiative.
  The continuous improvement cycle is described in Table 14.1.

14.3 CMMI Improvement Structure and Teams

The implementation of the CMMI requires several teams with specific responsibilities to be formed. These teams will oversee the initiative and actively participate in its implementation. The CMMI project manager is responsible for setting up the various teams, defining a charter to explain the purpose of each team, providing orientation to the team members, and actively working with each team.

The project manager needs to be active in monitoring progress, identifying potential roadblocks and resolving them, and escalating issues to the SPEG or Steering Group where appropriate. Table 14.2 suggests an improvement structure and teams for a CMMI implementation.

The CMMI project manager is responsible for running the CMMI initiative as a project. This involves tracking and managing the schedule, budget, effort, risks and issues during the project, and reporting progress to the SEPG team who will coordinate the day-to-day implementation of the CMMI. The project manager will report progress to the Steering Group who provide management sponsorship of the initiative, and who have the management influence to remove any roadblocks that may arise.

The project manager will work closely with the specific improvement teams that are set up and resourced by the SEPG. These teams are responsible for implementing one or more CMMI process areas such as project planning and project monitoring and

Table 14.1 Continuous improvement cycle

Activity	Description
Identify improvements to be made	The improvements to be made during an improvement cycle come from several sources:
	Improvement Suggestions from Staff
	Lessons Learned by Projects
	Periodic process reviews
	Recommendations from CMMI appraisals
	CMMI Implementation Strategy
Plan improvements	A project plan and schedule is prepared for a large improvement cycle (involving the implementation of several process areas).
	For a shorter improvement cycle an action plan (with owners and target completion dates) will often be sufficient.
Implement improvements	The plan will detail the resources required for to carry out the improvements.
	The improvements will generally be conducted by a dedicated improvement team and approved by the SEPG.
	The improvements will consist of new processes, standards, templates, procedures, guidelines checklists, and tools (where appropriate) to support the process.
Pilots/refine	Selected new processes and standards will often be piloted prior to their deployment to ensure that they are fit for purpose.
	The feedback from the pilot is used to refine the process prior to its general deployment.
Deploy	The processes and standards are deployed using a structured approach:
	Staff are trained on the new processes and standards
	Staff receive support during the deployment
	Audits are conducted to ensure that the new processes are followed.
Do it all again	Improvement is continuous and as soon as an improvement cycle is complete its effectiveness is considered, and a new improvement cycle is ready to commence.

The result from the pilot may be that the new process is not suitable to be deployed in the organization or that it needs to be significantly revised prior to deployment

control; requirements management; configuration management; and so on. The teams involved in a typical implementation of CMMI level 2 are described in Fig. 14.3.

14.3.1 Setting Up the SEPG Team

The SEPG team is one of the first teams to be set up in the initiative. It is responsible for day-to-day coordination of the improvement initiative, and it provides direction and support to the improvement teams working on the implementation of specific process areas.

Table 14.2 CMMI improvement structure and teams

Role/team	Members	Responsibility
CMMI Project Manager	CMMI Project Manager	Project Manage the CMMI improvement project.
		Provide leadership on process improvement
		Plan & coordinate CMMI improvements
		Ensure Steering Group, SEPG and Improvement Teams receive appropriate training on the CMMI.
		Chair the SEPG Team and report progress of improvement teams to SEPG
		Report progress to the Steering Group
		Facilitate review of improvement suggestions at SEPG
		Facilitate the review of Lessons Learned at the SEPG
		Facilitate periodic process reviews
		Facilitate independent appraisals
		Maintain continuous improvement cycle.
Steering Group (Project Board)	Senior Manager(s) and CMMI Project Manager	Provides management sponsorship of initiative
		Provides resources and funding for the initiative
		Meets monthly, bi-monthly or quarterly
		Reviews progress with initiative
		Uses influence to remove any roadblocks that arise with the improvement activities.
SEPG Team	Managers, Technical, and CMMI Project Manager	Coordinate day-to-day improvement activities.
		Generally meets every 2 weeks
		Provides direction and support to improvement teams
		Provides sufficient staff/resources to teams
		Review and approve new processes
		Coordinate pilots of new processes
		Coordinate training on new processes and standards.
		Coordinate rollout of new processes and standards.
Improvement Teams	Process users and CMMI Project Manager	Focus on specific process area(s)
		Teams will usually meet weekly (or bi-weekly)
		Review the current process "as is" and define the new process "to be" (Brainstorming/CMMI).
		Identify & create standards, templates, procedures and guidelines and tools needed to support the new process
		Get feedback from the SEPG on the new process
		Conduct pilots to ensure the new process is effective.
		Refine process as appropriate to address the feedback.
		Obtain approval from the SEPG on the new process
		Provide any required training on the new process
		Conduct rollout of new process

(continued)

Table 14.2 (continued)

Role/team	Members	Responsibility
Staff	All affected staff	Participate in improvement teams as directed by CMMI Project Manager and SEPG.
		Participate in pilots (as directed by CMMI project manager)
		Participate in training on new processes
		Adhere to new processes
External Consultancy	External Consultant	Conduct appraisal to determine initial maturity and assist in planning of first improvement cycle.
		Provide expertise on the CMMI and software engineering.
		Review progress made during the initiative and conduct periodic process reviews
		Provide training on the CMMI and software engineering disciplines.
		Conduct appraisal at end of each improvement cycle and identify strengths and weaknesses in the organization processes.

Improvement Structures / Teams

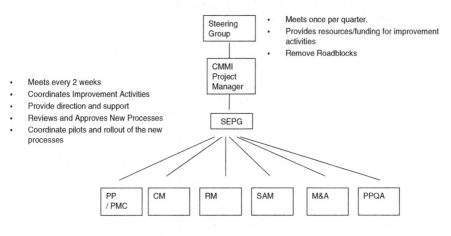

Fig. 14.3 CMMI Level 2 improvement structure and teams

The members of the SEPG will include management and technical representatives, and the team members will receive appropriate training on the CMMI. The CMMI training will typically include:

- Overview of Software Process Improvement
- Overview of the CMMI and Maturity Levels
- Overview of CMMI process areas.

The SEPG team will decide on the number of improvement teams to be initially set up as well as the members of each team. Typically, team members will need to spend a minimum of 3–4 h per week working on improvement activities as otherwise limited progress will be made. This requires that an appropriate balance is kept between the normal day-to-day project and support work that team members are involved in, and the software process improvement activities.

The SEPG team will review and approve the new processes and standards that are developed by the improvement sub-teams, and it will also coordinate pilots, rollout and training on the new processes and standards. The SEPG may decide to place processes and standards on an Intranet site in the company, and if so, the SEPG will review and approve the Intranet site prior to its deployment.

The CMMI project manager will chair the SEPG team and will report progress, risks and issues regularly during the initiative. The project manager will report any roadblocks to the Steering Group for resolution.

The SEPG team will generally meet to review progress every 2 weeks. The project manager will provide a regular status report to summarize the activities taking place, as well as listing the key risks and issues, and status with respect to the schedule and budget.

14.3.2 Setting Up the Steering Group

The Steering Group provides management sponsorship of the improvement initiative, and it authorises the funding and resources required to enable the improvement teams to implement their assigned process areas.

The steering group is typically composed of senior and middle managers, and it has sufficient influence to remove any roadblocks that may arise during the initiative. The team will resolve any issues that have been escalated by the SEPG team.

The steering group will not be involved in the day-to-day implementation of the CMMI, and so the team members do not require detailed training on the CMMI model. They will receive high-level training on the CMMI and process improvement, and the benefits that are gained from implementing the CMMI.

The team will ensure that a balance is kept between project work and process improvement activities. It approves the organization policy for software development, which states management expectations of the way that work will be done in the organization. All projects need to be carried out consistently with this policy.

The steering group is also responsible for reviewing and approving the project plan for the improvement initiative, as well as the schedule and budget. The CMMI project manager is a member of the Steering Group and will prepare regular status reports to provide visibility into progress with the improvement initiative, and also the status with respect to the allocated budget, schedule and effort, as well as documenting the key risks and issues.

The Steering Group typically meets less frequently than the SEPG and a frequency of bi-monthly or once per quarter is often sufficient. Extra meetings (in response to serious issues) may be scheduled where appropriate.

14.3.3 Setting Up Dedicated Improvement Sub-teams

The dedicated improvement teams are responsible for the implementation of one or more CMMI process areas. For example, the project management improvement team will usually implement the project planning and project monitoring and control process areas. The SEPG is responsible for setting up the improvement team; selecting team members; and providing orientation and training to the team members.

The team members will receive appropriate orientation on the CMMI model to enable them to implement their assigned process areas effectively. The CMMI project manager will conduct a kick-off session to commence work on the improvements and this includes introducing team members, communicating the objectives of the team and the planned deliverables, and the roles of the team members. The team will usually commence its work with process mapping and this involves defining and understanding the process as currently performed: i.e., the process "*as is*".

The team then critically examines the current process and brainstorms ways to improve it. Strengths and weaknesses in the current process are considered as well as best practice in the CMMI for the process area. The specific and generic practices in the CMMI for the process area will be considered, and used to guide the definition of the new process: i.e., the process "*to be*". Once the new process is agreed there will be a need to identify the standards, procedures, guidelines, checklists and templates required to support the new process.

The CMMI project manager may be a member of or may chair the specific improvement team. The project manager will facilitate the process mapping session, and will apply the CMMI specific and generic practices to the process area and verify that the specific and generic goals are satisfied.

The number of improvement teams set up at any period of time will depend on the size of the organization, and the amount of time that the organization can devote to software process improvement. Larger organizations have more resources available and are in a position to set up several improvement teams at the start of the initiative. Small organizations have fewer resources available and it may only be practical to set up only one or two improvement teams at any one time.

It is essential that sufficient time is available to team members to work on improvement activities, as otherwise little progress will be made in the initiative. The steering group is responsible for ensuring that the team members have 3–4 h of time available to them to work on their improvement activities.

The SEPG is responsible for reviewing and approving the new processes and standards, and it will coordinate the pilots, rollout and training on the new processes and standards.

The improvement team will act upon any feedback that the SEPG provides, and it will participate in pilots, training and rollout as directed by the SEPG team. The CMMI project manager will report progress and issues for all active improvement teams to the SEPG and the Steering Group.

14.3.4 Role of the CMMI Project Manager

The CMMI project manager plays a key role in managing the improvement initiative. This includes:
- Setting up the various teams (SEPG, Steering Group, and improvement teams)
- Providing training and orientation to the various teams.
- Managing the improvement initiative as a project
- Preparing the project plan and schedule.
- Tracking schedule, effort and budget
- Managing project risks and issues
- Reporting progress regularly to the steering group
- Chairing the SEPG team and discussing progress, risks and issues
- Recording minutes and actions from SEPG meetings.
- Providing guidance and direction to specific improvement teams
- Ensuring roadblocks are identified and resolved appropriately.

The CMMI project manager is required to have a strong background in the CMMI and software process improvement. The role requires a good understanding of SCAMPI appraisals as well as good verbal and written communication. The role requires skill in influencing people to change behaviour, as a software process improvement initiative involves changing the way that work is done in the organization. The project manager will need to be highly motivated to drive the improvement project to a successful conclusion.

14.3.5 Risks to Success

Software process improvement initiatives do not always succeed, and it is important to understand some of the reasons why, and to identify and manage risks. Senior management need to be fully behind the initiative, as this will ensure that middle managers and staff on the ground remain fully committed. Some common causes of failure include:
- Lack of senior management commitment to the initiative.
- Lack of buy-in from staff
- Insufficient time to perform the improvement activities
- Poor project management of the initiative
- Lack of participation from staff in defining the new processes.
- New processes may not meet the needs of the process users

- Lack of pilots on the new processes and standards.
- Inadequate training on new processes and standards.
- Lack of enforcement of new processes and standards.
- Lack of sense of ownership of processes and standards.
- Insufficient communication of issues to senior management.

It is essential that staff participate in the definition of the new processes and standards as this will help to promote ownership and buy-in of the processes. It also helps to ensure that the new processes and standards meet the needs of the process users.

14.4 Planning the Improvement Cycle

A major improvement cycle such as the implementation of a CMMI maturity level requires detailed planning and scheduling. However, the planning required for a small improvement cycle such as the implementation of a small number of process improvements may be as simple as an action plan. Large improvement cycles will require dedicated improvement teams to be set up to implement specific process areas, whereas improvement actions may be assigned to individuals for smaller cycles.

The roll of the project manager was discussed in Sect. 14.3.4, and the project manager is assigned to manage a major improvement cycle. The project plan records the key project planning information such as the business case, the key project goals and objectives for the initiative, the scope of the initiative as well as the process areas to be implemented. The roles and responsibilities of the various teams and individuals involved are recorded in the project plan. The project plan also documents the approved budget as well as the key project milestones and the high-level estimates for the work to be done.

The project manager will set up the risk and issue logs and will be proactive in identifying risks early in the project, and managing risks throughout the project. The project manager will work with the improvement teams to ensure successful delivery of the desired improvements, and will inform the SEPG of progress and any roadblocks that may impede progress.

For a shorter improvement cycle (e.g., such as the implementation of recommendations from an appraisal or the implementation of improvement suggestions from staff) it will usually be sufficient to employ an improvement action plan. Such an action plan will include target dates and owners for the various improvement actions, and the project manager and SEPG will track these to completion.

14.4.1 Appraisals

SCAMPI Appraisals were discussed in Sect. 13.7 and they play an important role in software process improvement. They allow an organization to understand its current software process maturity, as well as strengths and weaknesses in its processes.

The initial appraisal is conducted early in the initiative, and the improvements planned and implemented. An appraisal is conducted at the end of the improvement cycle to determine the progress made, and to identify strengths and opportunities for further improvement to the processes.

The SCAMPI appraisal is an independent evaluation of the practices in an organization against the CMMI model, and it is conducted by one or more experienced appraisers. The scope of the appraisal will often be the level 2 or level 3 process areas, and the appraisal will identify strengths and weaknesses and gaps with respect to the implementation of the CMMI.

The appraisal will typically consists of interviews and reviews of documentation, and the appraisal team[2] will determine the extent to which the CMMI goals and practices for each process area within the scope of the appraisal are satisfied.

The appraisal output will often be presented in a power-point presentation and documented in the appraisal report. The appraisal findings may include ratings of the process areas, as well as the overall CMMI rating for the organization and any gaps that exist with respect to the targeted CMMI maturity level.

The appraisal findings are valuable and will allow the CMMI project manager to plan and schedule the next improvement cycle. Appraisals are discussed in detail in the next chapter.

14.4.2 CMMI Project Plan

The CMMI project manager will prepare the project plan for the CMMI initiative. It will include the business case for the initiative, the approved budget and the key project milestones. It will document the approach taken, as well as the goals and objectives of the improvement initiative. The scope of the initiative including the process areas to be implemented will be defined in the plan. The stakeholders and teams involved will be documented as well as the key success factors, and any assumptions, risks and dependencies.

The project plan will include a section on estimation, and the estimation may be based on a work-breakdown structure where the estimates for the various phases of the project (and deliverables within the phase) are recorded. The knowledge, skills and tools required to carry out the improvement project are also recorded. The initial risks to the success of the initiative are documented, and the project manager will need to be proactive in identifying and managing risks during the project.

---

[2] The appraisal team could be the CMMI project manager only (if the project manager is a SCAMPI trained appraiser); alternatively, it could be an external appraiser and the project manager. For very large organizations interested in a very formal appraisal it could be a large team of 4–9 appraisers including a SCAMPI lead appraiser. There is a strict qualification process for a SCAMPI lead appraiser and it requires attending the official SEI CMMI and SCAMPI training as well as conducting two appraisals under the direction of a qualified SCAMPI lead appraiser.

The project plan will include sections on quality and communication planning. The quality planning covers how quality will be built into the deliverables, and communication planning covers how communication will take place during the project. The communication to the stakeholders will include project status reports and project meetings with the various stakeholders.

The plan will include a section on configuration management, and this will detail how changes will be controlled during the project. It will detail where the project deliverables will be placed, as well as defining how releases will be done. It will define how the deployment of the new processes and standards is done.

Once the project plan has been approved by the stakeholders, the project manager is in a position to prepare the project schedule. This will detail the various phases of the project lifecycle and the tasks and activities to be conducted.

14.4.3 CMMI Project Schedule

The project schedule details the tasks and activities to be carried out during the improvement project; the effort and duration of each task and activity; and the resources required. The schedule shows how the project will be delivered within the key project parameters such as time and cost without compromising quality in any way. A sample schedule was presented in Chap. 3 (Fig. 3.2).

The project manager will manage the schedule and will take corrective action when project performance deviates from expectations. The project schedule will be updated regularly during the improvement project (usually weekly or bi-weekly).

14.4.4 CMMI Kick-off Session

The implementation of the CMMI is a major initiative for an organization, and it is essential to raise its profile early in the initiative. This will allow senior management to state its importance, and to motivate the staff involved in its implementation. A CMMI kick-off meeting is important as it sets the scene for the activities in the CMMI implementation.

The meeting allows the CMMI project manager to give an introduction to the CMMI, its benefits, the improvement initiative planned for the organization, and the teams and people involved. A senior manager will typically open the kick off meeting and will introduce the CMMI project manager as well as stating the importance of the initiative to the organization, their commitment to it, and the expectation that all staff in the organization will give it full support. The project manager will give a presentation on the CMMI including:

- Introduction to the CMMI and Software Process Improvement
- Benefits of Software Process Improvement
- Goals and objectives of the initiative
- Teams involved in the improvement initiative
- Approach to CMMI implementation

- People involved and team composition.
- The timelines
- Next steps

Senior management will commit to making resources available to support the initiative, and senior management support is essential in ensuring that middle management and employees make the initiative a priority.

14.5 Implementation of Improvements

Once the specific improvement teams have been set up and the team members appropriately trained, the teams are ready to commence work on their assigned process areas. The improvement teams will generally meet weekly, and the first task is to prepare a plan for the implementation of its assigned process areas. The CMMI project manager will work closely[3] with the team to ensure that the plan is realistic and will address the CMMI requirements. The plan will detail the activities to be carried out and the deliverables to be produced. These include:

- Policy for the performance of the process
    (There will usually be one policy that covers all of the relevant process areas)
- Process Map to show the flow of activities for the process area.
- Procedure or Guidelines that describes the process in more detail
- Templates and Standards to assist in the performance of the process
- Checklists to assist in the performance of the process
- Evaluation and Selection of Tools to support the performance of the process
- Metrics to measure the effectiveness of performance of the process
- Training materials to assist in piloting and rollout of the process

The CMMI Project Manager may be a member of each improvement team, or may work closely with the teams to drive improvements and to determine progress on a regular basis. Any roadblocks that arise are first communicated to the SEPG, and if the SEPG is unable to resolve the issue is escalated to the Steering Group.

The project manager will report progress regularly to the SEPG and at appropriate intervals to the CMMI Steering Group.

14.5.1 Process Mapping

The starting point for each improvement team is to understand the process as it is currently performed and to determine the extent to which it is effective. The stakeholders of the process participate in the discussion of how it is currently performed, and the process is then sketched pictorially with activities and their

---

[3] The CMMI project manager may be a member or may chair the improvement team. It will depend on the experience of the team.

Fig. 14.4 Sample
process map

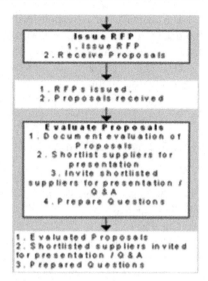

inputs and outputs recorded graphically. This graphical map is a representation of the process "as is".

We use the approach of representing activities in the process by rectangles (with tasks within an activity being numbered). Each activity has an input and an output and these are recorded in the process map. There may be standards to support the process (e.g., procedures and templates), and the tasks and activities are conducted by various roles. The process maps presented here are kept as simple and abstract as possible and focus on inputs, tasks and activities and outputs.

For example, Fig. 14.4 shows a simple process map that is part of supplier selection.

There are two activities listed in this process map. These are the "*Issue RFP*" activity that has two tasks, and the "*Evaluate Proposals*" activity that has four tasks associated with it. A more detailed process would specify standards to support the process and the roles involved in carrying out the tasks and activities. Entry and exit criteria could be specified as well as any verification steps and measures (Fig. 14.4).

Process mapping was discussed in an earlier chapter, and the process map is an abstraction of the way that work is done. The team critically examines the process map to determine how effective the process is, and weaknesses are identified. The CMMI specific and generic practices for the process area are considered, as they contain best practice for process performance.

This leads to modifications to the definition of the current process to yield the process "to be". Once the team has agreed the new process the templates required to support the process become clear from an examination of the input and output to the various activities. Templates will be prepared to standardize input and output from the process. Procedures or guidelines will be required to provide detailed information on how the process is to be carried out.

The SEPG team is responsible for approving the processes and deliverables produced by the improvement team. The SEPG may approve without comments, or it may require changes to the process and deliverables prior to approval.

Once the deliverables for a process area have been approved by the SEPG they are ready for piloting (where required) or deployment. The SEPG will decide whether a pilot is required prior to deployment.

14.5.2 Layout of Templates

Templates are employed to support the process and it is desirable that they have a common look and feel. The first 3–4 pages for each template should have identical headings such as:

- Title Page
  - This includes a unique document number, the date the current version was prepared, and the release status of the document.
  - It may include an abstract and an approval section.
- Version History
  - This includes the history of who modified the document, the reason for modification, and the date of modification.
- Table of Contents
- Introduction
  - This includes the purpose of the document, the definition of any acronyms, and references to other documents.
- Template Version No.
  - Each template has an associated version number

There are standard templates available (e.g., the IEEE standards) for various activities in software engineering. The organization may decide to use or tailor the IEEE standards to meet its needs, or it may decide to devise its own Templates.

14.5.3 Layout of Procedures and Guidelines

Processes are an abstraction of the way in which work is done. They need associated procedures or guidelines to describe in detail how the process is performed. It is desirable that these have a common look and feel with common sections such as:

- Title Page
- Version History
- Table of Contents
- Introduction
- Overview of Process
- Process Map
- Details
- Training and Metrics
- Roles and Responsibilities

14.6 Piloting the Process

The SEPG team will decide if the new processes and standards need to be piloted prior to their deployment. This involves:
- New process is approved for pilot by the SEPG.
- Project(s) and staff are selected for the pilot.
- Training is provided to all staff that will participate on the pilot.
- The CMMI project manager will communicate the objectives of the pilot to all participants.

The pilot then commences and the CMMI project manager will work closely with the participants to determine the effectiveness of the new process and standards.
- The participants will present feedback as to what went well and what went poorly during the pilot.
- The project manager and SEPG will consider the feedback and decide whether the process and standards are ready to be rolled out.
- The processes and standards are refined accordingly.
- If the pilot is unsuccessful the improvement team and the CMMI project manager will analyse the reasons why and develop an appropriate strategy for the process area.

14.7 Rolling Out Process

The SEPG team is responsible for approving the new process for rollout and for coordinating the activities for rollout. These include:
- New process is approved for rollout by the SEPG.
- Training Material on the process is prepared by the improvement team and approved by SEPG.
- Training is provided on the new process to all affected staff.
- The intranet site with the processes and standards will be updated to include the new process and standards.
- The induction checklist will be updated to include induction on the new process and standards.
- The audit checklist will be updated to audit the new process and standards.

The new process and standards will be deployed on all new projects (and possibly on projects that have recently commenced). The post-rollout activities may include:
- Induction to new staff on the new process
- Audits to verify that the new process is followed and effective.
- Metrics on the performance of the process are periodically reviewed to ensure that its performance is effective.

14.8   Review Questions

1. Discuss the approach suggested for software process improvement in this chapter.
2. Discuss the continuous software process improvement cycle.
3. Describe the teams involved in a typical software process improvement initiative.
4. Discuss the planning and scheduling required in a software process improvement initiative.
5. Describe the activities that take place during the kick-off session of a software process improvement initiative.
6. Describe the activities involved in process mapping.
7. Describe the purpose of pilots of new processes.
8. Describe how a new process may be rolled out to the staff in the organization.
9. Describe how appraisals fit into the software process improvement cycle.

14.9   Summary

This chapter discussed the activities and teams required to set up a CMMI improvement initiative, and an improvement programme involves identifying the improvements to be made; planning the improvements; implementing the improvements; pilots; deployment of the new processes; and doing it all again.

A CMMI project manager is assigned to run the initiative, and the project manager is responsible for defining the approach to implementation and setting up the teams involved. These include the Steering Group, the SEPG, and dedicated improvement teams. The CMMI project manager will ensure that all team members receive appropriate training.

The implementation consists of one or more improvement cycles. A major improvement cycle will implement several process areas, whereas minor improvement cycles may be concerned with implementing actions from an appraisal or improvement suggestions from staff.

One of the earliest activities in an appraisal is to determine the current maturity of the organization with respect to the CMMI model, as well as strengths and weaknesses in its processes. The first improvement cycle will often be concerned with the implementation of level 2 of the CMMI.

The PM will prepare the project plan and schedule, monitor and report progress, and will manage project risks and issues. The PM works closely with the improvement teams, and will participate in process mapping and in defining improved processes.

The SEPG will approve the new processes and templates and coordinate any pilots, as well as coordinating the rollout of the new processes and standards. A formal SCAMPI appraisal is conducted to confirm that the organization is performing at a higher level of maturity and that the improvements are successful.

SCAMPI Appraisals

15

Key Topics

Appraisal Plan
Conducting an Appraisal
Objective Evidence
SCAMPI (Class A, B, C) Appraisals
Reporting the results

15.1 Introduction

Appraisals (Fig. 15.1) play an essential role in the software process improvement programme. They allow an organization to understand its current software process maturity, including the strengths and weaknesses in its processes. An initial appraisal is conducted at the start of the initiative to allow the organization understand its current process maturity, and to plan and prioritize improvements for the first improvement cycle. Improvements are then implemented, and an appraisal is typically conducted at the end of the cycle to confirm progress.

An appraisal is an independent examination of the software engineering and management practices in the organization, and is conducted using the SCAMPI[1] appraisal methodology [63]. The appraisal will identify strengths and weaknesses in the processes and any gaps that exist with respect to the CMMI practices.

---

[1] There are three classes of SCAMPI appraisals and these are termed Class A, B, C. They differ in the level of formality, the cost and duration, and the reporting of the appraisal results.

G. O'Regan, *Introduction to Software Quality*, Undergraduate Topics
in Computer Science, DOI 10.1007/978-3-319-06106-1_15,
© Springer International Publishing Switzerland 2014

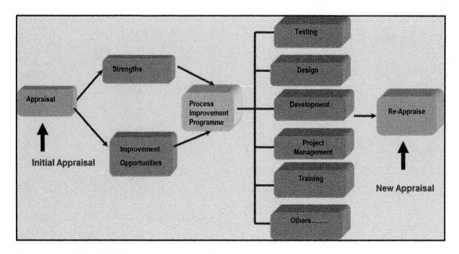

Fig. 15.1 Appraisals

The appraisal leader kicks off the appraisal with the opening presentation, and the leader introduces the appraisal team,[2] and presents the activities that will be carried out in the days ahead. These will include presentations, interviews, reviews of project documentation, and detailed analysis to determine the extent to which the specific and generic practices have been implemented, and whether the specific and generic goals for each process area within the scope of the appraisal are satisfied.

Sample output[3] from a SCAMPI Class A CMMI level 3 appraisal is presented in Fig. 15.2. Each column represents a CMMI process area and each row represents a specific or generic practice. Colour coding is employed to indicate the extent to which the specific or generic practices have been implemented. The extent of implementation may be:

- Fully satisfied
- Largely satisfied.
- Partially satisfied
- Not satisfied
- Not rated

The appraisal leader will present the appraisal findings, and the appraisal output may include a presentation and an appraisal report. The appraisal output summarises

---

[2] The appraisal team could be the CMMI project manager only (if the project manager is a SCAMPI trained appraiser); alternatively, it could be an external appraiser and the CMMI project manager. A SCAMPI Class A appraisal it could involve a large team of 4–9-appraisers (including a SCAMPI lead appraiser) for a large organization. There is a strict qualification process to become a SCAMPI lead appraiser, and it requires attending the official SEI CMMI and SCAMPI training and conducting two appraisals under the direction of a qualified SCAMPI lead appraiser.

[3] The type of output to be provided is agreed in discussions between the appraisal sponsor and the appraisal leader. The output may just be the strengths and improvement opportunities identified. In other cases, the ratings may just be of the specific and generic goals rather than of he practices.

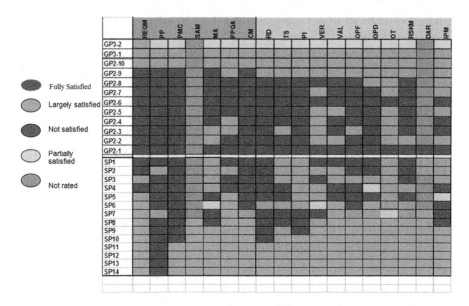

Fig. 15.2 SCAMPI CMMI L3 rating of practices

Table 15.1 Phases in a SCAMPI appraisal

Phase	Description
Planning and preparation	This involves identifying the sponsor's objectives and the requirements for the appraisal. A good appraisal plan is fundamental to the success of the appraisal.
Conducting the appraisal	The appraisal team interviews the participants and examines data to judge the extent to which the CMMI is implemented in the organization.
Reporting the results	The results of the appraisal are reported back to the sponsor. This will usually include a presentation of the findings and an appraisal report.

the strengths and opportunities for improvement identified, and ratings of the process areas will be provided (where ratings are a part of the appraisal). The ratings will indicate the current maturity of the organization's processes, and any gaps that exist with respect to the targeted CMMI maturity level.

The appraisal findings allow the CMMI project manager to plan and schedule the next improvement cycle, and to continue with the CMMI improvement programme. Appraisals allow an organization to

- Understand its current maturity (including strengths and weaknesses of its processes)
- Relate its strengths and weaknesses to the CMMI specific and generic practices
- Prioritize its improvements for the next improvement cycle
- Benchmark itself against other organizations (SCAMPI Class A)

There are three phases in an appraisal (Table 15.1).

15.2 Planning and Requirements for the Appraisal

Good planning is essential to the success of the appraisal. The appraisal leader[4] will determine the appraisal objectives in discussions with the sponsor. The type of appraisal to be conducted is determined, and an appraisal plan is developed to meet the sponsor's requirements. The appraisal leader then forms a team to conduct the appraisal.

There are three classes of SCAMPI appraisals [1] that may be conducted, and they vary in formality, the appraisal findings to be generated, and the output, duration and cost. The three classes of SCAMPI appraisals (Class A, B, and C) are defined in Fig. 15.3.

The initial evidence provided by the organization will often consist of questionnaires and Practice Implementation Indicator Descriptions (PIIDs[5]). The appraisal leader will analyse the initial evidence to get a preliminary understanding of the organization's processes and maturity.

15.2.1 Analyze Requirements

The appraisal leader will determine the goals and objectives of the appraisal in discussions with the sponsor. The appraisal leader may give an overview of the CMMI and appraisals to the sponsor and relevant members of the organization. This is to ensure that the purpose of appraisals, the various types of appraisals that

Requirements	Class A	Class B	Class C
Type of Objective Evidence	Documents and interviews	Documents and interviews	Documents or interviews
Ratings Generated	Goal ratings required	Not allowed	Not allowed
Organizational Unit Coverage	Required	Not required	Not required
Minimum Team Size	4	2	1
Appraisal Team Leader Requirements	Lead appraiser	Person trained and experienced	Person trained and experienced

Fig. 15.3 SCAMPI (classes of appraisals)

---

[4] For a formal SCAMPI Class A appraisals the appraisal team leader will need to be a qualified SEI- SCAMPI lead appraiser.

[5] The PIID is a mapping between the specific and generic practices in the CMMI model and the processes employed in the organization. It shows how the organization has implemented the CMMI. It is produced prior to the appraisal.

may be conducted and the output that may be produced are understood. This is essential when the organization is relatively new to software process improvement.

It will be explained where appraisals fit into software process improvement, and how the output from the appraisal is used in the next improvement cycle. The objectives of the appraisal should be realistic, and constraints such as cost, schedule and effort determined.

The business goals of the software process improvement initiative may influence the scope and type of appraisal to be conducted. The business goals may include:

- Reducing costs of software development
- Delivery software consistently on time
- Delivering high-quality software
- Delivering software fast to market ahead of competitors
- Marketing benefit of CMMI maturity level as a differentiator to its competitors

A software process improvement initiative will generally focus on improvements to those processes in the organization that will lead to the greatest business benefit. The appraisal is an objective way to determine if these processes have actually improved, as well as determining their actual maturity. Some companies may be interested in the marketing benefit of a CMMI maturity level rating, and may wish to benchmark themselves against other companies. They will generally be interested in a formal SCAMPI Class A appraisal.

The scope of the appraisal determines the CMMI process areas that will be appraised; the parts of the organization to be examined; the participants; and the projects and support functions involved.

The sponsor will decide on the appraisal outputs to be produced, and this may include strengths and weaknesses in the processes; ratings of the process areas appraised; a final findings presentation with recommendations; and an appraisal report. The appraisal input gathered from the discussions will include:

- Identity of appraisal sponsor
- Appraisal leader and team
- Participants in appraisal
- Objectives of appraisal
- Scope of appraisal
- Selected projects
- Constraints
- Confidentiality requirements
- Appraisal outputs

The sponsor and appraisal leader verbally agree the appraisal input which is then documented in the appraisal plan.

15.2.2 Develop Appraisal Plan

The appraisal plan is prepared by the appraisal leader, and it describes the scope of the appraisal and how it will be conducted. It includes the input gathered in discussions with the appraisal sponsor such as:

Time	Day 1	Day 2	Day 3
9:00	Kick Off	Planning/Consolidation	Gather Feedback
10:00	Interview (PM 1)	Interview (PM 3)	and
11:00	Notes	Notes	Prepare Feedback
11:30	Interview (Team 1)	Interview (Team 3)	Presentation
12:30	Notes & Lunch	Notes & Lunch	Lunch
13:30	Interview (PM 2)	Interview (Support)	Present Feedback
14:30	Notes	Notes	Close
15:00	Interview (Team 2)	Interview (QA/SEPG)	
16:00	Notes	Notes	
16:30	Demo Intranet	Interview (HR/Training)	
17:00	Notes & Close	Notes & Close	

Fig. 15.4 Sample schedule for SCAMPI Class C appraisal

- Identity of appraisal sponsor
- Appraisal leader and team
- Scope of the Appraisal
- Objectives and Constraints
- Projects to be examined
- Participants
- Appraisal Schedule
- Risks to success
- Appraisal outputs

The plan will detail the effort required, cost involved and the schedule for the appraisal. It will also document how the appraisal will be conducted as well as the resources required. The key personnel involved will include the appraisal leader, the appraisal team, the on-site coordinator and the participants.

The logistics requirements for the appraisal need to be determined and documented in the appraisal plan. These may include accommodation and meals, transportation, and access to rooms and equipment. The appraisal plan will describe how data is collected and validated. A sample appraisal schedule for a SCAMPI Class C appraisal is in Fig. 15.4.

The risks to the success of the appraisal need to be identified and managed. Finally, once the appraisal plan is complete it is reviewed and approved by the appraisal sponsor.

15.2.3 Select and Prepare Team

The appraisal leader is responsible for ensuring that the appraisal is conducted in accordance with the appraisal methodology. The leader will determine the size[6] and

---

[6] The minimum acceptable team size for a SCAMPI Class A appraisal (as in Fig. 15.3) is four and the maximum is nine. The minimum team size for Class A is one and for Class B is two.

composition of the team, and will select team members who are appropriately qualified and have sufficient knowledge and experience to conduct the appraisal effectively. Any knowledge and skill gaps will need to be identified, and addressed by training[7] prior to the appraisal.

The methodology requires that the team has sufficient software engineering and management experience. Team members also need good verbal and written communication skills to enable them to carry out their roles effectively.

The appraisal leader will introduce the team members to one another, and will give the team an overview of the goals of the appraisal; its scope; the appraisal plan; and the approach to the appraisal. This orientation will enable the appraisal team to carry out their assigned roles effectively.

The initial information provided by the organization (e.g., completed questionnaires and PIIDs) will be analyzed, and the data collection and validation methods and tools to be employed during the appraisal discussed. There are confidentiality requirements to be preserved during an appraisal. For example, everything that is said by individuals during the interviews is treated in the strictest confidence, and appraisal findings are not attributed to individuals.

There are several roles involved in the appraisal including the *on-site coordinator*[8] who takes care of the logistics to support the appraisal team leader; the *librarian* who manages the inventory of appraisal documents; *mini-teams* who are responsible for data collection for their assigned process areas; *facilitators* who conduct the interviews; and *timekeeper* who keeps the interview on time.

15.2.4 Obtain and Analyze Initial Evidence

The organization will provide initial information to the appraisal leader prior to the appraisal to show how it has implemented the CMMI. This helps the appraisal team to understand how the organization has implemented the various practices in the CMMI model, and assists the team in preparing a data collection plan to verify the implementation. The initial evidence may include completed questionnaires, relevant presentations, and a PIID mapping between the CMMI specific and generic practices and the process assets of the organization.

This initial evidence is analyzed by the team to enable them to understand the objective evidence available for the specific and generic practices. An inventory of the evidence available for the various CMMI practices is prepared, and the adequacy and completeness of the information provided is determined. This may result in the need for additional data which is then input into the data collection plan.

---

[7] The appraisers need to have received appropriate training on the CMMI reference model and on the SCAMPI appraisal methodology.

[8] The CMMI project manager is responsible for project managing the CMMI implementation , and may carry out the role of onsite coordinator.

Table 15.2 Indicators of practice implementation

Indicator	Description
Direct Artifact	Tangible output of the practice (e.g., typical work products in CMMI model).
Indirect Artifact	Artifacts that are a consequence of performing the process (e.g., meeting minutes), but not necessarily the purpose for which it is performed.
Affirmation	Oral or written statements confirming the performance of a practice.

There is a need for objective evidence to substantiate implementation of every practice within the scope of the appraisal, and for every project instance of that practice. The extent to which the practice has been implemented is judged by practice implementation indicators, given in Table 15.2.

It is important to collect as much objective evidence as possible prior to the appraisal, as this will reduce the time required for discovery activities during the appraisal. The discovery activities are concerned with looking for evidence to support practice implementation, and an efficient on-site appraisal will focus more on verification activities rather than on discovery activities.

15.2.5 Prepare for Conducting Appraisal

The appraisal leader will conduct an appraisal readiness review to judge the extent to which the organization is ready for the appraisal. There is no point in going ahead with the appraisal if the organization is not ready or is insufficiently prepared.

The sponsor and appraisal leader will consider the feasibility of the appraisal plan, and will decide on whether to continue with the appraisal as planned, to re-plan accordingly, or in a worst case scenario to cancel the appraisal.

The appraisal leader will judge whether the preliminary data is available, and whether the appraisal team has been formed and appropriately trained. The logistics will need to be suitably handled and the risks to the appraisal identified and managed.

The PIIDs will detail the coverage of the CMMI specific and generic practices, and it is reasonable to expect few significant coverage gaps prior to the appraisal. The PIID will refer to documents and evidence that need to be accessible to the appraisers. The appraisers need a verification strategy to verify the objective evidence that is available for practices, as well as a discovery strategy to find objective evidence for practices that have no available objective evidence. The verification and discovery activities to take place during the appraisal are documented in the data collection plan.

The data collection plan may be documented in a variety of deliverables (e.g., interview schedule and participants and scripted interview questions). It may include a spreadsheet with the CMMI practices or questions listed vertically and sources of information listed horizontally. Data on every practice within the scope of the appraisal is required.[9]

The appraisal leader will determine the participants required at each interview and the documents to be reviewed. The roles and responsibilities of team members in data collection activities will be documented in the data collection plan.

15.3   Conducting the Appraisal

This phase of the appraisal is concerned with on-site activities to gather data on the extent to which the specific and generic practices have been implemented. It involves gathering and examining the objective evidence, as well as documenting and verifying the data. The preliminary findings are generated and presented to the appraisal participants to get feedback in order to validate the data and findings. Additional data is then gathered and the final appraisal results prepared. The activities involved include:

- Prepare Participants
- Collect Objective Evidence
- Examine Objective Evidence
- Verify Objective Evidence
- Validate Objective Evidence
- Generate Appraisal Findings

The appraisal participants will receive appropriate training on the appraisal process and their role in it. The appraisal team members take notes and gather objective evidence during the various data collection activities. The objective evidence is then reviewed and consolidated, related to the specific and generic practices, critically examined and documented, and verified and validated. The extent to which the CMMI practices are implemented is determined.

Preliminary findings are prepared and validated and the final appraisal results are then prepared.

15.3.1 Prepare Participants

The onsite coordinator (this may be the CMMI project manager or the quality manager) will give appropriate orientation to the appraisal participants prior to the appraisal to ensure that they understand the purpose of the appraisal and their role in it. This will be the first experience of an appraisal for many in the organization, and so the participants need to understand the process and the required behaviours:

- Professional behaviour at all times
- Punctuality in attendance for interviews

---

[9] Data is required for every project instantiation for practices addressing processes at the project level. One instantiation is sufficient for practices addressing processes at the organization level.

- Openness and honesty in answering questions
- Acting promptly on requests to provide additional material
- Awareness of the confidentiality requirements
- Awareness that the appraisal findings will not be attributed to individuals or specific projects.

The participants need to be aware of the meetings and interviews that they need to attend. All participants will attend the opening and closing sessions, and will attend their own specific interview(s), and the feedback session(s).

The sponsor introduces the appraisal leader at the opening session, and the leader will set the context and expectations for the appraisal, and describes the activities that will take place in the days ahead. The leader gives a brief overview to the participants on the appraisal process and schedule, and the appraisal team is introduced. The opening presentation will typically cover:

- Overview of appraisal
- Appraisals and Process Improvement
- Process Areas within scope of appraisal
- Projects to be reviewed
- Activities in appraisal
- Participants in Appraisal
- Confidentiality
- Appraisal Schedule
- Output from appraisal

The information provided by participants will be treated in the strictest confidence by the appraisal team, and that none of the appraisal findings will be attributed to individuals or projects. This is important, as otherwise participants may be reluctant to share information.

15.3.2 Examine Objective Evidence

The accuracy of the appraisal findings is dependent on the accuracy of the information collected by the appraisal team. The team needs to collect adequate information on how the organization does its work, and the information gathered needs to be related to the CMMI specific and generic practices. This requires that the appraisal team understands how the organization has implemented the CMMI, and has objective evidence of specific and generic practice implementation.

The data collection needs to be well planned and tracked and it will be revised appropriately during the appraisal to reflect new information needs. The data collection plan consists of:

- Appraisal schedule
- Interview schedule
- Document list
- Interview questions

The appraisal team will continually manage the data collected, and plan new data collection in line with information needs. The data collection sources include:

- Interviews with appraisal participants
- Reviews of documentation
- Presentations from staff

The interviews need to be well planned as they have a limited amount of time to determine specific evidence (e.g., oral affirmation on the way the process is performed) from the participants. The planning requires the preparation of scripted questions to ensure that the interview is focused and achieves its objectives within the time constraints. Interviews also allow dynamic data gathering, with the interviewer able to branch off to discuss other related topics.

The information provided at an interview is treated in the strictest confidence, and the appraisal findings will not be attributed to individuals or projects. There will be separate interviews for:

- Project Managers
- Project Teams
- Functional Area Representatives (FAR)
- Managers
- Specific Groups (SEPG Team, QA, etc.).

Often, one of the appraisal team members will lead the interview with some or all of the other appraisers being present, listening and taking notes. The planned set of interviews will be defined in the data collection plan, and re-planning will take place as appropriate. There may be a need for extra on-call interviews or some of the planned interviews may be cancelled if sufficient objective evidence is available.

Documentation reviews give the appraisal team a clearer understanding of what practices are performed in the organization. This includes insight into how the process is performed, the extent to which it is performed, as well as allowing explicit deliverables produced to be examined. Most of the direct artefacts used as indicators of practice implementation are documents.

There are three levels of documents that will typically be examined during the appraisal. These are:

- Organization documents
- Project documents
- Implementation documents

The organization documents include policies, processes and procedures; the project documents include the deliverables produced during the project for each project instantiation; and the implementation documents provide an audit trail of the processes used. The appraisal team will maintain an inventory of the documents used.

Presentations allow the organization to explain how particular practices are performed. The appraisal team will need to analyse the information obtained during the various data collection activities to:

- Judge if the information collected is acceptable as objective evidence
- Relate it to the corresponding practices in the model.
- Relate evidence to the appropriate part of the organization unit

The results of data collection will often be recorded on electronic tools, as the inventory of the collected evidence. The appraisal team will closely monitor progress with the data collection activities, and as appraisals have a limited amount of time available it is essential that the data collection activities are focused and efficient.

Finally, once the team has examined, verified and validated all of the required data it is in a position to generate the appraisal findings, and where applicable, to generate ratings for the organization.

15.3.3 Document Objective Evidence

This part of the appraisal is concerned with note taking; reviewing and consolidating notes; relating the notes to the corresponding practices in the CMMI model; and documenting practice implementation and the strengths and weaknesses identified. The notes taken by the team members during the data gathering sessions are reviewed at the end of each session, and significant items relating to one or more practices tagged. The notes record the particular data gathering session as well as the participants.

The consolidation of the notes allows the appraisal team members to have a common understanding of the data collected to date, as well as identifying further data collection needs. The presence or absence of objective data for each model practice for each process area within scope needs to be done for each project instantiation. The gaps identified in the implemented processes with respect to the practices in the CMMI model are documented.

It is essential that the data collection, consolidation and documentation activities be conducted in a timely manner. An inventory (usually an electronic spreadsheet tool or a manual wall chart tool) of the objective evidence available for each specific and generic practice for each project instantiation within the scope of the appraisal is maintained.

The inventory allows the status of the data collection and consolidation activities to be determined, and this includes the practices for which there is sufficient objective evidence available, and those that have insufficient or missing evidence. The data collection plan needs to be updated appropriately to reflect additional data collection needs. The inventory will record:

- Project to which data applies
- Specific or Generic practice to which it applies
- Type of evidence (Direct, Indirect, Affirmation)
- Whether implies presence or absence of objective evidence

Often, in large formal appraisals, team members are assigned responsibilities for the collection and documentation of objective evidence for one or more process areas. This usually involves the formation of mini-teams with two or three members to obtain and document the objective evidence for their assigned process areas.

The raw notes taken by the appraisers are treated as confidential information and are not disclosed to anyone outside of the appraisal team. Team members will destroy their notes at the end of the appraisal to ensure that information cannot be attributed to individuals.

15.3.4 Verify Objective Evidence

This is concerned with verifying the implementation of the organization's practices for each project instantiation, as well as determining and documenting the extent to which the practices are implemented. The implementation of each practice is verified for each project instantiation, with exemplary implementations highlighted as strengths to be included in the appraisal findings.

The appraisal team uses the initial objective evidence provided by the organization to understand how the CMMI practices are implemented. The team then gathers data to confirm that the practices are actually implemented as defined, and this may reveal gaps in the implementation that were not apparent in the initial evidence provided. The implemented practices are then compared to the specific and generic practices in the CMMI model, and additional gaps may be identified. The gaps in the implementation are recorded, and become part of the appraisal findings.

The appraisal team must verify that each project within the scope of the appraisal has objective evidence of implementation of the specific or generic practices (reflecting project activities). The appraisal team will:

- Verify the appropriateness of each direct artefact provided for practices within appraisal scope
- Verify the appropriateness of each indirect artefact provided
- Verify appropriateness of affirmations
- Verify that implementation of each practice (within scope) is supported by direct artefacts and corroborated by indirect artefacts or affirmations
- Obtain oral affirmation corresponding to each specific and generic goal within scope of appraisal
- Generate the preliminary findings including the strengths identified and gaps in the implemented practices.

Much of the evidence required to perform verification is provided prior to the appraisal. The main focus of the data collection activities is to allow the appraisal team to verify that the intended practices are implemented across the organization unit and to identify any gaps in the implementation.

The appraisal team then characterizes the extent to which the CMMI practices are implemented for each project instantiation, and derives an aggregate rating to characterize the extent of implementation in the organization. The extent of implementation of a practice is:

- Fully implemented (FI)
- Largely implemented (LI)
- Partially implemented (PI)
- Not implemented (NI)

The extent of implementation of the practice is judged by:

- The presence or absence of direct artefacts and their adequacy.
- The presence or absence of indirect artefacts and affirmations to confirm the implementation
- Any weaknesses in practice implementation identified.

The aggregate organization rating for each practice is determined from the rating of the practice for each project instantiation. For example, if all project instantiations are fully implemented then the organization rating is fully implemented.

15.3.5 Validate Preliminary Findings

The appraisal team will present preliminary findings to members of the organization to ensure that they are an accurate reflection of the organization. This is mainly a data collection activity, and the goal is to validate the appraisal team's understanding of the processes implemented in the organization. Feedback and additional evidence will be requested and used in the formulation of the final findings.

The preliminary findings detail the practice implementation gaps identified as well as strengths noted by the appraisal team. Every model practice characterized at the organization level as not implemented, partially implemented or largely implemented will have a preliminary finding associated with it.

The appraisal team will issue a request for further information for areas where the appraisal team has insufficient objective evidence available.

15.3.6 Generate Appraisal Results

The appraisal team will rate specific and generic goal satisfaction based on the extent of practice implementation throughout the organization. The extent of practice implemented is judged by the validated data collected, including direct and indirect artefacts and oral affirmation objective evidence. Once the goals have been rated the process areas may be rated and then the overall maturity level determined.

A goal is considered satisfied if the practices associated with that goal are appropriately implemented. Any gaps are considered and the appraisal team makes a judgment made on whether these gaps threaten the ability to achieve the associated goal. All associated practices must be rated as largely or fully implemented, and any identified weaknesses must not have a significant impact on goal achievement. For any goals that are rated as not satisfied the appraisal team will detail how the weaknesses identified led to this rating.

Once the goals have been rated the team are then in a position to judge the satisfaction of the process areas within the appraisal scope. Process area satisfaction is closely related to goal satisfaction, and a process area is rated satisfied if all of its specific and generic goals up to the targeted maturity level are rated satisfied.

The appraisal team is then in a position to judge the maturity level of the organization. This is based on the ratings of the process areas within the scope of the appraisal. The maturity level determined is the highest level at which all process areas contained at that maturity level and lower levels are satisfied.[10]

---

[10] Generic goal 3 must also be rated for all of the level 2 process areas for a level 3 rating.

The appraisal team is then in a position to prepare the final appraisal findings including:

- Documenting the final findings
- Documenting the ratings (where ratings are part of the appraisal)
- Preparing (where applicable) the Appraisal Disclosure Statement (ADS) for the CMMI Stewart at the SEI.

15.4 Reporting the Results

The results of the appraisal are presented to the sponsor and the participants. The strengths and weaknesses of the processes are presented, as well as the ratings of the process areas (where these are part of the appraisal). The appraisal results need to be credible, as they will be used for continuous improvement.

The appraisal findings are intended to promote action and occasionally a separate executive session is conducted with senior management. The purpose of this session is to discuss the appraisal results, and to facilitate the preparation of an action plan to address the findings.

15.4.1 Deliver Appraisal Results

The findings will be presented to the appraisal participants. The appraisal sponsor is advised of the appraisal results prior to the presentation as a matter of courtesy and to prevent any surprises. The appraisal leader will provide the appraisal findings to the appraisal sponsor, and the findings will be signed by the appraisal leader and team. The appraisal findings will include:

- Summary of appraisal process
- Summary of strengths and weaknesses for each process area
- Ratings (where this is part of appraisal)

Any statements of weaknesses will adhere to the confidentiality requirements, and will not be attributed to projects or individuals. The appraisal leader and team will sign the appraisal findings to indicate their agreement with them.

An executive session may be conducted between the sponsor and appraisal leader to clarify any issues from the appraisal, and to help the sponsor and senior management understand the process weaknesses identified. This helps to ensure that management are sufficiently informed to act appropriately on the findings.

15.4.2 Archive Appraisal Results

Important data and records from the appraisal will be preserved and confidential information disposed of securely. Any lessons learned from the appraisal will be used to improve the appraisal process.

The information archived will include the appraisal plan and appraisal results. All notes taken by appraisers will be destroyed. The appraisal record will be delivered to the appraisal sponsor and will include:

- Dates of the appraisal
- Appraisal input
- Appraisal plan
- Objective evidence to support goal ratings
- Characterization of practice implementation
- Appraisal method
- Final findings
- All ratings (goals, practices and maturity levels)

The ADS record will be created and submitted to the CMMI steward at the SEI for formal SCAMPI Class A appraisals.

15.5 Review Questions

1. Discuss the purpose of appraisals and how they fit into the software process improvement cycle.
2. Describe the three phases in an appraisal.
3. Describe the three classes of SCAMPI appraisals.
4. Discuss the difference between data discovery and data verification activities in an appraisal.
5. Describe the activities that take place in planning the appraisal.
6. Describe the activities that take place during the appraisal.

15.6 Summary

Appraisals play a key role in software process improvement and are an essential part of the improvement programme. They allow an organization to understand its current software process maturity, including its strengths and opportunities for improvement. An initial appraisal is generally conducted at the start of the initiative to allow the organization plan and prioritize improvements for the first improvement cycle. Improvements are then implemented, and an appraisal is typically conducted at the end of the cycle to confirm progress.

An appraisal is an independent examination of the software engineering and management practices in the organization and will identify any gaps that exist with respect to the targeted level in the CMMI. There are three phases in an appraisal: planning the appraisal; conducting the appraisal; and reporting the results.

The appraisal leader will determine the appraisal requirements and objectives in discussions with the sponsor. The type of appraisal to be conducted is determined, and an appraisal plan is developed to meet the sponsor's requirements. The appraisal leader then forms a team to conduct the appraisal and the participants involved in the appraisal receive appropriate training on the appraisal process and their role in it.

The on-site activities will gather data to determine the extent to which the CMMI practices within the scope of the appraisal have been implemented. It involves gathering and examining the objective evidence, and documenting and verifying the data. The team makes notes and gathers objective evidence during the various data collection activities (e.g., interviews, presentations, and reviews of documentation). The objective evidence is then reviewed and consolidated, related to the CMMI practices, critically examined and documented, verified and validated. The extent to which the CMMI practices are implemented is determined. Preliminary findings are then prepared and validated by members of the organization. The final appraisal results are then prepared.

The results of the appraisal are then presented to the sponsor and the participants. The strengths and weaknesses identified with the processes will be presented, as well as the ratings of the process areas (where these are part of the appraisal). The appraisal results are used for continuous process improvement. An action plan is prepared to address the appraisal findings from the various.

Software Engineering Tools

16

> **Key Topics**
>
> Microsoft Project
> Cocomo
> Planview Enterprise
> IBM Rational Doors
> Rational Software Modeler
> LDRA Testbed
> Integrated Development Environment
> Sparx Enterprise Architect
> HP Quality Center

16.1 Introduction

The goal of this chapter is to give a flavour of a selection of tools[1] that can support the organization in various software engineering activities. Tools for project management, requirements management, configuration management, design and development, testing, and so on are considered. The organization will generally choose tools to support the process rather than choosing a process to support the tool.[2]

Mature organizations will employ a structured approach to the introduction of new tools. First, the requirements for a new tool are specified and the options to

---

[1] The list of tools discussed in this chapter is intended to give a flavour of what tools are available, and the inclusion of a particular tool is not intended as a recommendation of that tool. Similarly, the omission of a particular tool should not be interpreted as disapproval of that tool.

[2] That is, the process comes first then the tool rather than the other way around.

G. O'Regan, *Introduction to Software Quality*, Undergraduate Topics
in Computer Science, DOI 10.1007/978-3-319-06106-1_16,
© Springer International Publishing Switzerland 2014

Table 16.1 Tool evaluation table

	Tool 1	Tool 2	...	Tool k
Requirement 1	8	7		9
Requirement 2	4	6		8
....				
....				
Requirement n	3	6		8
Total	35	38	...	45

satisfy the requirements are considered. These may include developing a tool internally; outsourcing the development of a tool to a third party supplier; or purchasing a tool off the shelf from a vendor.

The sample tool evaluation in Table 16.1 lists all of the requirements vertically that the test tool is to satisfy, and the tools to be evaluated and rated against each requirement are listed horizontally. Various rating schemes may be employed and in the example presented here, a simple numeric rating scheme is employed to rate the effectiveness of the tool under evaluation, to indicate the extent to which the tool satisfies the particular requirement. The chosen tool in this example is Tool k as it is the most highly rated of the evaluated tools.

Several candidate tools will be identified and considered prior to selection, and each candidate tool will be evaluated to determine the extent to which it satisfies the specified requirements. An informed decision is then made and the proposed tool will be piloted prior to its deployment. The pilot provides feedback on its suitability, and the feedback will be considered prior to a decision on full deployment, and whether any customization is required prior to roll out.

Finally, the users are trained on the tool, and the tool is rolled out throughout the organization. Support is provided for a period post deployment. First, we consider tools for project management.

16.2 Tools for Project Management

There are several tools to support the various project management activities such as estimation and cost prediction, planning and scheduling, monitoring risks and issues, and managing a portfolio of projects. These include tools such as Microsoft Project which is a powerful project management scheduling tool widely used by project managers throughout the world. Small projects may employ a simpler tool such as Microsoft Excel for their project scheduling activities.

The Constructive Cost Model (COCOMO) is a cost prediction model developed by Barry Boehm [7] to estimate effort, schedule and cost for small and medium projects. It is based on an effort estimation equation that calculates the software development effort in person-months from the estimated project size. The effort estimation calculation is based on the estimate of a project's size in thousands of *source lines of code* (SLOC[3]). The accuracy of the tool is limited as there is a great deal of variation among teams due to differences in the expertise and experience of the personnel in the project team.

There are several commercial variants of the tool including the COCOMO Basic, Intermediate and Advanced Models. The Intermediate Model includes several cost drivers to model the project environment, and each cost driver is rated. There are over 15 cost drivers used and these include product complexity, reliability, and experience of personnel as well as programming language experience. The COCOMO parameters need to be calibrated to reflect the actual project development environment. The effort equation used in COCOMO is given by:

$$\text{Effort} = 2.94 * \text{EAF} * (\text{KSLOC})^E \tag{16.1}$$

In this equation, EAF refers to the effort adjustment factor that is derived from the cost drivers, and E is the exponent that is derived from the five scale drivers.[4] The Costar tool is a commercial tool that implements the COCOMO Mode, and it may be used on small or large projects. It needs to be calibrated to reflect the particular software engineering environment, and this will enable more accurate estimates to be produced.

Microsoft Project (Fig. 3.2) is a project management tool that is used for planning, scheduling and charting project information. It enables a realistic project plan to be created, and the plan is updated regularly during the project to reflect actual progress, and the project is re-planned as appropriate. We discussed project management in Chap. 3.

A project is defined as a series of steps or tasks to achieve a specific goal. The amount of time that it takes to complete a task is termed its duration, and tasks are performed in a sequence determined by the nature of the project. Resources such as people and equipment are required to perform a task. A project will typically consist of several phases such as planning and requirements; design; implementation; testing and closing the project.

The project schedule (Fig. 3.2) shows the tasks and activities to be carried out during the project; the effort and duration of each task and activity; the percentage complete of each task, and the resources needed to carry out the various tasks. The schedule shows how the project will be delivered within the key project parameters such as time, cost and functionality without compromising quality in any way.

The project manager is responsible for managing the schedule and will take corrective action when project performance deviates from expectations. The project schedule will be updated regularly to reflect actual progress made, and the project re-planned appropriately.

---

[3] SLOC includes delivered source lines of code created by project staff (excluding automated code generated and also code comments).

[4] The five scale drivers are factors contributing to duration and cost and they determine the exponent used in the Effort equation. Examples include team cohesion and process maturity.

Project portfolio management (PPM) is concerned with managing a portfolio of projects, and it allows the organization to choose the optimal mix and sequencing of its projects to yield the greatest business benefit to the organization.

It analyses the project's total expected cost, the resources required, the schedule, the benefits that will be realized as well as interdependencies with other projects in the portfolio. This allows project investment decisions to be made methodically to deliver the greatest benefit to the organization. The approach moves away from the normal once off analysis of an individual project proposal, to the analysis of a portfolio of projects. PPM tools aim to manage the continuous flow of projects from concept all the way to completion.

There are several commercial portfolio management tools available from various vendors. These include Clarity PPM from Computer Associates, Change Point from Compuware, RPM from IBM Rational, PPM Center from HP, and Planview Enterprise from Planview. It is not possible to discuss of all of these portfolio management tools, and the discussion in this section is limited to the Planview Enterprise tool.

Planview Enterprise Portfolio Management allows organizations to manage projects and resources across the enterprise, and to align their initiatives for maximum business benefit. It provides visibility into and control of project portfolios, and allows the organization to prioritize and manage its projects and resources. This allows it to make better investment decisions, and to balance its business strategy against its available resources. Planview helps an organization to optimize its business through eight key capabilities listed in Table 16.2.

Planview allows key project performance indicators to be closely tracked. This includes dashboard views of variances of cost, effort and schedule, and the analysis and reporting is described in Fig. 16.1.

Planview includes Process Builder (Fig. 16.2), which allows modelling and management of enterprise wide processes. It provides improved tracking, control and audit capabilities in key process areas such as requirements management and product development, as well as satisfying key regulatory requirements.

The organization may define and model its process in Process Builder, and this includes process adoption, compliance and continuous improvement. The functionality includes:
• Process Design
• Process Automation
• Process Measurement
• Process Auditing

Next, we will consider tools to support requirements development and management.

16.3   Tools for Requirements

There are several tools available to assist organizations in carrying out requirements development and management. These tools assist in eliciting requirements from the stakeholders; modelling requirements; verifying and validating the requirements; managing the requirements throughout the lifecycle; and providing traceability of

Table 16.2 Key capabilities of Planview Enterprise

Capability	Description
Strategic planning	Define mission, objectives and strategies.
	Allocate funding/staffing for chosen strategy
	Automate and manage strategic process
Investment analysis	Devise strategic long-term plans
	Identify key criteria to evaluate initiatives
	Optimize strategic and project investments to maximize business benefit
Capacity management	Balance resources with business demands
	Ensure capacity supports business strategy
	Align top down and bottom up planning
	Forecast resource capacity
Demand management	Request work and Check status
	Review lifecycles
Project management	Scope, schedule and execution of work
	Track/report time worked against projects
	Track and manage risks and issues
	Track/display performance and trend analysis
Financial management	Collaborate to better forecast cost
	Monitor spending
Resource management	Balance portfolios/assign people efficiently
	Improve forecasting
	Keep staff productive
Change management	Determine impact of change on schedule/cost
	Effectively manage change

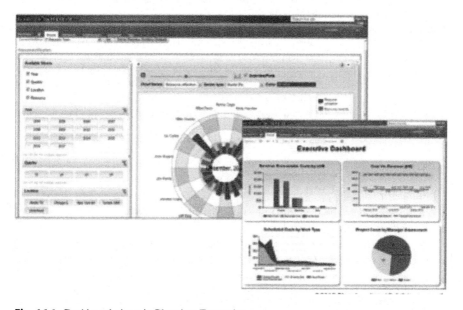

Fig. 16.1 Dashboard views in Planview Enterprise

PLANVIEW▼PROCESS BUILDER

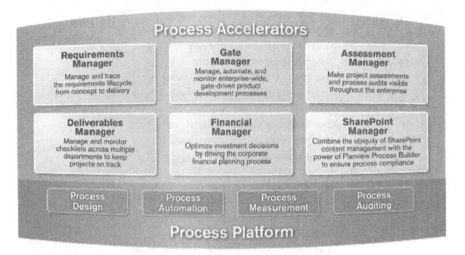

Fig. 16.2 Planview Process Builder

Table 16.3 Tools for requirements development and management

Tool	Description
DOORS (IBM/Rational)	This is a Requirements Management tool developed by Telelogic (which is now part of IBM/Rational).
Requisite Pro (IBM/Rational)	This is a Requirements Management and Use Case management tool developed by IBM/Rational
Enterprise Architect (Sparx Systems)	This is a UML analysis and design tool that covers requirements gathering, analysis and design, and testing and maintenance. It was developed by Sparx Systems and integrates requirements management with the other software development activities.
CORE (Vitech)	This is a requirements tool developed by Vitech and may be used for modelling and simulation.
Integrity (MKS)	This tool was developed by MKS and enables organizations to capture and validate software requirements, and to link them to downstream development and testing activities.

the requirements to the design and test cases. Table 16.3 gives a small selection of some of the tools that are available.

DOORS® (Dynamic Object-Oriented Requirements System) is a requirements management tool developed by IBM Rational. It allows the stakeholders to actively participate in the requirements process, and aims to optimize requirements communication, collaboration and verification. High-quality requirements help the organization in reducing costs[5] and in meeting their business objectives.

The tool can capture, link, trace, analyse, and manage changes to the requirements. It enhances communication and collaboration to ensure that the project conforms to the customer requirements, as well as compliance to regulations and standards.

Requirements are documented in a way that is easy to interpret and navigate. It is easy to locate information within the database, and the user requirements are recorded in a document style showing each individual requirement. It provides views of the list with assigned identifiers and also an Explorer-like navigation tree.

The tool employs links to support traceability of the requirements, and these are traversed with a simple click of the mouse to the corresponding object. The links are easy to create by dragging and dropping; e.g., a new link from the user requirements to the system requirements is created in this way. The tool provides dynamic reporting on traceability, and filters may be employed to ensure that traceability is complete. Traceability is essential in demonstrating that the requirements have been implemented and tested.

The management of change is an important part of the requirements process. The Doors tool supports changes to requirements and allows an impact analysis of the proposed changes to be performed. It allows changes that could impact other requirements or design items and test cases to be tagged. The Doors® tool (Fig. 16.3) provides:

- A comprehensive requirements management environment
- Web browser access to the requirements database
- Manages changes to requirements
- Scalable solution for managing project scope and cost
- Traceability to design items, test plans and test cases
- Active engagement from stakeholders
- Integrates with other IBM Rational tools

There are several other IBM Rational tools that may be integrated with Doors®. These include the IBM Rational System Architect, Requirements Composer, Rhapsody, and Quality Manager.

IBM Rational RequisitePro is a requirements management tool that allows requirements to be documented with familiar document-based methods, and it provides capabilities such as requirements traceability and impact analysis. Requirements are managed throughout the lifecycle, and changes to the requirements controlled.

The Core product suite (developed by Vitech) has functionality for requirements management, modelling and simulation, and verification and validation. It supports

---

[5] A good requirements process will enable high-quality requirements to be consistently produced, and the cost of poor quality is reduced as wastage and rework is minimized. The requirements are the foundation of the system and if they are incorrect then the delivered system will not be fit for purpose.

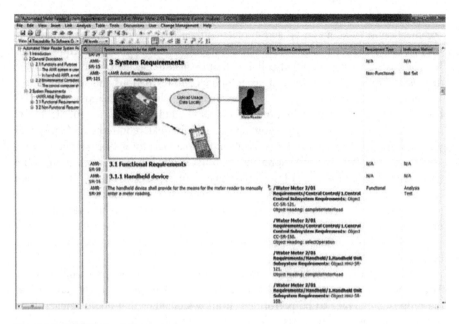

Fig. 16.3 IBM Rational DOORS tool

UML activity and sequence diagrams which enable the desired behaviour and flow of control to be captured and analysed. The tool provides:

- Comprehensive end-to-end system traceability
- Change impact analysis
- Multiple modelling notations with integrated graphical views
- System simulation based on behavioural models
- Generation of Documentation from the database

The Integrity tool was developed by MKS and it enables organizations to capture and validate software requirements. It enables them to link the requirements to downstream development and testing activities, and to manage changes to the requirements. Next, we will consider tools to support software design and development.

16.4 Tools for Design and Development

This section describes tools available to support software design and development activities. The software design includes the high-level architecture of the system, as well as the lower level design and algorithms. Table 16.4 gives a small selection of some of the tools that are available.

IBM Rational Software Modeler® (RSM) (Fig. 16.4) is a UML-based visual modelling and design tool. It promotes communication and collaboration during

Table 16.4 Tools for software design

Tool	Description
Microsoft Visio	This tool allows many types of drawings such as flowcharts, work flow diagrams and network diagrams to be created.
IBM Rational Software Modeler	This is a UML based visual modelling and software design tool.
IBM Rational Rhapsody	This modelling environment tool is based on UML and provides a visual development environment for software engineers. It uses graphical models and generates code in C, C++ and Java.
IBM Rational Software Architect	This modelling and development tool uses UML for designing architecture for C++ and Java applications.
Enterprise Architect (Sparx Systems)	This UML analysis and design tool is used for modelling systems with traceability from requirements to design and testing. It supports code generation.

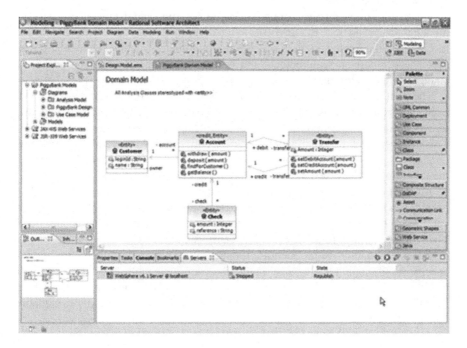

Fig. 16.4 IBM Rational Software Modeler

design and development, and allows information about development projects to be specified and communicated from several perspectives. It is used for model-driven development, and aligns the business needs with the product.

It gives the organization control over the evolving architecture, and provides an integrated analysis and design platform. Abstract UML specifications may be built with traceability and impact analysis shown.

It has an intuitive user interface and a diagram editor to create expressive and interactive diagrams. The tool may be integrated with other IBM Rational tools such as Clearcase, Clearquest and Requisite Pro.

BM Rational Rhapsody® is a visual development environment used in real-time or embedded systems. It helps teams collaborate to understand and elaborate requirements; abstract complexity using modelling languages such as UML; validate functionality early in development; and automate code generation to speed up the development process.

Enterprise Architect is a UML analysis and design tool used for modelling business and IT systems, and was developed by Sparx Systems. It covers the full product development lifecycle, including business modelling, requirements management, software design, code generation, testing, and so on. It supports automated document generation, code generation and reverse engineering of source code. Its reverse engineering feature allows a visual representation of the software application to be provided (Fig. 16.5).

It is a multi-user graphical tool with built in reporting and documentation. It can model, manage and trace requirements to the design, test cases and deployment, and its can trace the implementation of system requirements to model elements. It can search and report on requirements and perform an impact analysis on proposed changes to the requirements.

The tool allows deployments scripts to be built, debugged and tested and executed from within its development environment. UML and modelling are integrated into the development process and debugging capabilities are provided. This includes run time examination of the executing code for several programming languages, and NUnit and JUnit test classes may be generated and integrated directly into the test process.

An integrated development environment (IDE) is a software application that provides comprehensive support facilities to software developers. It includes specialized text editors; a compiler; build automation; and debugging capabilities. The features of an IDE are described in Table 16.5.

IDEs help to improve programmer productivity. They are usually dedicated to a specific programming language, although there are some multi-language tools such as Eclipse and Microsoft Visual Studio. There are many IDEs for languages such as Pascal, C, C++ and Java. The next section is concerned with tools to support configuration management.

16.5   Tools for Configuration Management and Change Control

Configuration management is concerned with identifying the work products that are subject to change control, and controlling changes to them. It involves creating and releasing baselines, maintaining their integrity, recording and reporting the status of the configuration items and change requests, and verifying the correctness and completeness of the configuration items with configuration audits.

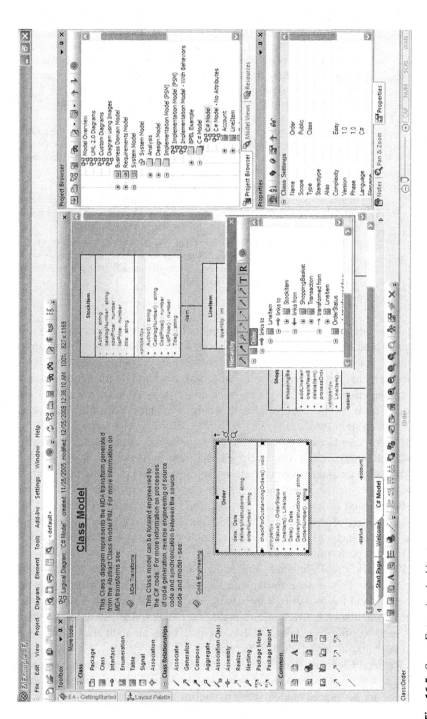

Fig. 16.5 Sparx Enterprise Architect

Table 16.5 Integrated development environment

Item	Description
Source code editor	This is a specialized text editor (e.g., Microsoft Visual Studio) designed for editing the source code. It includes features to speed up the input of source code, including syntax checking of the code while the programmer types.
Compiler or interpreter	A compiler is a computer program that translates the high-level programming language source code into object code to produce the executable code. A compiler carries out lexical analysis, parsing and code generation.
	An interpreter is a program that executes instructions written in a programming language. It may involve the direction execution of the code; translation of the code into an intermediate representation and immediate direct execution; or execution of stored precompiled code made by a compiler which is part of the Interpreter System.
Build automation tools	Build automation involves scripting to automate the build process. This includes tasks such as compiling the source code; linking the object code and building the executable software; performing automated tests and reporting results; reporting the build status; and generating release notes.
Debugger	A debugger is a software application that is used to debug and test other software programs. Debuggers offer step by step execution of the code or execution to breakpoints in the code. Examples include IBM Rational Purify and Microsoft Visual Studio Debugger.

Visual Source Safe (VSS) is a version control management system for source code and binary files. It was developed by the Microsoft Corporation and is used mainly by small software development organizations. It allows multiple users to place their source code and work products under version control management. It is fairly easy to use and may be integrated with the Microsoft Visual Studio tool. Microsoft plans to replace VSS with its Visual Studio Team System tool.

Polytron Version Control System (PVCS) is a version control system for software code and binary files. It was developed by Serena Software Inc., and is suitable for use by large or small teams. It allows multiple users to place their source code and project deliverables under version control management and it allows files to be checked in and checked out; baselines to be controlled; roll-back of code; and tracking of check-ins. It includes functionality for branching, merging and labelling. It includes the PV Tracker tool for tracking defects, and the PV Builder tool for performing builds and releases.

The PV Tracker tool automates the capture and communication of issues and change requests. This is done throughout the software development lifecycle for project teams, and the tool allows the developers to link the affected source code files with issues and changes. It allows managers to determine and report on team progress, and to prioritize tasks. PV Builder maintains an audit trail of the files included in the build as well as their versions.

IBM Rational Clearcase and Clearquest are popular configuration management tools with a rich feature set. Clearcase allows software code and other software deliverables to be placed under version control management, and it may be employed in large or medium projects. It can handle a large number of files and supports standard configuration management tasks such as checking in and checking out of the software assets as well as labelling and branching. Objects are stored in repositories called VOBs.

Clearquest may be linked to Clearcase as well as to other IBM Rational tools. It allows the defects in a project to be tracked, and it allows the versions of source code modules that were changed to be linked to a defect number in Clearquest.

16.6   Tools for Code Analysis and Code Inspections

Static code analysis is the analysis of software code without the actual execution of the code. It is usually performed with automated tools and the analysis conducted depends on the sophistication of the tools. Some tools may analyze individual statements or declarations, whereas others may analyze the whole source code. The objective of the analysis is to highlight potential coding errors early in the development lifecycle.

The LDRA Tools automatically determine the complexity of the source code, and provide metrics that give an indication of the maintainability of the code. A useful feature of LDRA is that it gives a visual picture of system complexity, and it has a re-factoring tool to assist with its reduction. It generates code assessment reports listing all of the files examined, and providing metrics of the clarity, maintainability and testability of the code. Other LDRA tools may be used for code coverage analysis (Fig. 16.6).

	Percentage	Success Limit
▲ 🗋 Productdatabase.cpp		
▲ ▰ Combined Coverage Run	Failed	
▰ Statement Coverage	99	100
▰ Branch/Decision Coverage	94	100
▰ Modified Condition / Decision Coverage	75	100
▷ 🔍 main		
▲ 🔍 ProductDatabase		
▲ ▰ Combined Coverage Run	Passed	
▰ Statement Coverage	100	100
▰ Branch/Decision Coverage	100	100
▰ Modified Condition / Decision Coverage	100	100
▲ 🔍 resetCountedProducts		
▲ ▰ Combined Coverage Run	Passed	
▰ Statement Coverage	100	100
▰ Branch/Decision Coverage	100	100
▰ Modified Condition / Decision Coverage	100	100
▲ ◊ countProduct		
▲ ▰ Combined Coverage Run	Failed	
▰ Statement Coverage	97	100
▰ Branch/Decision Coverage	86	100
▰ Modified Condition / Decision Coverage	50	100

Fig. 16.6 LDRA code coverage analysis report

Compliance to coding standards is important in producing readable code and in preventing error-prone coding styles. There are several tools available to check conformance to coding standards including the LDRA TBvision tool which has reporting capabilities to show code quality as well as fault detection and avoidance measures. It provides intuitive functionality to view the results in various graphs and reports.

Some static code analysis tools (e.g., tools for formal methods) aim to prove properties about a particular program. This may include reasoning about program correctness or that of a program meeting its specification. These tools often provide support for assertions, and a precondition is the assertion placed before the code fragment, and this predicate is true before execution of the code. The post-condition is the assertion placed after the code fragment, and this predicate is true after the execution of the code.

There are several open-source tools available for static code analysis, and these include the RATS tools which provide multi-language support for C, C++, Perl and PHP, and the PMD tool for Java. There are several commercial tools available and these include the LDRA Testbed tool which provides support for C, C++ and Java; The Fortify tool helps developers to identify security vulnerabilities in C, C++ and Java; and the Parasoft tools helps developers to identify coding issues that lead to security, reliability, performance, and maintainability issues later.

16.7   Tools for Testing

Testing plays a key role in verifying that the software system satisfies the requirements and is fit for purpose. There are various tools to support testing such as test management tools; defect tracking tools; regression test automation tools; performance tools; and so on. The tools considered in this section include:
- Test Director
- Winrunner
- Load Runner

Test Director (now called Quality Center) is a web-based test management tool developed by Mercury.[6] It provides a consistent repeatable process for gathering requirements; planning and scheduling tests; analysing results; and managing defects. It consists of four modules namely:
- Requirements
- Test Plan
- Test Lab
- Defect Management.

The Requirements module supports requirements management and traceability of the test cases to the requirements. The Test Plan module supports the creation

---

[6] Mercury is now part of HP.

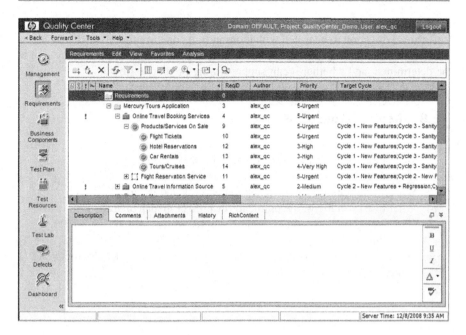

Fig. 16.7 HP Quality Center

and update of test cases. The Test Lab module supports execution of the test cases defined in the Test Plan module. The Defect Management module supports the logging of defects and these defects can be linked back to the test cases that failed.

Test Director supports a high-level of collaboration and communication between the stakeholders. It allows the business analysts to define the application requirements and testing objectives. The test managers and testers may then design test plans, test cases and automated scripts. The testers then run the manual and automated tests, report results and log the defects. The developers review and correct the logged defects. Project and test managers can create status reports and manage test resources. Test and product managers decide objectively whether the application is ready to be released.

Test Director is now a part of Quality Center™ (Fig. 16.7) developed by HP. This tool standardizes and manages the entire test and quality process, and is a web-based system for automated software quality management and testing. It employs dashboard technology to give visibility into the process.

Mercury developed the Winrunner tool which automatically captures, verifies and replays user interactions. It is used mainly used to automate regression testing, which improves productivity and allows defects to be identified in a timely manner. This provides confidence that enhancements to the software have had no negative impact on the integrity of the system. The Winrunner tool has been replaced by HP Unified Functional Testing Software which includes HP Quick Test Professional and HP Service Test.

Mercury developed the LoadRunner performance testing tool, which allows a software application to be tested with thousands of concurrent users to determine its performance under heavy loads. It allows the scalability of the software system to be determined, and whether it can support future predicted growth.

16.8   Review Questions

1. Why are tools used in software engineering?
2. How should a tool be selected for an organization?
3. What is the relationship between the process and the tool?
4. What tools would you recommend for project management?
5. Describe how you would go about selecting a tool for requirements development.
6. Describe various tools that are available for design and development and which are your preferred tools?

16.9   Summary

The objective of this chapter was to give a flavour of various tools available to support the organization in engineering software. These included tools for project management, configuration management, design and development, test management, and so on. The tools are chosen to support the process.

The project management tools included a discussion of the cocoma Cost Model which may be employed to estimate the cost and effort for a project; the Microsoft Project tool which is used extensively by project managers to schedule and track their projects. The Planview Portfolio Management Tool was also discussed and this tool allows an organization to manage a portfolio of projects.

The tools to support requirements development and management included IBM Rational Doors, Requisite Pro and Core. The Doors tool allows all stakeholders to actively participate in the requirements process, and aims to optimize requirements communication, collaboration and verification.

The tools to support design and development included the IBM Rational Software Modeler tool, the Sparx Enterprise Architect tool and Integrated Developer Environments to support software developers. The Rational Software Modeler® (RSM) is a UML-based visual modelling and design tool. Enterprise Architect is a UML analysis and design tool, and provides traceability from requirements to design, testing and deployment. The tools discussed to support configuration management included PVCS and Clearcase.

The tools to support testing included Quality Center™, Winrunner and Loadrunner tools. Quality Center™ standardizes and manages the entire test process. It has modules for requirements management, test planning, test lab and defect management.

Tool selection is done in a controlled manner. First, the organization needs to determine its requirements for the tool. Various candidate tools are evaluated and a decision on the proposed tool is made. Next, the tool is piloted to ensure that it meets the needs of the organization, and feedback from the pilot may lead to changes or customizations of the tool. Finally, the end users are trained on the use of the tool and it is rolled out throughout the organization.

Formal Methods

17

Key Topics

Vienna Development Method
Z Specification Language
B Method
Process Calculus
Finite State Machines
Model-oriented approach
Axiomatic approach
Usability of Formal Methods

17.1 Introduction

The term "*formal methods*" refer to various mathematical techniques used for the formal specification and development of software. They consist of a formal specification language, and employ a collection of tools to support the syntax checking of the specification, as well as the proof of properties of the specification. They allow questions to be asked about what the system does independently of the implementation.

The use of mathematical notation avoids speculation about the meaning of phrases in an imprecisely worded natural language description of a system. Natural language is inherently ambiguous, whereas mathematics employs a precise rigorous notation. Spivey [62] defines formal specification as:

Definition 5.1 (Formal Specification) *Formal specification is the use of mathematical notation to describe in a precise way the properties that an information system must have, without unduly constraining the way in which these properties are achieved.*

G. O'Regan, *Introduction to Software Quality*, Undergraduate Topics
in Computer Science, DOI 10.1007/978-3-319-06106-1_17,
© Springer International Publishing Switzerland 2014

The formal specification thus becomes the key reference point for the different parties involved in the construction of the system. It may be used as the reference point for the requirements; program implementation; testing and program documentation. It promotes a common understanding for all those concerned with the system. The term *"formal methods"* is used to describe a formal specification language and a method for the design and implementation of computer systems.

The specification is written in a mathematical language, and the implementation may be derived from the specification via step-wise refinement.[1] The refinement step makes the specification more concrete and closer to the actual implementation. There is an associated proof obligation to demonstrate that the refinement is valid, and that the concrete state preserves the properties of the abstract state. Thus, assuming that the original specification is correct and the proofs of correctness of each refinement step are valid, then there is a very high degree of confidence in the correctness of the implemented software. Step-wise refinement is illustrated as follows: the initial specification S is the initial model M_0; it is then refined into the more concrete model M_1, and M_1 is then refined into M_2, and so on until the eventual implementation $M_n = E$ is produced.

$$S = M_0 \subseteq M_1 \subseteq M_2 \subseteq M_3 \subseteq \ldots \ldots \subseteq M_n = E$$

Requirements are the foundation of the system to be built, and irrespective of the best design and development practices, the product will be incorrect if the requirements are incorrect. The objective of requirements validation is to ensure that the requirements reflect what is actually required by the customer (in order to build the right system). Formal methods may be employed to model the requirements, and the model exploration yields further desirable or undesirable properties. The ability to prove that certain properties are true of the specification is very valuable, especially in safety critical and security critical applications. These properties are logical consequences of the definition of the requirements, and, where appropriate, the requirements may be amended. Thus, formal methods may be employed in a sense to debug the requirements during requirements validation.

The use of formal methods generally leads to more robust software and to increased confidence in its correctness. The challenges involved in the deployment of formal methods in an organization include the education of staff in formal specification, as the use of these mathematical techniques may be a culture shock to many staff.

Formal methods have been applied to a diverse range of applications, including the security critical field; the safety critical field; the railway sector; microprocessor verification; the specification of standards, and the specification and verification of

---

[1] It is questionable whether step-wise refinement is cost effective in mainstream software engineering, as it involves re-writing a specification *ad nauseum*. It is time-consuming to proceed in refinement steps with significant time also required to prove that the refinement step is valid. It is more relevant to the safety-critical field. Others in the formal methods field may disagree with this position.

Table 17.1 Criticisms of formal methods

No.	Criticism
1.	Often the formal specification is as difficult to read as the program[a].
2.	Many formal specifications are wrong[b].
3.	Formal methods are strong on syntax but provide little assistance in deciding on what technical information should be recorded using the syntax[c].
4.	Formal specifications provide a model of the proposed system. However, a precise unambiguous mathematical statement of the requirements is what is needed[d].
5.	Step-wise refinement is unrealistic. It is like, for example, deriving a bridge from the description of a river and the expected traffic on the bridge. There is always a need for the creative step in design[e].
6.	Much unnecessary mathematical formalisms have been developed rather than using the available classical mathematics[f].

[a]Of course, others might reply by saying that some of Parnas's tables are not exactly intuitive, and that the notation he employs in some of his tables is quite unfriendly. The usability of all of the mathematical approaches needs to be enhanced if they are to be taken seriously by industrialists

[b]Obviously, the formal specification must be analysed using mathematical reasoning and tools to provide confidence in its correctness. The validation of a formal specification can be carried out using mathematical proof of key properties of the specification; software inspections; or specification animation

[c]Approaches such as VDM include a method for software development as well as the specification language

[d]Models are extremely valuable as they allow simplification of the reality. A mathematical study of the model demonstrates whether it is a suitable representation of the system. Models allow properties of the proposed requirements to be studied prior to implementation

[e]Step-wise refinement involves rewriting a specification with each refinement step producing a more concrete specification (that includes code and formal specification) until eventually the detailed code is produced. However, tool support may make refinement easier

[f]Approaches such as VDM or Z are useful in that they add greater rigour to the software development process. They are reasonably easy to learn, and there have been some good results obtained by their use. Classical mathematics is familiar to students and therefore it is desirable that new formalisms are introduced only where absolutely necessary

programs. Parnas and others have criticized formal methods on the grounds mentioned in Table 17.1.

However, formal methods are potentially quite useful and reasonably easy to use. The use of a formal method such as Z or VDM forces the software engineer to be precise and helps to avoid ambiguities present in natural language. Clearly, a formal specification should be subject to peer review to provide confidence in its correctness. New formalisms need to be intuitive to be usable by practitioners. The advantage of classical mathematics is that it is familiar to students.

17.2   Why Should We Use Formal Methods?

There is a strong motivation to use best practice in software engineering in order to produce software adhering to high quality standards. Quality problems with software may cause minor irritations or major damage to a customer's business including loss of life. Formal methods are a leading-edge technology that may be of benefit to companies in reducing the occurrence of defects in software products. Brown [55] argues that for the safety critical field that:

Comment 17.1 (Missile Safety) *Missile systems must be presumed dangerous until shown to be safe, and that the absence of evidence for the existence of dangerous errors does not amount to evidence for the absence of danger.*

This suggests that companies will need to demonstrate that every reasonable practice was taken to prevent the occurrence of defects. One such practice is the use of formal methods, and its exclusion may need to be justified in some domains. It is quite possible that a software company may be sued for software which injures a third party, and this suggests that companies will need a rigorous quality assurance system to prevent the occurrence of defects.

There is some evidence to suggest that the use of formal methods provides savings in the cost of the project. For example, a 9 % cost saving is attributed to the use of formal methods during the CICS project; the T800 project attributes a 12-month reduction in testing time to the use of formal methods. These are discussed in more detail in chapter one of [26].

The use of formal methods is mandatory in certain circumstances. The Ministry of Defence in the United Kingdom issued two safety-critical standards[2] in the early 1990s related to the use of formal methods in the software development lifecycle.

The first is Defence Standard 00-55, *"The Procurement of safety critical software in defense equipment"* [44] which makes it mandatory to employ formal methods in safety-critical software development in the UK; and mandates the use of formal proof that the most crucial programs correctly implement their specifications.

The other is Def. Stan 00-56 *"Hazard analysis and safety classification of the computer and programmable electronic system elements of defense equipment"* [45]. The objective of this standard is to provide guidance to identify which systems or parts of systems being developed are safety-critical and thereby require the use of formal methods. This proposed system is subject to an initial hazard analysis to determine whether there are safety-critical parts.

The reaction to these defence standards 00-55 and 00-56 was quite hostile initially, as most suppliers were unlikely to meet the technical and organization requirements of the standard. This is described in [65].

17.3   Applications of Formal Methods

Formal methods have been employed to verify correctness in the nuclear power industry, the aerospace industry, the security technology area, and the railroad domain. These sectors are subject to stringent regulatory controls to ensure safety

[2] The U.K. Defence Standards 0055 and 0056 have been revised in recent years to be less prescriptive on the use of formal methods.

and security. Several organizations have piloted formal methods with varying degrees of success. These include IBM, who developed VDM at its laboratory in Vienna; IBM (Hursley, England) piloted the *Z* formal specification language on the CICS (Customer Information Control System) project.

The mathematical techniques developed by Parnas (i.e., requirements model and tabular expressions) have been employed to specify the requirements of the A-7 aircraft as part of a research project for the US Navy.[3] Tabular expressions have also been employed for the software inspection of the automated shutdown software of the Darlington Nuclear power plant in Canada.[4] These are two successful uses of mathematical techniques in software engineering.

There are examples of the use of formal methods in the railway domain, and examples dealing with the modelling and verification of a railroad gate controller and railway signalling are described in [26]. Clearly, it is essential to verify safety critical properties such as *"when the train goes through the level crossing then the gate is closed"*.

17.4 Tools for Formal Methods

A key criticism of formal methods is the limited availability of tools to support the software engineer in writing the formal specification and in conducting proof. Many of the early tools were criticized as not being of industrial strength. However, in recent years more advanced tools to support the software engineer's work in formal specification and formal proof have become available, and this is likely to continue in the coming years.

The tools include syntax checkers that determine whether the specification is syntactically correct; specialized editors which ensure that the written specification is syntactically correct; tools to support refinement; automated code generators that generate a high-level language corresponding to the specification; theorem provers to demonstrate the presence or absence of key properties and to prove the correctness of refinement steps, and to identify and resolve proof obligations; and specification animation tools where the execution of the specification can be simulated.

The *B*-Toolkit from *B*-Core is an integrated set of tools that supports the *B*-Method. These include syntax and type checking, specification animation, proof obligation generator, an auto-prover, a proof assistor, and code generation. This allows, in theory, a complete formal development from initial specification to

---

[3] However, the resulting software was never actually deployed on the A-7 aircraft.

[4] This was an impressive use of mathematical techniques and it has been acknowledged that formal methods must play an important role in future developments at Darlington. However, given the time and cost involved in the software inspection of the shutdown software some managers have less enthusiasm in shifting from hardware to software controllers [22].

final implementation to be achieved, with every proof obligation justified, leading to a provably correct program.

The IFAD Toolbox[5] is a support tool for the VDM-SL specification language, and it includes support for syntax and type checking, an interpreter and debugger to execute and debug the specification, and a code generator to convert from VDM-SL to C++. It also includes support for graphical notations such as the OMT/UML design notations.

17.5   Approaches to Formal Methods

There are two key approaches to formal methods: namely the *model-oriented approach* of VDM or Z, and the *algebraic* or *axiomatic approach* of the process calculi such as the calculus communicating systems (CCS) or communicating sequential processes (CSP).

17.5.1 Model-Oriented Approach

The model-oriented approach to specification is based on mathematical models, and a model is a mathematical representation or abstraction of a physical entity or system. The model aims to provide a mathematical explanation of the behaviour of the physical world, and it is considered suitable if its properties closely match those of the system, and if its calculations match and simplify calculations in the real world. A model will allow predictions of future behaviour to be made. There are many models employed in the physical world such as models of the weather system that allow weather predictions to be made.

It is fundamental to explore the model to determine its adequacy, and to determine the extent to which it explains the underlying physical behaviour, and allows predictions of future behaviour to be made. This will determine its acceptability as a representation of the physical world. Models that are ineffective will be replaced with models that offer a better explanation of the manifested physical behaviour. There are many examples in science of the replacement of one theory by a newer one. For example, the Copernican model of the universe replaced the older Ptolemaic model, and Newtonian physics was replaced by Einstein's theories on relativity. The structure of the revolutions that take place in science are described in [36].

The model-oriented approach to software development involves defining an abstract model of the proposed software system. The model acts as a representation of the proposed system, and the model is then explored to assess its suitability. The exploration of the model takes the form of model interrogation, i.e., asking questions and determining the effectiveness of the model in answering the

---

[5] The IFAD Toolbox has been renamed to VDM Tools as IFAD sold the VDM Tools to CSK in Japan. The tools are expected to be available worldwide and to be improved further.

questions. The modelling in formal methods is typically performed via elementary discrete mathematics, including set theory, sequences, functions and relations.

VDM and Z are model-oriented approaches to formal methods. VDM arose from work done in the IBM laboratory in Vienna in formalizing the semantics for the PL/1 compiler, and it was later applied to the specification of software systems. The origin of the Z specification language is in work done at Oxford University in the early 1980s.

17.5.2 Modelling

The world is dominated by models: for example, models of weather systems as used by meteorologists; models of the economy as used by Economists; models of population growth; and models of the solar system, for example, the Ptolemaic model and the Copernican model. Modelling can play a key role in computer science, as computer systems tend to be highly complex, whereas a model allows simplification or abstraction of the underlying complexity, and enables a richer understanding of the underlying reality to be gained.

There may be more than one model of a particular entity, for example, the Ptolemaic model and the Copernican model are different models of the solar system. This leads to the question as to which is the best or most appropriate model to use, and to what criteria should be employed to determine whether a model is good. The choice is generally influenced by the ability of the model to explain the behaviour, its simplicity, and its elegance.

The importance of models is that they serve to explain the behaviour of a particular entity and may also be used to predict future behaviour. Different models may vary in their ability to explain aspects of the entity under study. One model may be good at explaining some aspects of the behaviour under study, whereas another model might be good at explaining other aspects. The adequacy of a model is a key concept in modelling, and the adequacy is determined by the effectiveness of the model in representing the underlying behaviour, and its ability to predict future behaviour. Model exploration consists of asking questions, and determining whether the model is able to give an effective answer to the particular question. A good model is chosen as a representation of the real world, and is referred to whenever there are questions in relation to the aspect of the real world.

The model is a simplification or abstraction of the real world and will contain only the essential details. For example, the model of an aircraft is hardly likely to include the colour of the aircraft and instead the objective may be to model the aerodynamics of the aircraft. The principle of *"Ockham's Razor"* is used in modelling and in model simplification. The objective is to choose only those entities in the model which are absolutely necessary to explain the behaviour of the world.

The software domain has applied models of software development to assist with the complexities in software development. These include the Capability Maturity Model (CMM), which is employed as a framework to enhance the capability of the

organization in software development; UML which is employed to model
requirements with graphical notations; and mathematical models derived from
formal specifications.

17.5.3 Axiomatic Approach

The axiomatic approach focuses on the properties that the proposed system is to
satisfy, and there is no intention to produce an abstract model of the system. The
required properties and behaviour of the system are stated in mathematical notation.
The difference between the axiomatic specification and a model-based approach is
may be seen in the example of a stack.

The stack includes operators for pushing an element onto the stack and popping
an element from the stack. The properties of *pop* and *push* are explicitly defined in
the axiomatic approach. The model-oriented approach constructs an explicit model
of the stack and the operations are defined in terms of the effect that they have on
the model. The specification of the *pop* operation on a stack is given by axiomatic
properties, for example, *pop(push(s, x)) = s*.

Comment 17.2 (Axiomatic Approach) *The property-oriented approach has the
advantage that the implementer is not constrained to a particular choice of
implementation, and the only constraint is that the implementation must satisfy
the stipulated properties.*

The emphasis is on specifying the required properties of the system, and
implementation issues are avoided. The properties are typically stated using mathematical logic or higher-order logics. Mechanized theorem-proving techniques may
be employed to prove results.

One potential problem with the axiomatic approach is that the properties
specified may not be realized in any implementation. Thus, whenever a "formal
axiomatic theory" is developed a corresponding "model" of the theory must be
identified, in order to ensure that the properties may be realized in practice. That is,
when proposing a system that is to satisfy some set of properties, there is a need to
prove that there is at least one system that will satisfy the set of properties.

17.6   Proof and Formal Methods

The word "*proof*" has several connotations in various disciplines; for example, in a
court of law, the defendant is assumed innocent until proven guilty. The proof of the
guilt of the defendant may take the form of certain facts in relation to the
movements of the defendant, the defendant's circumstances, the defendant's alibi,
statements taken from witnesses, rebuttal arguments from the defence, and certain

theories produced by the prosecution or defence. Ultimately, in the case of a trial by jury, the defendant is judged guilty or not guilty depending on the extent to which the jury has been convinced by the arguments made by the prosecution and defence.

A mathematical proof typically includes natural language and mathematical symbols, and often many of the tedious details of the proof are omitted. The proof may employ a "*divide and conquer*" technique; i.e., breaking the conjecture down into sub-goals and then attempting to prove the sub-goals. Many proofs in formal methods are concerned with crosschecking the details of the specification or checking the validity of refinement steps, or checking that certain properties are satisfied by the specification. There are often many tedious lemmas to be proved, and theorem provers[6] are essential in assisting with this. Machine proof needs to be explicit, and reliance on some brilliant insight is avoided. Proofs by hand are notorious for containing errors or jumps in reasoning, while machine proofs are explicit but are often extremely lengthy and unreadable. For example, the actual machine proof of correctness of the VIPER microprocessor[7] [65] consisted of several million formulae.

A formal mathematical proof consists of a sequence of formulae, where each element is either an axiom or derived from a previous element in the series by applying a fixed set of mechanical rules.

Theorem provers are invaluable in resolving many of the thousands of proof obligations that arise from a formal specification, and the application of formal methods in an industrial environment requires the use of machine-assisted proof. Automated theorem proving is difficult, as often mathematicians prove a theorem with an initial intuitive feeling that the theorem is true. Human intervention to provide guidance or intuition improves the effectiveness of the theorem prover.

The proof of various properties about a program increases confidence in its correctness. However, an absolute proof of correctness[8] is unlikely except for the most trivial of programs. A program may consist of legacy software that is assumed to work; a compiler that is assumed to work correctly creates it. Theorem provers are programs that are assumed to function correctly. The best that formal methods can claim is increased confidence in correctness of the software, rather than an absolute proof of correctness.

---

[6] Most existing theorem provers are difficult to use and are for specialist use only. There is a need to improve the usability of theorem provers.

[7] This verification was controversial with RSRE and Charter overselling VIPER as a chip design that conforms to its formal specification.

[8] This position is controversial with others arguing that if correctness is defined mathematically then the mathematical definition (i.e., formal specification) is a theorem, and the task is to prove that the program satisfies the theorem. They argue that the proofs for non-trivial programs exist, and that the reason why there are not many examples of such proofs is due to a lack of mathematical specifications.

17.7   The Future of Formal Methods

The debate concerning the level of use of mathematics in software engineering is still ongoing. Many practitioners are against the use of mathematics and avoid its use. They tend to employ methodologies such as software inspections and testing to improve confidence in the correctness of the software. They argue that in the current competitive industrial environment where time to market is a key driver that the use of such formal mathematical techniques would seriously impact the market opportunity. Industrialists often need to balance conflicting needs such as quality; cost; and delivering on time. They argue that the commercial necessities require methodologies and techniques that allow them to achieve their business goals effectively.

The other camp argues that the use of mathematics is essential in the delivery of high-quality and reliable software, and that if a company does not place sufficient emphasis on quality it will pay the price in terms of poor quality and its reputation in the market place.

It is generally accepted that mathematics and formal methods must play a role in the safety critical and security critical fields. Apart from that the extent of the use of mathematics is a hotly disputed topic. The pace of change in the world is extraordinary, and companies face significant competitive forces in a global market place. It is unrealistic to expect companies to deploy formal methods unless they have clear evidence that it will support them in delivering commercial products to the market place ahead of their competition, at the right price and with the right quality. Formal methods need to prove that it can do this if it wishes to be taken seriously in mainstream software engineering. The issue of technology transfer of formal methods to industry is discussed in [48].

17.8   The Vienna Development Method

VDM dates from work done by the IBM research laboratory in Vienna. This group was specifying the semantics of the PL/1 programming language using an operational semantic approach. That is, the semantics of the language were defined in terms of a hypothetical machine which interprets the programs of that language [5, 6]. Later work led to the Vienna Development Method (VDM) with its specification language, Meta IV. This was used to give the denotational semantics of programming languages; i.e., a mathematical object (set, function, etc.) is associated with each phrase of the language [6]. The mathematical object is termed the *denotation* of the phrase.

VDM is a *model-oriented approach* and this means that an explicit model of the state of an abstract machine is given, and operations are defined in terms of this state. Operations may act on the system state, taking inputs, and producing outputs as well as a new system state. Operations are defined in a precondition and post-condition style. Each operation has an associated proof obligation to ensure that if the precondition is true, then the operation preserves the system invariant. The initial state itself is, of course, required to satisfy the system invariant.

VDM uses keywords to distinguish different parts of the specification, e.g., preconditions, post-conditions, as introduced by the keywords *pre* and *post* respectively. In keeping with the philosophy that formal methods specifies *what* a system does as distinct from *how*, VDM employs post-conditions to stipulate the effect of the operation on the state. The previous state is then distinguished by employing *hooked variables*, e.g., v¬, and the post-condition specifies the new state which is defined by a logical predicate relating the pre-state to the post-state.

VDM is more than its specification language VDM-SL, and is, in fact, a software development method, with rules to verify the steps of development. The rules enable the executable specification, i.e., the detailed code, to be obtained from the initial specification via refinement steps. Thus, we have a sequence $S = S_0$, $S_1, \ldots, S_n = E$ of specifications, where S is the initial specification, and E is the final (executable) specification.

Retrieval functions enable a return from a more concrete specification to the more abstract specification. The initial specification consists of an initial state, a system state, and a set of operations. The system state is a particular domain, where a domain is built out of primitive domains such as the set of natural numbers, etc., or constructed from primitive domains using domain constructors such as Cartesian product, disjoint union, etc. A domain-invariant predicate may further constrain the domain, and a *type* in VDM reflects a domain obtained in this way. Thus, a type in VDM is more specific than the signature of the type, and thus represents values in the domain defined by the signature, which satisfy the domain invariant. In view of this approach to types, it is clear that VDM types may not be "statically type checked".

VDM specifications are structured into modules, with a module containing the module name, parameters, types, operations, etc. Partial functions occur frequently in computer science as many functions, may be undefined, or fail to terminate for some arguments in their domain. VDM addresses partial functions by employing nonstandard logical operators, namely the logic of partial functions (LPFs) discussed in [48].

VDM has been used in industrial projects, and its tool support includes the IFAD Toolbox.[9] VDM is described in more detail in [48]. There are several variants of VDM, including VDM++, the object-oriented extension of VDM, and the Irish school of the VDM, which is discussed in the next Section.

17.9   VDM*, the Irish School of VDM

The Irish School of VDM is a variant of standard VDM, and is characterized by [39] its constructive approach, classical mathematical style, and its terse notation. This method aims to combine the *what* and *how* of formal methods in that its terse

---

[9] The VDM Tools are now available from the CSK Group in Japan.

specification style stipulates in concise form *what* the system should do; furthermore, the fact that its specifications are constructive (or functional) means that the *how* is included with the *what*. However, it is important to qualify this by stating that the how as presented by VDM⁺ is not directly executable, as several of its mathematical data types have no corresponding structure in high-level programming languages or functional languages. Thus, a conversion or reification of the specification into a functional or higher-level language must take place to ensure a successful execution. Further, the fact that a specification is constructive is no guarantee that it is a good implementation strategy, if the construction itself is naive.

The Irish school follows a similar development methodology as in standard VDM, and is a model-oriented approach. The initial specification is presented, with initial state and operations defined. The operations are presented with preconditions; however, no post-condition is necessary as the operation is "functionally" (i.e., explicitly) constructed.

There are proof obligations to demonstrate that the operations preserve the invariant. That is, if the precondition for the operation is true, and the operation is performed, then the system invariant remains true after the operation. The philosophy is to exhibit existence *constructively* rather than a theoretical proof of existence that demonstrates the existence of a solution without presenting an algorithm to construct the solution.

The school avoids the existential quantifier of predicate calculus and reliance on logic in proof is kept to a minimum, and emphasis instead is placed on equational reasoning. Structures with nice algebraic properties are sought, and one nice algebraic structure employed is the monoid, which has closure, associativity, and a unit element. The concept of isomorphism is powerful, reflecting that two structures are essentially identical, and thus we may choose to work with either, depending on which is more convenient for the task in hand.

The school has been influenced by the work of Polya and Lakatos. The former [54] advocated a style of problem solving characterized by first considering an easier sub-problem, and considering several examples. This generally leads to a clearer insight into solving the main problem. Lakatos's approach to mathematical discovery [37] is characterized by heuristic methods. A primitive conjecture is proposed and if global counter-examples to the statement of the conjecture are discovered, then the corresponding *hidden lemma* for which this global counterexample is a local counter example is identified and added to the statement of the primitive conjecture. The process repeats, until no more global counterexamples are found. A sceptical view of absolute truth or certainty is inherent in this.

Partial functions are the norm in VDM⁺, and as in standard VDM, the problem is that functions may be undefined, or fail to terminate for several of the arguments in their domain. The logic of partial functions (LPFs) is avoided, and instead care is taken with recursive definitions to ensure termination is achieved for each argument. Academic and industrial projects have been conducted using the method of the Irish school, but at this stage tool support is limited.

17.10 The Z Specification Language

Z is a formal specification language founded on Zermelo set theory, and Abrial developed it at Oxford University in the early 1980s. It is used for the formal specification of software and is a model-oriented approach. An explicit model of the state of an abstract machine is given, and the operations are defined in terms of the effect on the state. It includes a mathematical notation that is similar to VDM and the visually striking schema calculus. The latter consists essentially of boxes (or schemas), and these are used to describe operations and states. The schema calculus enables schemas to be used as building blocks and combined with other schemas. The Z specification language was published as an ISO standard (ISO/IEC 13568:2002) in 2002.

The schema calculus is a powerful means of decomposing a specification into smaller pieces or schemas. This helps to make Z specification highly readable, as each individual schema is small in size and self-contained. The exception handling is done by defining schemas for the exception cases, and these are then combined with the original operation schema. Mathematical data types are used to model the data in a system and these data types obey mathematical laws. These laws enable simplification of expressions and are useful with proofs.

Operations are defined in a precondition/post-condition style. However, the precondition is implicitly defined within the operation; i.e., it is not separated out as in standard VDM. Each operation has an associated proof obligation to ensure that if the precondition is true, then the operation preserves the system invariant. The initial state itself is, of course, required to satisfy the system invariant. Post-conditions employ a logical predicate which relates the pre-state to the post-state, and the post-state of a variable v is given by priming, e.g., v'. Various conventions are employed, e.g., $v?$ indicates that v is an input variable and $v!$ indicates that v is an output variable. The symbol $\Xi\,Op$ operation indicates that this operation does not affect the state, whereas $\Delta\,Op$ indicates that this operation affects the state.

Many data types employed in Z have no counterpart in standard programming languages. It is therefore important to identify and describe the concrete data structures that will ultimately represent the abstract mathematical structures. The operations on the abstract data structures may need to be refined to yield operations on the concrete data structure that yield equivalent results. For simple systems, direct refinement (i.e., one step from abstract specification to implementation) may be possible; in more complex systems, deferred refinement is employed, where a sequence of increasingly concrete specifications are produced to yield the executable specification eventually.

Z has been successfully applied in industry, and one of its well-known successes is the CICS project at IBM Hursley in England. Z is described in more detail in the next chapter.

17.11 The *B* Method

The *B-Technologies* [42] consist of three components: a method for software development, namely the *B*-Method; a supporting set of tools, namely, the *B*-Toolkit; and a generic program for symbol manipulation, namely, the *B*-Tool (from which the *B*-Toolkit is derived). The *B*-Method is a model-oriented approach and is closely related to the *Z* specification language. Abrial developed the B specification language, and every construct in the language has a set theoretic counterpart, and the method is founded on Zermelo set theory. Each operation has an explicit precondition.

A key role of the *abstract machine* in the *B*-Method is to provide encapsulation of variables representing the state of the machine and operations which manipulate the state. Machines may refer to other machines, and a machine may be introduced as a refinement of another machine. The abstract machines are specification machines, refinement machines, or implementable machines. The *B*-Method adopts a layered approach to design where the design is gradually made more concrete by a sequence of design layers. Each design layer is a refinement that involves a more detailed implementation in terms of the abstract machines of the previous layer. The design refinement ends when the final layer is implemented purely in terms of library machines. Any refinement of a machine by another has associated proof obligations, and proof is required to verify the validity of the refinement step.

Specification animation of the Abstract Machine Notation (AMN) specification is possible with the *B*-Toolkit, and this enables typical usage scenarios n to be explored for requirements validation. This is, in effect, an early form of testing, and it may be used to demonstrate the presence or absence of desirable or undesirable behaviour. Verification takes the form of a proof to demonstrate that the invariant is preserved when the operation is executed within its precondition, and this is performed on the AMN specification with the *B*-Toolkit.

The *B*-Toolkit provides several tools that support the *B*-Method, and these include syntax and type checking; specification animation, proof obligation generator, auto prover, proof assistor, and code generation. Thus, in theory, a complete formal development from initial specification to final implementation may be achieved, with every proof obligation justified, leading to a provably correct program.

The *B*-Method and toolkit have been successfully applied in industrial applications, including the CICS project at IBM Hursley in the United Kingdom [28]. The automated support provided has been cited as a major benefit of the application of the *B*-Method and the *B*-Toolkit.

17.12 Predicate Transformers and Weakest Preconditions

The precondition of a program S is a predicate, i.e., a statement that may be true or false, and it is usually required to prove that if the precondition Q is true then execution of S is guaranteed to terminate in a finite amount of time in a state satisfying R. This is written as $\{Q\}\ S\ \{R\}$.

The weakest precondition (cf. p. 109 of [25]) of a command S with respect to a post-condition R represents the set of all states such that if execution begins in any one of these states, then execution will terminate in a finite amount of time in a state with R true. These set of states may be represented by a predicate Q', so that wp $(S,R) = wp_S(R) = Q'$, and so wp_S is a predicate transformer: i.e., it may be regarded as a function on predicates. The weakest precondition is the precondition that places the fewest constraints on the state than all of the other preconditions of (S,R). That is, all of the other preconditions are stronger than the weakest precondition.

The notation $Q\{S\}R$ is used to denote partial correctness and indicates that if execution of S commences in any state satisfying Q, and if execution terminates, then the final state will satisfy R. Often, a predicate Q which is stronger than the weakest precondition $wp(S,R)$ is employed, especially where the calculation of the weakest precondition is nontrivial. Thus, a stronger predicate Q such that $Q \Rightarrow wp$ (S,R) is often employed.

There are many properties associated with the weakest preconditions, and these may be used to simplify expressions involving weakest preconditions, and in determining the weakest preconditions of various program commands such as assignments, iterations, etc. Weakest preconditions may be used in developing a proof of correctness of a program in parallel with its development [48].

An imperative program may be regarded as a predicate transformer. This is since a predicate P characterises the set of states in which the predicate P is true, and an imperative program may be regarded as a binary relation on states, which may be extended to a function F, leading to the Hoare triple $P\{F\}Q$. That is, the program F acts as a predicate transformer with the predicate P regarded as an input assertion, i.e., a Boolean expression that must be true before the program F is executed, and the predicate Q is the output assertion, which is true if the program F terminates (where F commenced in a state satisfying P).

17.13   The Process Calculii

The objectives of the process calculi [27] are to provide mathematical models which provide insight into the diverse issues involved in the specification, design, and implementation of computer systems which continuously act and interact with their environment. These systems may be decomposed into sub-systems that interact with each other and their environment.

The basic building block is the *process*, which is a mathematical abstraction of the interactions between a system and its environment. A process that lasts indefinitely may be specified recursively. Processes may be assembled into systems they may execute concurrently, or communicate with each other. Process communication may be synchronized, and this takes the form of one process outputting a message simultaneously to another process inputting a message. Resources may be shared among several processes. Process calculi such as CSP [27] and CCS [43] have been developed to enrich the understanding of communication and concurrency, and these calculi obey a rich collection of mathematical laws.

The expression (a ? P) in CSP describes a process which first engages in event a, and then behaves as process P. A recursive definition is written as (μX)•$F(X)$ and an example of a simple chocolate vending machine is:

$$\mathrm{VMS} = \mu x : \{\mathrm{coin}, \mathrm{choc}\} \bullet (\mathrm{coin?}(\mathrm{choc?X}))$$

The simple vending machine has an alphabet of two symbols, namely, *coin* and *choc*. The behaviour of the machine is that a coin is entered into the machine, and then a chocolate selected and provided, and the machine is ready for further use.

CSP processes use channels to communicate values with their environment, and input on channel c is denoted by ($c?.x\,P_x$). This describes a process that accepts any value x on channel c, and then behaves as process P_x. In contrast, ($c!e\,P$) defines a process which outputs the expression e on channel c and then behaves as process P.

The π-calculus is a process calculus based on names. Communication between processes takes place between known channels, and the name of a channel may be passed over a channel. There is no distinction between channel names and data values in the π-calculus. The output of a value v on channel a is given by $\bar{a}v$; i.e., output is a negative prefix. Input on a channel a is given by $a(x)$, and is a positive prefix. Private links or restrictions are denoted by (x)P.

17.14 Finite State Machines

The neurophysiologists Warren McCulloch and Walter Pitts published early work on finite state automata in 1943. They were interested in modelling the thought process for humans and machines. Moore and Mealy developed this work further, and these finite-state machines are referred to as the "*Moore machine*" and the "*Mealy machine*". The Mealy machine determines its outputs through the current state and the input, whereas the output of Moore's machine is based upon the current state alone.

Definition 17.2 (Finite State Machine) *A finite state machine (FSM) is an abstract mathematical machine that consists of a finite number of states. It includes a start state q_0 in which the machine is in initially; a finite set of states Q; an input alphabet Σ; a state transition function δ; and a set of final accepting states F (where $F \subseteq Q$).*

The state transition function takes the current state and an input and returns the next state. That is, the transition function is of the form:

$$\delta : Q \times \Sigma \to Q$$

The transition function provides rules that define the action of the machine for each input, and it may be extended to provide output as well as a state transition. State diagrams are used to represent finite state machines, and each state accepts a

Fig. 17.1 Deterministic
finite state machine

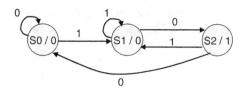

finite number of inputs. A finite state machine may be deterministic or non-deterministic, and a *deterministic machine* changes to exactly one state for each input transition, whereas a *non-deterministic machine* may have a choice of states to move to for a particular input (Fig. 17.1).

Finite state automata can compute only very primitive functions and are not an adequate model for computing. There are more powerful automata such as the *Turing machine* [50] that is essentially a finite automaton with an infinite storage (memory). Anything that is computable is computable by a Turing machine.

The memory of the Turing machine is a tape that consists of a potentially infinite number of one-dimensional cells. The Turing machine provides a mathematical abstraction of computer execution and storage, as well as providing a mathematical definition of an algorithm.

17.15   The Parnas Way

Parnas has been influential in the computing field, and his ideas on the specification, design, implementation, maintenance, and documentation of computer software remain important. He advocates a solid engineering approach and argues that the role of the engineer is to apply scientific principles and mathematics to design and develop products. He argues that computer scientists need to be educated as engineers to ensure that they have the appropriate background to build software correctly. His contributions to software engineering include:

- *Tabular Expressions*
  These are mathematical tables for specifying requirements and enable complex predicate logic expressions to be represented in a simpler form.
- *Mathematical Documentation*
  He advocates the use of precise mathematical documentation for requirements and design.
- *Requirements Specification*
  He advocates the use of mathematical relations to specify the requirements precisely.
- *Software Design*
  He developed *information hiding* that is used in object-oriented design,[10] and allows software to be designed for change. Every information-hiding module has

---

[10] It is surprising that many in the object-oriented world seem unaware that information hiding goes back to the early 1970s and many have never heard of Parnas.

an interface that provides the only means to access the services provided by the modules. The interface hides the module's implementation.

- *Software Inspections*
  His approach requires the reviewers to take an active part in the inspection. They are provided with a list of questions by the author and their analysis involves the production of mathematical table to justify the answers.
- *Predicate Logic*
  He developed an extension of the predicate calculus to deal with partial functions. This approach preserves the classical two-valued logic and deals with undefined values that may occur in predicate logic expressions.

17.16 Usability of Formal Methods

There are practical difficulties associated with the use of formal methods. It seems to be assumed that programmers and customers are willing to become familiar with the mathematics used in formal methods. There is little evidence to suggest that customers would be prepared to use formal methods.[11] Customers are concerned with their own domain and speak the technical language of that domain.[12] Often, the use of mathematics is an alien activity that bears little resemblance to their normal work. Programmers are interested in programming rather than in mathematics, and generally are not interested in becoming mathematicians.[13]

However, the mathematics involved in most formal methods is reasonably elementary, and, in theory, if both customers and programmers are willing to learn the formal mathematical notation, then a rigorous validation of the formal specification can take place to verify its correctness. Both parties can review the formal specification to ensure its correctness, and the code can be verified to be correct with respect to the formal specification. It is usually possible to get a developer to learn a formal method, as a programmer has some experience of mathematics and logic; however, in practice, it is more difficult to get a customer to learn a formal method.

This often means that a formal specification of the requirements and an informal definition of the requirements using a natural language are maintained. It is essential that both of these are consistent and that there is a rigorous validation of the formal specification. Otherwise, if the programmer proves the correctness of the code with respect to the formal specification, and the formal specification is

---

[11] The domain in which the software is being used will influence the willingness or otherwise of the customers to become familiar with the mathematics required. Certainly, in mainstream software engineering the author does not detect any interest from customers and the perception is that formal methods are unusable; however, in some domains such as the regulated sector there is a greater willingness of customers to become familiar with the mathematical notation.

[12] The author's experience is that most customers have a very limited interest and even less willingness to use mathematics. There are exceptions to this especially in the regulated sector.

[13] Mathematics that is potentially useful to software engineers is discussed in [13, 47].

Table 17.2 Techniques for validation of formal specification

Technique	Description
Proof	This involves demonstrating that the formal specification satisfies key properties of the requirements. The implementation will need to preserve these properties.
Software inspections	This involves a Fagan like inspection to compare an informal set of requirements (unless the customer has learned the formal method) with the formal specification, and to ensure consistency between them.
Specification animation	This involves program (or specification) execution as a way to validate the formal specification. It is similar to testing.
Tools	Tools provide some limited support in validating a formal specification.

Table 17.3 Why are formal methods difficult?

Factor	Description
Notation/Intuition	The notation employed differs from that employed in mathematics. Intuition varies from person to person. Many programmers find the notation in formal methods to be unintuitive.
Formal specification	It is easier to read a formal specification than to write one.
Validation of formal specification	The validation of a formal specification using proof techniques or a Fagan like inspection is difficult.
Refinement[a]	The refinement of a formal specification into successive more concrete specifications with proof of validity of each refinement step is difficult and time consuming.
Proof	Proof can be difficult and time consuming.
Tool support	Many of the existing tools are difficult to use.

[a]The author doubts that refinement is cost effective for mainstream software engineering. However, it may be useful in the regulated environment

incorrect, then the formal development of the software is incorrect. There are several techniques to validate a formal specification and these are described in [66] Table 17.2.

17.16.1 Why Are Formal Methods difficult?

Formal methods are perceived as being difficult to use and of providing limited value in mainstream software engineering. Programmers receive some training in mathematics as part of their education. However, in practice, most programmers who learn formal methods at university never use formal methods again once they take an industrial position.

It may well be that the very nature of formal methods is such that it is suited only for specialists with a strong background in mathematics. Some of the reasons why formal methods are perceived as being difficult are given in Table 17.3.

Table 17.4 Characteristics of a usable formal method

Characteristic	Description
Intuitive	A formal method should be intuitive.
Teachable	A formal method needs to be teachable to the average software engineer. The training should include (at least) writing practical formal specifications.
Tool support	Good tools to support formal specification, validation, refinement and proof are required.
Adaptable to change	Change is common in a software engineering environment. A usable formal method should be adaptable to change.
Technology transfer path	The process for software development needs to be defined to include formal methods. The migration to formal methods needs to be managed.
Cost[a]	The use of formal methods should be cost effective with a return on investment. There should be benefits in time, quality and productivity.

[a] A commercial company will expect a return on investment from the use of a new technology. This may be reduced software development costs, improved quality and improved timeliness of projects, and improvements in productivity. A company does not go to the trouble of deploying a new technology just to satisfy academic interest

17.16.2 Characteristics of a Usable Formal Method

It is important to investigate ways by which formal methods can be made more usable to software engineers. This may involve designing more usable notations and better tools to support the process. Practical training and coaching to employees can help. Some of the characteristics of a usable formal method are given in Table 17.4.

17.17 Review Questions

1. What are formal methods and describe their potential benefits? How essential is tool support?
2. What is stepwise refinement and is it realistic in mainstream software engineering?
3. Discuss Parnas's criticisms of formal methods and discuss whether his views are valid.
4. Discuss the applications of formal methods and which areas have benefited most from their use? What problems have arisen?
5. Describe a technology transfer path for the potential deployment of formal methods in an organization.
6. Explain the difference between the model-oriented approach and the axiomatic approach.
7. Discuss the nature of proof in formal methods and tools to support proof.
8. Discuss the Vienna Development Method and explain the difference between standard VDM and VDM$^{\clubsuit}$.
9. Discuss Z and B ? Describe the tools in the B-Toolkit.
10. Discuss process calculi such as CSP, CCS or π–calculus.

17.18 Summary

This chapter discussed formal methods which offer a rigorous approach to the development of high-quality software. Formal methods employ mathematical techniques for the specification and formal development of software, and are useful in the safety critical field. They consist of formal specification languages or notations; a methodology for formal software development; and a set of tools to support the syntax checking of the specification, as well as the proof of properties of the specification.

Formal methods may be model oriented or axiomatic oriented. The model-oriented approach includes formal methods such as VDM, Z and B. The axiomatic approach includes the process calculi such as CSP, CCS and the π calculus. VDM was developed at the IBM lab in Vienna, and has been used in academia and industry. CSP was developed by C.A.R. Hoare and CCS by Robin Milner.

Formal methods allow questions to be asked and answered about what the system does independently of the implementation. They offer a way to debug the requirements, and to show that certain desirable properties are true of the specification, whereas certain undesirable properties are absent.

The use of formal methods generally leads to more robust software and to increased confidence in its correctness. There are challenges involved in the deployment of formal methods, as the use of these mathematical techniques may be a culture shock to many staff.

The usability of existing formal methods was considered, and reasons for their perceived difficulty considered. The characteristics of a usable formal method were explored.

There are various tools to support formal methods including syntax checkers; specialized editors; tools to support refinement; automated code generators that generate a high-level language corresponding to the specification; theorem provers; and specification animation tools where the execution of the specification can be simulated.

Z Formal Specification Language

18

Key Topics

Sets, relations and functions
Bags and sequences
Data Reification and Refinement
Schema Calculus
Proof in Z

18.1 Introduction

Z is a formal specification language based on Zermelo set theory. It was developed at the Programming Research Group at Oxford University in the early 1980s [18], and became an ISO standard in 2002. Z specifications are mathematical and employ a classical two-valued logic. The use of mathematics ensures precision, and allows inconsistencies and gaps in the specification to be identified. Theorem provers may be employed to demonstrate the correctness of the refinement steps, and that the software implementation meets its specification.

Z is a '*model oriented*' approach with an explicit model of the state of an abstract machine given, and operations are defined in terms of this state. Its mathematical notation is used for formal specification, and the schema calculus is used to structure the specifications. The latter is visually striking, and consists essentially of boxes, with these boxes or schemas used to describe operations and states. The schema calculus enables schemas to be used as building blocks and combined with other schemas. The simple schema in Fig. 18.1 is the specification of the positive square root of a real number.

G. O'Regan, *Introduction to Software Quality*, Undergraduate Topics
in Computer Science, DOI 10.1007/978-3-319-06106-1_18,
© Springer International Publishing Switzerland 2014

Fig. 18.1 Specification
of positive square root

$$
\begin{array}{|l}
\hline
\lnot SqRoot \rule{3em}{0.4pt} \\
\text{num?, } root! : \mathbb{R} \\
\hline
num? \geq 0 \\
root!^2 = num? \\
root! \geq 0 \\
\hline
\end{array}
$$

The schema calculus is a powerful means of decomposing a specification into smaller pieces or schemas. This helps to make Z specifications highly readable, as each individual schema is small in size and self-contained. Exception handling is addressed by defining schemas for the exception cases. These are then combined with the original operation schema. Mathematical data types are used to model the data in a system, these data types obey mathematical laws. These laws enable simplification of expressions, and are useful with proofs.

Operations are defined in a precondition/post-condition style. A precondition must be true before the operation is executed, and the post-condition must be true after the operation has executed. The precondition is implicitly defined within the operation. Each operation has an associated proof obligation to ensure that if the precondition is true, then the operation preserves the system invariant. The system invariant is a property of the system that must be true at all times. The initial state itself is, of course, required to satisfy the system invariant.

The precondition for the specification of the square root function above is that $num? \geq 0$; i.e., the function $SqRoot$ may be applied to positive real numbers only. The post-condition for the square root function is $root!^2 = num?$ and $root! \geq 0$. That is, the square root of the number is positive and its square gives the number. Post-conditions employ a logical predicate which relates the pre-state to the post-state, and the post-state of a variable being distinguished by priming the variable, e.g., v'.

Z is a typed language and whenever a variable is introduced its type must be given. A type is simply a collection of objects, and there are several standard types in Z. These include the natural numbers $\mathbb{N}$, the integers $\mathbb{Z}$ and the real numbers $\mathbb{R}$. The declaration of a variable x of type X is written $x : X$. It is also possible to create your own types in Z.

Various conventions are employed within Z specification, for example $v?$ indicates that v is an input variable; $v!$ indicates that v is an output variable. The variable $num?$ is an input variable and $root!$ is an output variable in the square root example above. The notation Ξ in a schema indicates that the operation Op does not affect the state; whereas the notation Δ in the schema indicates that Op is an operation that affects the state.

Many of the data types employed in Z have no counterpart in standard programming languages. It is therefore important to identify and describe the concrete data structures that ultimately will represent the abstract mathematical structures. As the concrete structures may differ from the abstract, the operations on the abstract data structures may need to be refined to yield operations on the concrete data that yield equivalent results. For simple systems, direct refinement (i.e., one step from abstract specification to implementation) may be possible; in more complex

Fig. 18.2 Specification
of a library system

$$
\begin{array}{l}
\text{--}Library\text{------} \\
\hline
on\text{-}shelf,\ missing,\ borrowed : \mathbb{P}\ Bkd\text{-}Id \\
\hline
on\text{-}shelf \cap missing = \varnothing \\
on\text{-}shelf \cap borrowed = \varnothing \\
borrowed \cap missing = \varnothing
\end{array}
$$

Fig. 18.3 Specification
of borrow operation

$$
\begin{array}{l}
\text{--}Borrow\text{------} \\
\Delta\ Library \\
b?\ :Bkd\text{-}Id \\
\hline
b? \in on\text{-}shelf \\
on\text{-}shelf' = on\text{-}shelf \setminus \{b?\} \\
borrowed' = borrowed \cup \{b?\}
\end{array}
$$

systems, deferred refinement[1] is employed, where a sequence of increasingly concrete specifications are produced to yield the executable specification. There is a calculus for combining schemas to make larger specifications, and this is discussed later in the chapter.

Example 18.1

Figure 18.2 gives a *Z* specification to borrow a book from a library system. The library is made up of books that are on the shelf; books that are borrowed; and books that are missing. The specification models a library with sets representing books on the shelf, on loan or missing. These are three mutually disjoint subsets of the set of books *Bkd-Id*.

The system state is defined in the *Library* schema in Fig. 18.2, and operations such as *Borrow* and *Return* affect the state. The *Borrow* operation is specified in Fig. 18.2.

The notation $\mathbb{P}\ Bkd\text{-}Id$ is used to represent the power set of *Bkd-Id* (i.e., the set of all subsets of *Bkd-Id*). The disjointness condition for the library is expressed by the requirement that the pairwise intersection of the subsets *on-shelf, borrowed, missing* is the empty set (Fig. 18.3).

The precondition for the *Borrow* operation is that the book must be available on the shelf to borrow. The post-condition is that the borrowed book is added to the set of borrowed books and is removed from the books on the shelf.

Z has been successfully applied in industry including the CICS project at IBM Hursley in the UK.[2] Next, we describe various parts of the *Z* specification language including sets, relations, functions, sequences and bags.

---

[1] Step-wise refinement involves producing a sequence of increasingly more concrete specifications until eventually the executable code is produced. Each refinement step has associated proof obligations to prove that the refinement step is valid.

[2] This project claimed a 9 % increase in productivity attributed to the use of formal methods.

18.2   Sets

Sets may be enumerated by listing all of their elements. Thus, the set of all even natural numbers less than or equal to 10 is:

$$\{2, 4, 6, 8, 10\}$$

Sets can be created from other sets using set comprehension: i.e., stating the properties that its members must satisfy. For example, the set of even natural numbers less than 10 is given by set comprehension as:

$$\{n : \mathbb{N} \mid n \neq 0 \wedge n < 10 \wedge n \bmod 2 = 0 \bullet n\}$$

There are three main parts to the set comprehension above. The first part is the signature of the set and this is given by $n : \mathbb{N}$ above. The first part is separated from the second part by a vertical line. The second part is given by a predicate, and for this example the predicate is $n \neq 0 \wedge n < 10 \wedge n \bmod 2 = 0$. The second part is separated from the third part by a bullet. The third part is a term, and it is simply n for this simple example. The term is often a more complex expression: e.g., $\log(n^2)$.

In mathematics, there is just one empty set. However, since Z is a typed set theory, there is an empty set for each type of set. Hence, there are an infinite number of empty sets in Z. The empty set is written as $\varnothing$ [X] where X is the type of the empty set. In practice, X is omitted when the type is clear.

Various set operations such as union, intersection, set difference, and symmetric difference are employed in Z. The power set of a set X is the set of all subsets of X, and is denoted by $\mathbb{P}X$. The set of non-empty subsets of X is denoted by $\mathbb{P}_1X$ where

$$\mathbb{P}_1X == \{U : \mathbb{P}\,X \mid U \neq \varnothing[X]\}$$

A finite set of elements of type X (denoted by F X) is a subset of X that cannot be put into a one to one correspondence with a proper subset of itself. This is defined formally as:

$$F\,X == \{U : \mathbb{P}\,X \mid \neg \exists V : \mathbb{P}\,U \bullet V \neq U \wedge (\exists f{:}V \rightarrowtail\!\!\!\rightarrow U)\}$$

The expression $f : V \rightarrowtail\!\!\!\rightarrow U$ denotes that f is a bijection from U to V and injective, surjective and bijective functions are discussed in [50].

The fact that Z is a typed language means that whenever a variable is introduced (e.g., in quantification with $\forall$ and $\exists$) it is first declared. For example, $\forall j{:}J \bullet P \Rightarrow Q$. There is also the unique existential quantifier $\exists_1 j{:}J \mid P$ which states that there is exactly one j of type J that has property P.

18.3   Relations

Relations are used extensively in Z and are discussed in [50]. A relation R between X and Y is any subset of the Cartesian product of X and Y; i.e., $R \subseteq (X \times Y)$, and the relation is denoted by $R : X \leftrightarrow Y$. The notation $x \mapsto y$ indicates that the pair $(x, y) \in R$.

Consider, the relation *home_owner : Person* ↔ *Home* that exists between people and their homes. An entry *daphne* ↦ *mandalay* ∈ *home_owner* if *daphne* is the owner of *mandalay*. It is possible for a person to own more than one home:

$$rebecca \mapsto nirvana \in home\_owner$$

$$rebecca \mapsto tivoli \in home\_owner$$

It is possible for two people to share ownership of a home:

$$rebecca \mapsto nirvana \in home\_owner$$

$$rebecca \mapsto nirvana \in home\_owner$$

There may be some people who do not own a home, and there is no entry for these people in the relation *home_owner*. The type *Person* includes every possible person, and the type *Home* includes every possible home. The domain of the relation *home_owner* is given by:

$$x \in \mathrm{dom}\ home\_owner \Leftrightarrow \exists h : Home \bullet x \mapsto h \in home\_owner.$$

The range of the relation *home_owner* is given by:

$$h \in \mathrm{ran}\ home\_owner \Leftrightarrow \exists x : Person \bullet x \mapsto h \in home\_owner.$$

The composition of two relations *home_owner: Person* ↔ *Home* and *home_value: Home* ↔ *Value* yields the relation *owner_wealth: Person* ↔ *Value* and is given by the relational composition *home_owner ; home_value* where:

$$p \mapsto \upsilon \in home\_owner; home\_owner \Leftrightarrow$$
$$\left(\exists h : Home \bullet p \mapsto h \in home\_owner \wedge h \mapsto \upsilon \in home\_value \right.$$

The relational composition may also be expressed as:

$$owner\_wealth = home\_value \; o \; home\_owner$$

The union of two relations often arises in practice. Suppose a new entry *aisling* ↦ *muckross* is to be added. Then this is given by

$$home\_owner' = home\_owner \cup \{aisling \mapsto muckross\}$$

Suppose that we are interested in knowing all females who are house owners. Then we restrict the relation *home_owner* so that the first element of all ordered pairs have to be female. Consider *female* : $\mathbb{P}$ *Person* with $\{aisling, rebecca\} \subseteq$ *female*.

$$home\_owner = \{aisling \mapsto muckross, rebecca \mapsto nirvana, \; lawrence \mapsto nirvana\}$$

$$female \lhd home\_owner = \{aisling \mapsto muckross, rebecca \mapsto nirvana\}$$

That is, *female* ▷ *home_owner* is a relation that is a subset of *home_owner*, and the first element of each ordered pair in the relation is female. The operation ▷ is termed domain restriction and its fundamental property is:

$$x \mapsto y \in U \lhd R \Leftrightarrow \left(x \in U \land x \mapsto y \in R \right\}$$

where R : X $\leftrightarrow$Y and $U : \mathbb{P}\, X$.

There is also a domain anti-restriction (subtraction) operation and its fundamental property is:

$$x \mapsto y \in U \lhd R \Leftrightarrow \left(x \in U \land x \mapsto y \in R \right\}$$

where R : X $\leftrightarrow$Y and $U : \mathbb{P}X$.

There are also range restriction (the ▷ operator) and the range anti-restriction operator (the ▷ operator). These are discussed in [18].

18.4   Functions

A function [18] is an association between objects of some type X and objects of another type Y such that given an object of type X, there exists only one object in Y associated with that object. That is, a function is a set of ordered pairs where the first element of the ordered pair has at most one element associated with it. A function is therefore a special type of relation, and a function may be *total* or *partial*.

A total function has exactly one element in Y associated with each element of X, whereas a partial function has at most one element of Y associated with each element of X (there may be elements of X that have no element of Y associated with them).

A partial function from X to Y (denoted $f : X \nrightarrow Y$) is a relation $f : X \leftrightarrow Y$ such that:

$$\forall x : X; y, z{:}Y \bullet (x \mapsto y \in f \land x \rightarrow z \in f \Rightarrow y = z)$$

The association between x and y is denoted by $f(x) = y$, and this indicates that the value of the partial function f at x is y. A total function from X to Y (denoted $f : X \rightarrow Y$) is a partial function such that every element in X is associated with some value of Y.

$$f : X \rightarrow Y \Leftrightarrow f : X \nrightarrow Y \land \operatorname{dom} f = X$$

Clearly, every total function is a partial function but not vice versa.

One operation that arises quite frequently in specifications is the function override operation. Consider the following specification of a temperature map:

```
-TempMap-----
  CityList : PCity
  temp : City --+> Z
  -----
  dom temp = CityList
```

Suppose the temperature map is given by $temp = \{Cork \mapsto 17, Dublin \mapsto 19, London \mapsto 15\}$. Then consider the problem of updating the temperature map if a new temperature reading is made in Cork say $\{Cork \mapsto 18\}$. Then the new temperature chart is obtained from the old temperature chart by function override to yield $\{Cork \mapsto 18, Dublin \mapsto 19, London \mapsto 15\}$. This is written as:

$$temp' = temp \oplus \{Cork \mapsto 18\}$$

The function override operation combines two functions of the same type to give a new function of the same type. The effect of the override operation is that the entry $\{Cork \mapsto 17\}$ is removed from the temperature chart and replaced with the entry $\{Cork \mapsto 18\}$.

Suppose $f, g : X \nrightarrow Y$ are partial functions then $f \oplus g$ is defined and indicates that f is overridden by g. It is defined as follows:

$$(f \oplus g)(x) = g(x) \text{where } x \in \operatorname{dom} g$$

$$(f \oplus g)(x) = f(x) \quad \text{where } x \notin \operatorname{dom} g \land x \in \operatorname{dom} f$$

This may also be expressed (using function override) as:

$$f \oplus g = ((\operatorname{dom} g) \ntriangleleft f) \cup g$$

There is notation in Z for injective, surjective and bijective functions. An injective function is one to one: i.e.,

$$f(x) = f(y) \Rightarrow x = y.$$

A surjective function is onto: i.e.,

$$\text{Given } y \in Y, \exists x \in X \text{ such that } f(x) = y$$

A bijective function is one to one and onto, and it indicates that the sets X and Y can be put into one to one correspondence with one another. Z includes lambda calculus notation (λ-notation) to define functions. For example, the function cube $== \lambda x:\mathbf{N} \bullet x * x * x$. Lambda calculus is discussed in [50]. Function composition $f \, ; g$ is similar to relational composition.

18.5 Sequences

The type of all sequences of elements drawn from a set X is denoted by Seq X. Sequences are written as $\langle x_1, x_2, \dots x_n \rangle$ and the empty sequence is denoted by $\langle \rangle$. Sequences may be used to specify the changing state of a variable over time with each element of the sequence representing the value of the variable at a discrete time instance.

Sequences are functions and a sequence of elements drawn from a set X is a finite function from the set of natural numbers to X. A finite partial function f from X to Y is denoted by $f: X \nrightarrow Y$. A finite sequence of elements of X is given by $f: \mathbf{N} \nrightarrow X$, and the domain of the function consists of all numbers between 1 and $\#f$. It is defined formally as:

$$\text{seq } X == \{ f: \mathbf{N} \nrightarrow X \mid \mathrm{dom}\, f = 1 \mathinner{\ldotp\ldotp} \#f \bullet f \}$$

The sequence $\langle x_1, x_2, \dots x_n \rangle$ above is given by:

$$\{ 1 \mapsto x_1, 2 \mapsto x_2, \dots n \mapsto x_n \}$$

There are various functions to manipulate sequences. These include the sequence concatenation operation. Suppose $\sigma = \langle x_1, x_2, \dots x_n \rangle$ and $\tau = \langle y_1, y_2, \dots y_m \rangle$ then:

$$\sigma ^\frown \tau = \langle x_1, x_2, \dots x_n, y_1, y_2, \dots y_m \rangle$$

The head of a non-empty sequence gives the first element of the sequence.

$$\text{head } \sigma = \text{head} \langle x_1, x_2, \dots x_n \rangle = x_1$$

The tail of a non-empty sequence is the same sequence except that the first element of the sequence is removed.

$$\text{tail } \sigma = \text{tail} \langle x_1, x_2, \dots x_n \rangle = \langle x_2, \dots x_n \rangle$$

Given $f : X \rightarrow Y$ and a sequence $\sigma :$ Seq X then the map function applies f to each element of σ:

$$\text{map} f \, \sigma = \text{map} f \langle x_1, x_2, \ldots x_n \rangle = \langle f(x_1), f(x_2), \ldots f(x_n) \rangle$$

The map function may also be expressed via function composition as:

$$\text{map} f \, \sigma = \sigma; f$$

The reverse order of a sequence is given by the rev function:

$$\text{rev} \, \sigma = \text{rev} \langle x_1, x_2, \ldots x_n \rangle = \langle x_n, \ldots x_2, x_1 \rangle$$

18.6   Bags

A bag is similar to a set except that it may contain multiple occurrences of each element. A bag of elements of type X is defined as a partial function from the type of the elements of the bag to positive whole numbers. Its definition is:

$$\text{bag} \, X == X \twoheadrightarrow \mathbb{N}_1.$$

For example, a bag of marbles may contain 3 blue marbles, 2 red marbles, and 1 green marble. This is denoted by $B = [b, b, b, g, r, r]$. The bag of marbles is thus denoted by:

$$\text{bag} \, Marble == Marble \twoheadrightarrow \mathbb{N}_1.$$

The function count determines the number of occurrences of an element in a bag. For the example above, count $Marble \, b = 3$, and count $Marble \, y = 0$ since there are no yellow marbles in the bag. This is defined formally as:

$$\text{count bag} X \, y = 0 \qquad\qquad y \notin \text{bag } X$$

$$\text{count bag} X \, y = (\text{bag} X)(y) \quad y \in \text{bag } X$$

An element y is in bag X if and only if y is in the domain of bag X.

$$y \text{ in bag} X \Leftrightarrow y \in \text{dom}(\text{bag} X)$$

The union of two bags of marbles $B_1 = [b, b, b, g, r, r]$ and $B_2 = [b, g, r, y]$ is given by $B_1 \uplus B_2 = [b, b, b, b, g, g, r, r, r, y]$. It is defined formally as:

$$(B_1 \uplus B_2) \, (y) = B_2(y) \qquad\qquad y \notin \text{dom } B_1 \wedge y \in \text{dom } B_2$$

$$(B_1 \uplus B_2) \, (y) = B_1(y) \qquad\qquad y \in \text{dom } B_1 \wedge y \notin \text{dom } B_2$$

$$(B_1 \uplus B_2) \, (y) = B_1(y) + B_2(y) \quad y \in \text{dom } B_1 \wedge y \in \text{dom } B_2$$

Fig. 18.4 Specification of
vending machine using bags

$$
\begin{array}{|l}
-\Delta Vending\ Machine\text{————} \\
stock\ :\ \text{bag}\ Good \\
price\ :\ Good \rightarrow \mathbb{N}_1 \\
\hline
\text{dom}\ stock \subseteq \text{dom}\ price
\end{array}
$$

A bag may be used to record the number of occurrences of each product in a warehouse as part of an inventory system. It may model the number of items remaining for each product in a vending machine (Fig. 18.4).

The operation of a vending machine would require other operations such as identifying the set of acceptable coins, checking that the customer has entered sufficient coins to cover the cost of the good, returning change to the customer, and updating the quantity on hand of each good after a purchase. A more detailed examination is in [18].

18.7   Schemas and Schema Composition

The schemas in Z are visually striking and the specification is presented in two-dimensional graphic boxes. Schemas are used for specifying states and state transitions, and they employ notation to represent the before and after state (e.g., s and s' where s' represents the after state of s). They group all relevant information that belongs to a state description.

There are a number of useful schema operations such as schema inclusion, schema composition, and the use of propositional connectives to link schemas together. The Δ convention indicates that the operation affects the state whereas the Ξ convention indicates that the state is not affected. These operations and conventions allow complex operations to be specified concisely, and assist with the readability of the Z specification. Schema composition is analogous to relational composition, and allows new schemas to be derived.

A schema name S_1 may be included in the declaration part of another schema S_2. The effect of the inclusion is that the declarations in S_1 are now part of S_2 and the predicates of S_1 are S_2 are joined together by conjunction. If the same variable is defined in both S_1 and S_2, then it must be of the same type in both schemas.

$$
\begin{array}{|l}
-S_1\text{——} \\
x,\ y\ :\ \mathbb{N} \\
\hline
x + y > 2
\end{array}
\qquad
\begin{array}{|l}
-S_2\text{——} \\
S_1\ ;\ z\ :\ \mathbb{N} \\
\hline
z = x + y
\end{array}
$$

The result is that S_2 includes the declarations and predicates of S_1 (Fig. 18.5).

Two schemas may be linked by propositional connectives such as $S_1 \wedge S_2$, $S_1 \vee S_2$, $S_1 \Rightarrow S_2$, and $S_1 \Leftrightarrow S_2$. The schema $S_1 \vee S_2$ is formed by merging the declaration parts of S_1 and S_2, and then combining their predicates with the logical $\vee$ operator. For example, Fig. 18.6 gives the result of $S = S_1 \vee S_2$.

Fig. 18.5 Schema inclusion

$$
\begin{array}{|l}
\hline
S_2 \\
x,\ y : \mathbb{N} \\
z : \mathbb{N} \\
\hline
x + y > 2 \\
z = x + y \\
\hline
\end{array}
$$

Fig. 18.6 Merging schemas
($S_1 \vee S_2$)

$$
\begin{array}{|l}
\hline
S \\
x,\ y : \mathbb{N} \\
z : \mathbb{N} \\
\hline
x + y > 2 \vee z = x + y \\
\hline
\end{array}
$$

Schema inclusion and the linking of schemas use normalization to convert sub-types to maximal types, and predicates are employed to restrict the maximal type to the sub-type. This involves replacing declarations of variables (e.g., $u : 1 .. 35$ with $u : \mathbb{Z}$, and adding the predicate $u > 0$ and $u < 36$ to the predicate part of the schema).

The Δ and Ξ conventions are used extensively, and the notation Δ *TempMap* is used in the specification of schemas that involve a change of state. The notation Δ *TempMap* represents:

$$\Delta TempMap = TempMap \wedge TempMap'$$

The longer form of Δ *TempMap* is written as:

$$
\begin{array}{|l}
\hline
\Delta TempMap \\
CityList,\ CityList' : \mathbb{P}\,City \\
temp,\ temp' : City \nrightarrow \mathbb{Z} \\
\hline
\text{dom } temp = CityList \\
\text{dom } temp' = CityList' \\
\hline
\end{array}
$$

The notation Ξ *TempMap* is used in the specification of operations that do not involve a change to the state. It represents:

$$
\begin{array}{|l}
\hline
\Xi\ TempMap \\
\Delta TempMap \\
\hline
CityList = CityList' \\
temp = temp' \\
\hline
\end{array}
$$

Schema composition is analogous to relational composition and it allows new specifications to be built from existing ones. It allows the after state variables of one schema to be related with the before variables of another schema. The composition of two schemas S and T (S ; T) is described in detail in [18] and involves four steps, as given in Table 18.1.

Table 18.1 Schema composition

Step	Procedure
1.	Rename all *after* state variables in S to something new: S $[s^+/s']$.
2.	Rename all *before* state variables in T to the same new thing: i.e., T $[s^+/s]$.
3.	Form the conjunction of the two new schemas: S $[s^+/s'] \wedge$ T $[s^+/s]$.
4.	Hide the variable introduced in step 1 and 2. S ; T $= (S\ [s^+/s'] \wedge T\ [s^+/s])\backslash(s^+)$

Fig. 18.7 Schema
composition

$$
\begin{array}{l}
\text{—}S_1 \wedge T_1\text{———}\\
x,\ x^+,\ x',\ y?\ :\mathbb{N}\\
\hline
x^+ = y? - 2\\
x' = x^+ + 1\\
\hline
\end{array}
\qquad
\begin{array}{l}
\text{—}S\ ;\ T\text{———}\\
x,\ x',\ y?\ :\mathbb{N}\\
\hline
\exists x^+ : \mathbb{N}\ \bullet\\
\quad(x^+ = y? - 2\\
\quad\ \ x' = x^+ + 1)\\
\hline
\end{array}
$$

The example in Fig. 18.7 should make schema composition clearer. Consider the composition of S and T where S and T are defined as follows:

$$
\begin{array}{l}
\text{—}S\text{———}\\
x,\ x',\ y?\ :\mathbb{N}\\
\hline
x' = y? - 2\\
\hline
\end{array}
\qquad
\begin{array}{l}
\text{—}T\text{———}\\
x,\ x' : \mathbb{N}\\
\hline
x' = x + 1\\
\hline
\end{array}
$$

$$
\begin{array}{l}
\text{—}S_1\text{———}\\
x,\ x^+,\ y?\ :\mathbb{N}\\
\hline
x^+ = y? - 2\\
\hline
\end{array}
\qquad
\begin{array}{l}
\text{—}T_1\text{———}\\
x^+,\ x' : \mathbb{N}\\
\hline
x' = x^+ + 1\\
\hline
\end{array}
$$

S_1 and T_1 represent the results of step 1 and step 2, with x' renamed to x^+ in S, and x renamed to x^+ in T. Step 3 and step 4 yield the result shown in Fig. 18.7.

Schema composition allows new specifications to be created from existing ones.

18.8   Reification and Decomposition

A Z specification involves defining the state of the system and then specifying the required operations. The Z specification language employs many constructs that are not part of conventional programming languages, and it is therefore not directly executable on a computer. A programmer implements the formal specification, and mathematical proof may be employed to prove that a program meets its specification.

Often, there is a need to write an intermediate specification that is between the original Z specification and the eventual program code. This intermediate specification is more algorithmic and uses less abstract data types than the Z specification. It is termed the design and needs to be correct with respect to the specification, and the program needs to be correct with respect to it. The design is a refinement

Fig. 18.8 Refinement
commuting diagram

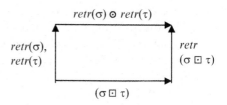

(reification) of the specification, and the operations of the specification have been decomposed into those of the design.

The representation of an abstract data type such as a set by a sequence is termed data reification, and this is concerned with the process of transforming an abstract data type into a concrete data type. The abstract and concrete data types are related by the retrieve function, which maps the concrete data type to the abstract data type. There are typically several possible concrete data types for a particular abstract data type (i.e., refinement is a relation), whereas there is one abstract data type for a concrete data type (i.e., retrieval is a function). For example, sets are often reified to unique sequences; however, more than one unique sequence can represent a set whereas a unique sequence represents exactly one set.

The operations defined on the concrete data type are related to the operations defined on the abstract data type. That is, the commuting diagram property is required to hold; i.e., the operation $\boxdot$ on the concrete data type correctly refines the operation $\odot$ on the abstract data type if the diagram in Fig. 18.8 commutes, and this property requires proof.

That is, it is required to prove that:

$$ret(\sigma\boxdot\tau) = (ret\,\sigma) \odot (ret\,\tau)$$

In Z, the refinement and decomposition is done with schemas. It is required to prove that the concrete schema is a valid refinement of the abstract schema, and this gives rise to a number of proof obligations. It needs to be proved that the initial states correspond to one another, and that each operation in the concrete schema is correct with respect to the operation in the abstract schema, and also that it is applicable (i.e., whenever the abstract operation may be performed the concrete operation may also be performed).

18.9   Proof in Z

Mathematicians conduct rigorous proof of theorems using technical and natural language. Logicians employ formal proofs to prove theorems using propositional and predicate calculus. Formal proofs generally involve a long chain of reasoning with every step of the proof justified. Rigorous proofs involve precise reasoning using a mixture of natural and mathematical language. Rigorous proofs [18] have been described as being analogous to high level programming languages, whereas formal proofs are analogous to machine language.

A mathematical proof includes natural language and mathematical symbols and often many of the tedious details of the proof are omitted. Many proofs in formal methods such as Z are concerned with crosschecking on the details of the specification, or on the validity of the refinement step, or proofs that certain properties are satisfied by the specification. There are often many tedious lemmas to be proved, and tool support is essential as proof by hand often contain errors or jumps in reasoning. Machine proofs are lengthy and largely unreadable; however, they provide extra confidence as every step in the proof is justified.

A formal mathematical proof consists of a sequence of formulae, where each element is either an axiom or derived from a previous element in the series by applying a fixed set of mechanical rules. The proof of various properties about the programs increases confidence in its correctness. Mathematical proof is discussed in more detail in [50].

18.10 Review Questions

1. Describe the main features of the Z specification language.
2. Explain the difference between $\mathbb{P}_1 X$, $\mathbb{P} X$ and FX.
3. Give an example of a set derived from another set using set comprehension. Explain the three main parts of set comprehension in Z.
4. Discuss the applications of Z and which areas have benefited most from their use? What problems have arisen?
5. Give examples to illustrate the use of domain and range restriction operators and domain and range anti-restriction operators with relations in Z.
6. Give examples to illustrate relational composition.
7. Explain the difference between a partial and total function and give examples to illustrate function override.
8. Give examples to illustrate the various operations on sequences including concatenation, head, tail, map and reverse operations.
9. Give examples to illustrate the various operations on bags.
10. Discuss the nature of proof in Z and tools to support proof.
11. Explain the process of refining an abstract schema to a more concrete representation, the proof obligations that are generated, and the commuting diagram property.

18.11 Summary

Z was developed at Oxford University and it has been employed in both industry and academia. Its specifications are·mathematical and this allows properties to be proved about the specification, and any gaps or inconsistencies in the specification may be identified.

Z is a "model oriented" approach and an explicit model of the state of an abstract machine is given, and the operations are defined in terms of their effect on the state. Its main features are the schema calculus and a mathematical notation that is similar to VDM. The former consists essentially of boxes and are used to describe operations and states.

The schema calculus enables schemas to be used as building blocks to form larger specifications. It is a powerful means of decomposing a specification into smaller pieces, and helps with the readability of Z specifications, as each individual schema is small in size and self-contained.

Z is a highly expressive specification language and includes notation for sets, functions, relations, bags, sequences, predicate calculus and schema calculus. A Z specification may be refined into the detailed code. This involves producing intermediate specifications between the Z specification and the eventual program code. Mathematical proof is required to demonstrate the validity of the refinement step, and this involves a proof of the commuting diagram property.

Tool support is essential to carry out formal proof, as hand proofs often involve jumps in reasoning, and are extremely time consuming due to the volume of proof obligations.

Unified Modelling Language

19

Key Topics

Use Cases
Classes and Objects
Sequence diagrams
Statecharts
Collaboration diagrams
Rational Unified Process

19.1 Introduction

The unified modelling language (UML) is a visual modelling language for software systems. It was developed by Jim Rumbaugh, Grady Booch, and Ivar Jacobson [32] at Rational Corporation as a notation for modelling object-oriented systems. It provides a visual means of specifying, constructing and documenting object-oriented systems, and facilitates the understanding of the architecture of the system, and managing the complexity of a large system. The language was strongly influenced by three methods: the *Object Modelling Technique* (OMT) developed by Rumbaught; the *Booch Method* developed by Booch, and *Object-Oriented Software Engineering* (OOSE) developed by Jacobson. UML unifies and improves upon these methods, and it has become a popular formal approach to modelling software systems.

Models provide a better understanding of the system to be developed, and a UML model allows the system to be visualized prior to its implementation, and simplifies the underlying reality. Large complex systems are difficult to understand in their entirety, and the use of a UML model is an aid to simplifying complexity.

G. O'Regan, *Introduction to Software Quality*, Undergraduate Topics
in Computer Science, DOI 10.1007/978-3-319-06106-1_19,
© Springer International Publishing Switzerland 2014

The choice of the model is fundamental, and a good model will provide a good insight into the system. Models need to be explored and tested to ensure their adequacy as a representation of the system. Models simplify the reality, but it is important to ensure that the simplification does not exclude any important details. The chosen model affects the view of the system, and different roles require different viewpoints of the proposed system.

An architect will design a house prior to its construction, and the blueprints will contain details of the plan of each room, as well as plans for electricity and plumbing. That is, the plans for a house include floor plans, electrical plans, and plumping plans. These plans provide different viewpoints of the house to be constructed, and are used to provide estimates of the time and materials required to construct it.

A database developer will often focus on entity-relationship models, whereas a systems analyst will often focus on algorithmic models. An object-oriented developer will focus on classes and interactions of classes. Often, there is a need to be able to view the system at different levels of detail. No single model in itself is sufficient for this, and a small set of interrelated models is employed.

UML provides a formal model the system, and it allows the same information to be presented in several ways, and at different levels of detail. The requirements of the system are expressed in terms of use cases; the design view captures the problem space and solution space; the process view models the systems processes; the implementation view addresses the implementation of the system; and the deployment view models the physical deployment of the system.

There are nine main diagrams providing different viewpoints of the system, and these UML diagrams provide the blueprint of software.

19.2 Overview of UML

UML is an expressive graphical modelling language for visualizing, specifying, constructing and documenting a software system. It provides several views of the software's architecture, and it has a clearly defined syntax and semantics. Each stakeholder (e.g., project manager, developers, and testers) has a different perspective, and looks at the system in different ways at different times during the project. UML is a way to model the software system before implementing it in a programming language.

A UML specification consists of precise, complete and unambiguous models. The models may be employed to generate code in a programming language such as Java or C++. The reverse is also possible and so it is possible to work with either the graphical notation of UML or the textual notation of a programming language. UML expresses things that are best expressed graphically, whereas a programming language expresses things that are best expressed textually, and tools are employed to keep both views consistent. UML may be employed to document the software system, and it has been employed in many domains including the banking sector, defence, and telecommunications.

Table 19.1 Classification of UML things

Thing	Kind	Description
Structural	Class	A class is a description of a set of objects that share the same attributes and operations.
	Interface	An interface is a collection of operations that specify a service of a class or component. It specifies externally visible behaviour of the element.
	Collaboration	A collaboration defines an interaction between software objects.
	Use Case	A use case is a set of actions that define the interaction between an actor and the system to achieve a particular goal.
	Active Class	An active class is used to describe concurrent behaviour of a system.
	Component	A component is used to represent any part of a system for which UML diagrams are made.
	Node	A node is used to represent a physical part of the system (e.g., server, network, etc).
Behavioural	Interaction	These comprise interactions (message exchange between components) expressed as sequence diagrams or collaboration diagrams.
	State Machine	A state machine is used to describe different states of system component.
Grouping	Packages	These are the organization parts of UML models. A package organizes elements into groups and is a way to organize a UML model.
Annotation		These are the explanatory parts (notes) of UML.

The use of UML requires an understanding of its basic building blocks, the rules for combining the building blocks, and the common mechanisms that apply throughout the language. There are three kinds of building blocks employed:
• Things
• Relationships
• Diagrams

Things are the object-oriented building blocks of the UML. They include *structural things, behavioural things, grouping things* and *annotational things*. Structural things are the nouns of the UML models; behavioural things are the dynamic parts and represent behaviour over time; grouping things are the organization parts of UML; and annotation things are the explanatory parts. Things, relationships and diagrams are all described graphically and are discussed in [32] (Table 19.1).

There are four kinds of relationship in UML:
• Dependency
• Association
• Generalization
• Extensibility

Dependency is used to represent a relationship between two elements of a system, in which a change to one thing affects the other thing (dependent thing). *Association* describes how elements in the UML diagram are associated, and describes a set of connections among elements in a system. *Aggregation* is an association that represents a structural relationship between a whole and its parts. A *generalization* is a parent/child relationship in which the objects of the specialized element (child) are substituted for objects of the generalized element (the parent). *Extensibility* refers to a mechanism to extend the power of the language to represent extra behaviour of the system. Next, we describe the key UML diagrams.

19.3   UML Diagrams

The UML diagrams provide a graphical visualization of the system from different viewpoints, and there are nine key UML diagrams (Table 19.2).

The concept of class and objects are taken from object-oriented design, and classes are the most important building block of any object-oriented system. A class is a set of objects that share the same attributes, operations, relationships and semantics [32]. Classes may represent software things and hardware things. For example, walls, doors, and windows are all classes, whereas individual doors and windows are objects. A class represents a set of objects rather than an individual object.

Automated bank teller machines (ATMs) include two key classes: customers and accounts. The class definition includes both the data structure for customers and accounts, and the operations on customers and accounts. These include operations to add or remove a customer, operations to debit or credit an account, or to transfer from one account to another. There are several instances of customers and accounts, and these are the actual customers of the bank and their accounts.

Table 19.2 UML diagrams

Diagram	Description
Class	This shows a set of classes, interfaces and collaborations and their relationships. They address the static design view of a system.
Object	This shows a set of objects and their relationships. An object diagram is an instance of a class diagram.
Use Case	These describe the functionality of the system, and the relationship between the use cases and the actors.
Sequence	These diagrams show the interaction among the components of a system, and the sequence of messages flowing from one object to another.
Collaboration	This is an interaction diagram that emphasizes the structural organization of objects that send and receive messages.
State chart	This is used to represent the event driven change of state of a system, and consists of a state machine with states, events and transitions.
Activity	This diagram is used to illustrate the flow of control in a system.
Component	This diagram represents the implementation view of a system, and consists of a set of components and their relationships.
Deployment	This diagram is used for visualizing the deployment view of a system.

Table 19.3 Simple class diagram

Customer	Account
Name: String	Balance:Real
Address: String	Type:String
Add()	Debit()
Remove()	Credit()
	CheckBal()
	Transfer()

Every class has a name (e.g., Customer and Account) to distinguish it from other classes. There will generally be several objects associated with the class. The class diagram describes the name of the class, its attributes and its operations. An attribute represents some property of the class that is shared by all objects; for example, the attributes of the class 'Customer' are name and address. Attributes are listed below the class name, and the operations are listed below the attributes. The operations may be applied to any object in the class. The responsibilities of a class may also be included in the definition (Table 19.3).

Class diagrams typically include various relationships between classes. In practice, very few classes are stand alone, and most collaborate with others in various ways. The relationship between classes needs to be considered and these provide different ways of combining classes to form new classes. The relationships include dependencies (a change to one thing affects the dependent thing); generalizations (these link generalized classes to their specializations in a subclass/superclass relationship); and associations (these represent structural relationships among objects).

A dependency is a relationship that states that a change in the specification of one thing affects the dependent thing. It is indicated by a dashed line (---->). Generalizations allow a child class to be created from one or more parent classes (single or multiple inheritance). A class that has no parents is termed a base class, e.g., there are three children of the base class Shape namely Rectangle, Circle and Polygon. There is one child of Rectangle namely Square. Generalization is indicated by a solid directed line that points to the parent (—▶). Association is a structural relationship that specifies that objects of one thing are connected to objects of another thing. It is indicated by a solid line connecting the same or different classes.

The object diagram (Fig. 19.1) shows a set of objects and their relationships at a point of time. It is related to the class diagram in that the object is an instance of the class. The ATM example in Table 19.3 had two classes (customers and accounts), and the objects of these classes are the actual customers and their corresponding accounts. Each customer may have several accounts, and the names and addresses of the customers are detailed as well as the corresponding balance in the customer's accounts. There is one instance of the customer class and two instances of the account class in this example.

An object has a state which has a given value at each time instance. Operations on the object will typically (with the exception of query operations) change its state.

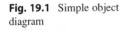

Fig. 19.1 Simple object
diagram

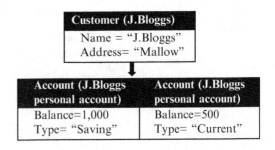

An object diagram contains objects and links to other objects, and gives a snapshot
of the system at a particular moment of time.

A use case diagram model the dynamic aspects of the system, and it shows a set of
use cases and actors and their relationships. It describes scenarios (or sequences of
actions) in the system from the user's viewpoint (actor), and shows how the actor
interacts with the system. An actor represents the set of roles that a user can play, and
the actor may be human or an automated system. Actors are connected to use cases by
association, and they may communicate by sending and receiving messages.

A use case diagram shows a set of use cases and each use case represents a
functional requirement. Use cases are employed to model the visible services that
the system provides within the context of its environment, and for specifying the
requirements of the system as a black box. Each use case carries out some work that
is of value to the actor, and the behaviour of the use case is described by the flow of
events in text. The description includes the main flow of events for the use case and
the exceptional flow of events. These flows may also be represented graphically.
There may also be alternate flows as well as the main flow of the use case. Each
sequence is termed a scenario and a scenario is one instance of a use case.

Use cases provide a way for the end users and developers to share a common
understanding of the system. They may be applied to all or part of the system
(subsystem), and the use cases are used as the basis for development and testing. A
use case is represented graphically by an ellipse. The benefits of use cases include:

- Enables the stakeholders (e.g., domain experts, developers, testers and end users)
  to share a common understanding
- Models the requirements (specifies what the system should do).
- Models the context of a system (identifies actors and their roles)
- Used for development and testing.

Figure 19.2 presents a simple example of the definition of the use cases for an
ATM application. The typical user operations at an ATM machine include the
balance inquiry operation, cash withdrawal, and the transfer of funds from one
account to another. The actors for the system include 'customer' and 'admin', and
these actors have different needs and expectations of the system.

The behaviour from the user's viewpoint is described, and the use-cases include
"withdraw cash", "balance enquiry", "transfer" and "maintain/reports". The use
case view of the system includes the actors who are performing the sequence of
actions.

Fig. 19.2 Use-Case diagram
of ATM machine

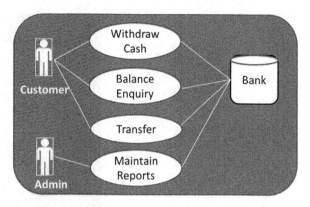

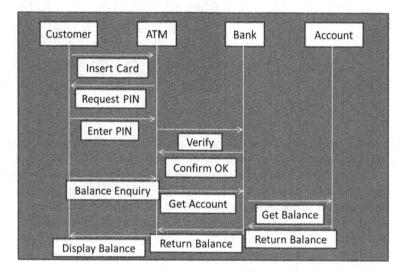

Fig. 19.3 UML sequence diagram

The next UML diagram considered is the sequence diagram which models the dynamic aspects of the system, and shows the interaction between objects/classes in the system for each use case. The interactions model the flow of control that characterises the behaviour of the system, and the objects that play a role in the interaction are identified. A sequence diagram emphasizes the time ordering of messages, and the interactions may include messages that are dispatched from object to object, with the messages ordered in sequence by time. The example in Fig. 19.4 considers the sequences of interactions between objects for the "Balance Enquiry" use case. This sequence diagram is specific to the case of a valid balance enquiry, and a sequence diagram is needed to handle the exception cases as well (Fig. 19.3).

Fig. 19.4 UML activity
diagram

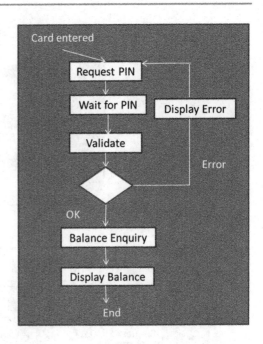

Fig. 19.4 UML activity
diagram

The behaviour of the "balance enquiry" operation is evident from the diagram. The customer inserts the card into the ATM machine and the PIN number is requested by the ATM. The customer then enters the number and the ATM machine contacts the bank for verification of the number. The bank confirms the validity of the number and the customer then selects the balance enquiry operation. The ATM contacts the bank to request the balance of the particular account, and the bank sends the details to the ATM machine. The balance is displayed on the screen of the ATM machine. The customer then withdraws the card. The actual sequence of interactions is evident from the sequence diagram.

The example in Fig. 19.3 has four objects (Customer, ATM, Bank and Account) and these are laid out from left to right at the top of the sequence diagram. Collaboration diagrams are interaction diagrams that consist of objects and their relationships. However, while sequence diagrams emphasize the time ordering of messages, a collaboration diagram emphasizes the structural organization of the objects that send and receive messages. Sequence diagrams and collaboration diagrams may be converted to the other without loss of information. Collaboration diagrams are described in more detail in [32].

The activity diagram is considered in Fig. 19.4, and this is essentially a flow chart showing the flow of control from one activity to another. It is used to model the dynamic aspects of a system, and this involves modelling the sequential and possibly concurrent steps in a computational process. It is different from a sequence diagram in that it shows the flow from activity to activity, whereas a sequence diagram shows the flow from object to object.

Table 19.4 Advantages of UML

Advantages of UML
Visual modelling language with a rich expressive notation.
Mechanism to manage complexity of a large system
Enables the proposed system to be studied before implementation.
Visualization of architecture design of the system.
The UML diagrams provide different views of the system.
Visualization of system from different viewpoints.
Use cases allow the description of typical user behaviour.
Better understanding of implications of user behaviour.
Use cases provide a mechanism to communicate the proposed behaviour of the software system
Use cases are the basis of development and testing.

State diagrams or state charts show the dynamic behaviour of a class, and how different operations result in a change of state. There is an initial state and a final state, and the operations result in different states being entered and exited. There are several other UML diagrams including component and deployment diagrams. The reader is referred to [32].

19.3.1 Advantages of UML

UML offers a rich notation to model software systems and to understand the proposed system from different viewpoints. The main advantages of UML are given in Table 19.4.

19.4   Rational Unified Process

Software projects need a well-structured development process to achieve their objectives. The *Rational Unified Development Software Process* (RUP) [57] has become important in recent years, and RUP and UML are often used together. It is

- Use case driven
- Architecture centric
- Iterative and incremental

It includes iterations, phases, workflows, risk mitigation, quality control, project management, and configuration control. Software projects may be complex, and there are risks that requirements may be missed in the process, or that the interpretation of a requirement may differ between the customer and developer. RUP gathers requirements as use cases, which describe the functional requirements from the point of view of the users of the system.

The use case model describes what the system will do at a high-level, and there is user focus in defining the scope the project. Use cases drive the development

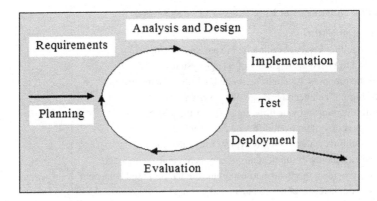

Fig. 19.5 Rational unified process

process, and the developers create a series of design and implementation models that realize the use cases. The developers review each successive model for conformance to the use-case model. The testers verify that the implementation model correctly implements the use cases.

The software architecture concept embodies the most significant static and dynamic aspects of the system. The architecture grows out of the use cases and factors such as the platform that the software is to run on, deployment considerations, legacy systems, and non-functional requirements.

A commercial software product is a large undertaking and the work is decomposed into smaller slices or mini-projects, where each mini-project is a manageable chunk. Each mini-project is an iteration that results in an increment (Fig. 19.5).

Iterations refer to the steps in the workflow, and an increment leads to the growth of the product. If the developers need to repeat the iteration, the organization loses only the misdirected effort of a single iteration, rather than the entire product. Therefore, the unified process is a way to reduce risk in software engineering.

Rup consists of four phases, and these are inception, elaboration, construction and transition. Each phase consists of one or more iterations, and the iteration consists of several workflows. The workflows may be requirements, analysis, design, implementation and test. Each phase terminates in a milestone with one or more project deliverables (Fig. 19.6).

The inception identifies and prioritizes the most important risks, and it is concerned with initial project planning, cost estimation and early work on the architecture and functional requirements for the product. The elaboration phase specifies most of the use cases in detail. The construction phase is concerned with building the product, and implements all agreed use cases. The transition phase covers the period during which the product moves into the customer site and includes activities such as training customer personnel, providing help-line assistance and correcting defects found after delivery.

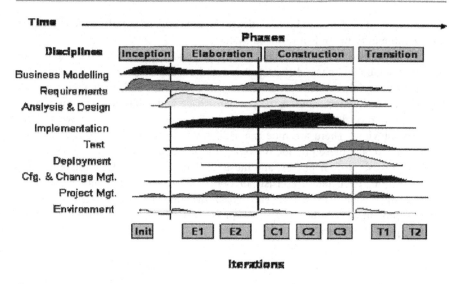

Fig. 19.6 Phases and workflows in rational unified process

The waterfall lifecycle has the disadvantage that the risk is greater towards the end of the project, where it is costly to undo mistakes from earlier phases. Iterative processes were developed as a response to this, with the waterfall steps applied in the iteration. Instead of developing the whole system in one step, an increment (i.e., a subset of the system functionality) is selected and developed, then another increment, and so on.

19.5   Review Questions

1. What is UML? Explain its main features.
2. Explain the difference between an object and a class.
3. Describe the various UML diagrams.
4. What are the advantages and disadvantages of UML?
5. What is the Rational Unified Process?
6. Describe the workflows in a typical iteration.
7. Describe the phases in the Rational Unified Process.

19.6   Summary

The unified modelling language is a visual modelling language for software systems, and it facilitates the understanding of the architecture, and management of the complexity of large systems. It was developed as a notation for modelling object-oriented systems, and it provides a visual means of specifying, constructing and documenting the object-oriented system.

UML is applied to formally model the system and it allows the same information to be presented in many different ways and at different levels of detail. The requirements of the system are expressed in use cases; and other views include the design view which captures the problem space and solution space; the process view which models the systems processes; the implementation view and the deployment view. There are nine main diagrams providing different viewpoints of the system, and these provide the blueprint of the software.

RUP consists of four phases, and these are inception, elaboration, construction and transition. Each phase consists of one or more iterations, and the iteration consists of several workflows. The workflows may be requirements, analysis, design, implementation and test. Each phase terminates in a milestone with one or more project deliverables.

Epilogue

20

We embarked on a long journey is this book and set ourselves the objective of providing an introduction to the software quality field to students and practitioners. The book was based on the author's experience in software quality and software process improvement at leading industrial companies. The principles of software quality management and software process improvement were discussed.

The goal was to cover both theory and practice, and to give the reader a grasp of the fundamentals of the software quality field, as well as guidance on how to apply the theory in an industrial environment.

We noted that companies today need to focus on customer satisfaction and software quality, and need to ensure that the desired quality is built into the software product. Customers today have very high expectations on quality, and expect high-quality software products to be consistently delivered on time. The focus on quality requires that the organization define a sound software development infrastructure to enable quality software to be consistently produced.

Quality improvement also requires that the organization be actively aware of industrial best practice, as well as emerging technologies from various research programs. Piloting or technology transfer of innovative technology is an important part of continuous improvement.

We started our journey with a discussion of some key figures in the history of quality including well-known quality gurus such as Shewhart, Deming, Juran, and Crosby. These grandfathers of quality played an important role in promoting quality in business, and in helping companies to change and to be more effective in delivering high-quality products. We also discussed the contributions of Watts Humphrey, who is considered the father of software quality.

We described approaches used in current software engineering to build quality into software. We discussed project planning and tracking, software lifecycles, software inspections and testing, configuration management, software quality assurance, etc. The capability maturity model integrated (CMMI) was discussed and it provides a framework that assists organizations in software process improvement. It allows them to assess the current capability or maturity of selected software processes and to prioritize improvements.

G. O'Regan, *Introduction to Software Quality*, Undergraduate Topics
in Computer Science, DOI 10.1007/978-3-319-06106-1_20,
© Springer International Publishing Switzerland 2014

The assessment (or *SCAMPI appraisal*) of an organization against the CMMI reveals strengths and weaknesses of the management and engineering processes in the organization. The output from the appraisal is used to formulate an improvement plan, which is then tracked to completion. The execution of the plan may take 1 or more years of effort.

We provided an introduction to project management and discussed project estimation, project planning and scheduling, project monitoring and control, risk management, and managing project quality.

We then discussed requirements and design, and discussed requirements elicitation, software design, and implementation. We then moved on to discuss the configuration management, and the concept of a baseline. Configuration management is concerned with identifying those deliverables that are subject to change control, and controlling changes to them.

We then discussed software inspections including Fagan inspections, as well as the less formal review and walkthrough methodologies. Software testing was then discussed, including the various types of testing that may be carried out, and we discussed test planning, test case definition, test tracking, test metrics, test reporting, and testing in an e-commerce environment.

We then discussed the selection and management of a software supplier, and described how candidate suppliers may be formally evaluated, and how the selected supplier may be managed during the project.

We then discussed software quality assurance and the importance of process quality. This chapter explained audits and described how they are carried out. We then discussed metrics and problem solving, including the balanced score card and GQM. We presented a collection of sample metrics for an organization.

We then discussed the ISO 9000 standard, which is an important standard for product and service delivery. The main features of the standard were discussed as well as guidance on its implementation.

We then discussed the important field of software process improvement. It began with a discussion of a software process, and discussed the benefits that may be gained from software process improvement.

We then gave an overview of the CMMI model, and discussed its five maturity levels and their constituent process areas. We discussed both the staged and continuous representations.

We then discussed the activities and teams required to set up a CMMI improvement initiative for an organization. These include the CMMI Steering Group, the SEPG team and process specific teams.

We then discussed the SCAMPI appraisal methodology, and this included a discussion of the formal SCAMPI Class A appraisal used large organizations to obtain a CMMI rating, as well as the less formal SCAMPI Class B and C appraisals.

We then examined various tools to support the organizations in improving their software engineering maturity. The focus is first to define the process, and then to find tools to support the process.

We then discussed formal methods which are often employed in the safety critical and security critical fields. These consist of a set of mathematical techniques to specify and derive a program from its specification. Formal methods may be employed to rigorously state the requirements of the proposed system; they may be employed to derive a program from its mathematical specification; and they provide a rigorous proof that the implemented program satisfies its specification.

We then presented the Z specification language, which is one of the most widely used formal methods. It was developed at Oxford University in the U.K.

Finally, we presented the unified modelling language (UML) which presents various views of the system architecture. Finally, we consider the future of software quality.

20.1   The Future of Software Quality

Quality will continue to be fundamental to the success of the company. There is likely to be an increased focus on achieving approved quality systems such as ISO 9001, or to achieve a specific CMMI maturity level. Many companies are ISO 9001 certified or are working towards certification, or have been assessed to be performing at a particular CMMI maturity level. Customer expectations are increasing all the time, and in the future it is likely that software companies will need to have a minimal quality standard such as ISO 9001 or CMM level 3 to be taken seriously by potential customers.

The cost of poor quality is currently measured in mature companies. It is likely to be measured in many more software companies in the future, as driving down the cost of poor quality will become a key goal for many organizations to improve their profitability and long-term survival.

Software components and the verification of software components may become increasingly important, as companies will wish to speed up development to shorten the time to market, which is a key driver in today's competitive environment. However, software organizations will need to have confidence in the correctness of the components, and there may be an independent certification body to verify that components are correct.

Glossary

ADS	Appraisal Disclosure Statement
AMN	Abstract Machine Notation
AQL	Acceptable Quality Level
ATM	Automated Teller Machine
BRS	Business Requirements Specification
BSC	Balanced Score Card
CAR	Causal Analysis and Resolution
CCB	Change Control Board
CCS	Calculus Communicating Systems
CICS	Customer Information Control System
CM	Configuration Management
CMM®	Capability Maturity Model
CMMI®	Capability Maturity Model Integration
COCOMO	Constructive Cost Model
COPQ	Cost of Poor Quality
COTS	Customized Off the Shelf
CSP	Communicating Sequential Processes
DAR	Decision Analysis and Resolution
DMAIC	Define, Measure, Analyse, Improve, Control
DMADV	Define, Measure, Analyse, Design, Verify
DOORS	Dynamic Object-Oriented Requirements System
DSDM	Dynamic Systems Development Method
EAF	Effort Adjustment Factor
ESA	European Space Agency
ESI	European Software Institute
FAR	Functional Area Representatives
FI	Fully Implemented
FMEA	Failure Mode and Effects Analysis
FSM	Finite State Machine
GG	Generic Goal
GP	Generic Practice
GQM	Goal, Question, Metric
GUI	Graphical User Interface
HP	Hewlett Packard

G. O'Regan, *Introduction to Software Quality*, Undergraduate Topics
in Computer Science, DOI 10.1007/978-3-319-06106-1,
© Springer International Publishing Switzerland 2014

HR	Human Resources
HTML	Hyper Text Mark-up Language
IBM	International Business Machines
IDE	Integrated Development Environment
IDEAL	Initiating, Diagnosing, Establishing, Acting and Learning
IEC	International Electro technical Commission
IEEE	Institute of Electrical and Electronic Engineers
IPM	Integrated Project Management
ISEB	Information System Examination Board
ISO	International Standards Organization
JAD	Joint Application Development
KLOC	Thousand Lines of Code
LCL	Lower Control Limit
LDRA	Liverpool Data Research Associates
LI	Largely Implemented
LOC	Lines of Code
MA	Measurement and Analysis
MOD	Ministry of Defence
MTTF	Mean Time to Failure
MTTR	Mean Time to Repair
NATO	North Atlantic Treaty Organization
NI	Not Implemented
ODC	Orthogonal Defect Classification
OID	Organization Innovation and Deployment
OMT	Object Modelling Technique
OOSE	Object-Oriented Software Engineering
OPD	Organization Process Definition
OPF	Organization Process Focus
OPP	Organization Process Performance
OSSP	Organization Set of Standard Processes
OT	Organization Training
PB	Project Board
PCE	Phase Containment Effectiveness
PCMM	People Capability Maturity Model
PDCA	Plan, Do, Check, Act
PI	Product Integration
PI	Partially Implemented
PIID	Practice Implementation Indicator Description
PL/1	Programming Language 1
PMBOK	Project Management Book of Knowledge
PMI	Project Management Institute
PMC	Project Monitoring and Control
PMP	Project Management Professional
PP	Project Planning

PPM	Project Portfolio Management
PPQA	Process and Product Quality Assurance
Prince	Projects In a Controlled Environment
PSP	Personal Software Process
PVCS	Polytron Version Control System
QA	Quality Assurance
QCC	Quality Control Circle
QMS	Quality Management System
QPM	Quantitative Project Management
RAD	Rapid Application Development
RAG	Red, Amber, Green
RCA	Root Cause Analysis
RD	Requirements Development
RFP	Request for Proposal
RM	Requirements Management
ROI	Return on Investment
RPM	Rational Portfolio Manager
RSM	Rational Software Modeller
RSKM	Risk Management
RUP	Rational Unified Process
SAM	Supplier Agreement Management
SCAMPI	Standard CMMI Appraisal Method for Process Improvement
SEI	Software Engineering Institute
SEPG	Software Engineering Process Group
SG	Specific Goal
SLA	Service Level Agreement
SLOC	Source lines of code
SOW	Statement of Work
SP	Specific Practice
SPC	Statistical Process Control
SPI	Software Process Improvement
SPICE	Software Process Improvement Capability dEtermination
SQA	Software Quality Assurance
SSADM	Structured Systems Analysis and Design Method
TQM	Total Quality Management
TS	Technical Solution
TSP	Team Software Process
UAT	User Acceptance Testing
UCL	Upper Control Limit
UK	United Kingdom
UML	Unified Modelling Language
VAL	Validation
VDM	Vienna Development Method
VDM✤	Irish School of VDM

VER	Verification
VOB	Version Object Base
VSS	Visual Source Safe
Y2K	Year 2000

References

1. Appraisal Requirements for CMMI V1.2. (ARC V1.2) (2006) SCAMPI Upgrade Team. TR CMU/SEI-2006-TR-011. August, 2006
2. Basili V, Rombach H (1988) The TAME project. Towards improvement-oriented software environments. IEEE Trans Softw Eng 14(6):758–773
3. Beck K (2000) Extreme Programming explained. Embrace change. Addison-Wesley, Reading
4. Bhandari I (1993) A case study of software process improvement during development. IEEE Trans Softw Eng 19(12):1157–1170
5. Bjorner D, Cliff J (1978) The Vienna development method. The meta language, vol 61, Lecture notes in computer science. Springer, New York
6. Bjorner D, Jones C (1982) Formal specification and software development, Prentice Hall International series in computer science. Prentice Hall International, Englewood Cliffs
7. Boehm B (1981) Software engineering economics. Prentice Hall, Englewood Cliffs
8. Boehm B (1988) A spiral model for software development and enhancement. Computer 21:61–72
9. Brassard M, Ritter D (1994) The Memory Jogger. A pocket guide of tools for continuous improvement and effective planning. Goal/QPC, Methuen
10. Brooks F (1975) The mythical man month. Addison Wesley, Reading
11. Brooks F (1986) No silver bullet. Essence and accidents of software engineering. In: Information processing. Elsevier, Amsterdam
12. Buxton JN, Naur P, Randell B (1975) Software Engineering. Petrocelli. Report on two NATO conferences held in Garmisch, Germany (October1968) and Rome, Italy (October 1969)
13. Chrissis MB, Conrad M, Shrum S (2011) CMMI for development. Guidelines for process integration and product improvement, 3rd edn, SEI series in software engineering. Addison Wesley, Boston
14. Crosby P (1979) Quality is free. The art of making quality certain. McGraw Hill, New York
15. Deming WE (1986) Out of crisis. MIT Press, Cambridge, MA
16. Dijkstra EW (1972) Structured programming. Academic, London
17. Dijkstra EW (1976) A disciple of programming. Prentice Hall, Englewood Cliffs
18. Diller A (1990) Z. An introduction to formal methods. Wiley, England
19. Dunaway DK, Masters S (1996) CMM Based Appraisal for Internal Process Improvement (CBA IPI): method description. Technical report CMU/SEI-96-TR-007. Software Engineering Institute, Pittsburgh
20. Fagan M (1976) Design and code inspections to reduce errors in software development. IBM Syst J 15(3):182–210
21. Fenton N (1995) Software metrics: A rigorous approach. Thompson Computer Press, Boston
22. Gerhart S, Craighen D, Ralston T (1994) Experience with formal methods in critical systems. IEEE Software, January 1994
23. Gilb T (1976) Software metrics. Winthrop Publishers, Inc., Cambridge
24. Gilb T, Graham D (1994) Software inspections. Addison-Wesley, Reading
25. Gries D (1981) The science of programming. Springer, Berlin

26. Hinchey M, Bowen J (eds) (1995) Applications of formal methods, Prentice Hall International series in computer science. Prentice Hall, New York
27. Hoare CAR (1985) Communicating sequential processes, Prentice Hall International series in computer science. Prentice Hall International, Englewood Cliffs
28. Hoare JP (1995) Application of the B-method to CICS. In: Hinchey M, Bowen JP (eds) Applications of formal methods, Prentice Hall International series in computer science. Prentice Hall, New York
29. Humphry W (1989) Managing the software process. Addison-Wesley, Reading
30. Ince D, Andrews D (1991) Practical formal methods with VDM, McGraw Hill International series in software engineering. McGraw Hill, New York
31. ISO/IEC (1991) ISO/IEC 9126: Information Technology. Software Product Evaluation: quality characteristics and guidelines for their use. ISO/IEC, Geneva
32. Jacobson I, Booch G, Rumbaugh J (1999) The unified software modelling language user guide. Addison-Wesley, Reading
33. Juran J (1951) Juran's quality handbook. McGraw Hill, New York
34. Kaplan RS, Norton DP (1996) The balanced scorecard. Translating strategy into action. Harvard Business School Press, Boston
35. Keeni G et al (2000) The evolution of quality processes at Tate Consultancy Services. IEEE Software 17(4):79–88
36. Kuhn T (1970) The structure of scientific revolutions. University of Chicago Press, Chicago
37. Lakatos I (1976) Proof and refutations. The logic of mathematical discovery. Cambridge University Press, Cambridge
38. Lions JL (1996) Ariane 5. Flight 501. Failure report by enquiry board, The MathWorks, Inc., Natick
39. Mac An Airchinnigh M (1990) Conceptual models and computing. PhD thesis, Department of Computer Science, University of Dublin. Trinity College, Dublin
40. Manley E (1995) Taurus: how I lived to tell the tale. Am Program Softw Fail 8:17
41. Manns T, Coleman M (1996) Software quality assurance. Macmillan Press Ltd., Hampshire
42. McDonnell E (1994) The development of a multiplex bundling system using formal methods, vols I & II. MSc thesis. Department of Computer Science, Trinity College, Dublin
43. Milner R et al (1989) A calculus of mobile processes (Part 1). LFCS report series. ECS-LFCS-89-85. Department of Computer Science. University of Edinburgh, Edinburgh
44. Ministry of Defence (1991) 00-55 (PART 1)/Issue 1, The procurement of safety critical software in defence equipment, PART 1: Requirements. Ministry of Defence, Interim Defence Standard, UK
45. Ministry of Defence (1991) 00-55 (PART 2)/Issue 1, The procurement of safety critical software in defence equipment, PART 2: Guidance. Ministry of Defence, Interim Defence Standard, UK
46. O'Hara F (1998) Peer reviews – the key to cost effective quality. European SEPG, Amsterdam
47. O'Regan G (2002) A practical approach to software quality. Springer, New York
48. O'Regan G (2006) Mathematical approaches to software quality. Springer, London
49. O'Regan G (2010) Introduction to software process improvement. Springer, London
50. O'Regan G (2013) Mathematics in computing. Springer, London
51. Office of Government Commerce (2004) Managing successful projects with PRINCE2. TSO, London
52. Parnas D (1972) On the criteria to be used in decomposing systems into modules. Commun ACM 15(12):1053–1058
53. Peterson B (1995) The IDEAL model. Software Engineering Institute. Software process improvement and practice (Pilot Issue), Wiley, New York, August. 1995
54. Polya G (1957) How to solve it. A new aspect of mathematical method. Princeton University Press, Princeton
55. Rational for the development of the U.K. defence standards for safety critical software. COMPASS conference, June 1990. Ministry of Defence

56. Royce W (1970) The software lifecycle model (Waterfall Model). In: Proceedings of the WESTCON, Los Angeles, August, 1970
57. Rumbaugh J et al (1999) The unified software development process. Addison-Wesley, Reading
58. Shewhart W (1931) The economic control of manufactured products. Van Nostrand, New York
59. Software Engineering Institute (2006) CMMI executive overview. Presentation by the SEI. Software Engineering Institute
60. Software Engineering Institute (2009) CMMI impact. Presentation by Anita Carleton. Software Engineering Institute. August 2009
61. Sommerville I (2011) Software engineering, 9th edn. Pearson, Boston
62. Spivey JM (1992) The Z notation. A reference manual, Prentice Hall International series in computer science. Prentice Hall, Englewood Cliffs
63. Standard CMMI Appraisal Method for Process Improvement (2006) CMU/SEI-2006-HB-002. V1.2. August 2006
64. Standish Group (1999) Estimating: art or science. Featuring Morotz Cost Expert. Standish Group Research Note
65. Tierney M (1991) The evolution of Def Stan 00-55 and 00-56: an intensification of the "Formal Methods debate" in the UK. Research Centre for Social Sciences, University of Edinburgh, Edinburgh
66. Wichmann BA (2000) A personal view of formal methods. National Physical Laboratory, March 2000

Index

CPSIA information can be obtained at www.ICGtesting.com
Printed in the USA
LVOW03s2127221015

459348LV00002B/16/P